Eisenhower and the
Management of Prosperity

STUDIES IN GOVERNMENT
AND PUBLIC POLICY

Eisenhower and the Management of Prosperity

John W. Sloan

080664

 University Press of Kansas

To my parents,
Alice and John Sloan

Published by the University Press of Kansas (Lawrence, Kansas 66049),
which was organized by the Kansas Board of Regents and is operated and
funded by Emporia State University, Fort Hays State University, Kansas
State University, Pittsburg State University, the University of Kansas, and
Wichita State University

Library of Congress Cataloging-in-Publication Data

Sloan, John W., 1940–
    Eisenhower and the management of prosperity / John W. Sloan.
        p.   cm.—(Studies in government and public policy)
    Includes bibliographical references and index.
    ISBN 0–7006–0489–8   ISBN 0–7006–0587–8 (pbk.)
    1. United States—Economic policy—1945–1960. I. Title. II. Series.
HC106.5.S476   1991
338.973'009'045—dc20   90–22749

British Library Cataloguing in Publication Data is available.

Printed in the United States of America

10 9 8 7 6 5 4 3 2

The paper used in this publication meets the minimum requirments of the
American National Standard for Permanence of Paper for Printed Library
Materials Z39.48–1984.

Contents

List of Illustrations, Figures, and Tables   vii

1   Introduction   1

2   Economic Philosophy and Administration
in the Eisenhower Presidency   12

3   The Political Economy of the 1950s   48

4   The Battle over the Budget   69

5   Monetary Policy – The Battle against Inflation   105

6   The Struggle against Recession: 1953–54 and 1957–58   133

7   Conclusion   152

Notes   163

Bibliography   179

Index   185

Illustrations, Figures, and Tables

Illustrations

George Humphrey arriving at Camp David   21

President Eisenhower, Robert Anderson, Douglas Dillon   25

Percival Brundage being sworn in as director of the BOB   30

Joseph Dodge   31

Arthur Burns being sworn in as chairman of the CEA   33

Sherman Adams, Raymond Saulnier, and Arthur Burns   39

Rowland Hughes being sworn in as director of the BOB   84

Maurice Stans being sworn in as director of the BOB   89

William McChesney Martin   109

Eisenhower and BOB director Percival Brundage   153

Figures

3.1   The Goals of National Economic Policy, 1952–1960   51

Tables

3.1   Results of National Elections, 1948–1960   57

4.1   The Budgetary Record of the Eisenhower Administration   79

4.2   National Defense Spending, 1950–1960   81

4.3   Gross National Product and National Defense
Spending, 1950–1960   82

4.4   Total Budget Expenditures and Major National Security
Expenditures, FY 1950–FY 1960   83

1
Introduction

The initial scholarly evaluation of the Eisenhower presidency was generally negative. The critics of the 1950s charged that Eisenhower self-indulgingly maintained his popularity by *not* using the full powers of his office to resolve the growing problems of the decade. By being "above politics," Eisenhower avoided many political battles, but problems were allowed to grow and fester beneath the superficial calm of the 1950s, problems that would inevitably be more difficult to deal with in the 1960s. Liberal critics charged that the times required the challenging leadership of another FDR to complete the liberal agenda of the New Deal, but the reforms were being blocked by Eisenhower.

For many students of the presidency, Franklin D. Roosevelt had created the "one best way" to be president, to run the White House, and to manage the nation's problems. Since Dwight D. Eisenhower handled these tasks differently, observers of the presidency believed he performed poorly in the White House. One participant observer of the Eisenhower presidency wrote,

> The Eisenhower who rose to fame in the 1940s . . . brought to the White House of the 1950s a view of the presidency so definite . . . as to seem almost a studied retort and rebuke to a Roosevelt. Where Roosevelt had sought and coveted power, Eisenhower distrusted and discounted it: one man's appetite was the other man's distaste. Where Roosevelt had avidly grasped and adroitly manipulated the abundant authorities of the office, Eisenhower fingered them almost hesitantly and always respectfully—or generously dispersed them. Where Roosevelt had been an extravagant partisan, Eisenhower was a tepid partisan. Where Roosevelt had trusted no one and nothing so confidently as his own judgment and his own instinct, Eisenhower trusted and required a consensus of Cabinet or staff to shape the supreme judgments and determinations.

1

Where Roosevelt had sought to goad . . . the processes of government toward the new and the untried, Eisenhower sought to be both guardian of old values and healer of old wounds.[1]

Eisenhower's critics conceded that he was a popular president, as evidenced by his two landslide elections in 1952 and 1956 and his generally high ratings in the polls, but they attributed this popularity to nonperformance factors. That is, Eisenhower was well liked because he was a war hero; he had a warm, infectious grin; he was lucky; he was treated uncritically by the Republican-controlled press; and he was living off the intellectual capital of the Roosevelt and Truman presidencies. Many of his critics were frustrated that Eisenhower did not use his popularity to promote liberal reforms. They accused him of blowing an "uncertain trumpet" when a clear call was required to mobilize the nation to meet what were considered the unprecedented challenges of the 1950s. These critics believed that Eisenhower was more concerned with hoarding his popularity than with "spending it" to confront Joe McCarthy, expand black civil rights, promote more rapid economic growth, and imaginatively challenge the expanding power of the Soviet Union.

For some critics Eisenhower resembled a nineteenth-century president whose popularity dominated the political stage but who had a negligible impact on the economy and important historical trends. In a widely read essay written in 1958, William Shannon suggested that Eisenhower symbolized the 1950s in the way that Calvin Coolidge epitomized the 1920s — they both reigned but were not able to rule the diverse forces of their decade. "Eisenhower is a transitional figure. He has not shaped the future nor tried to repeal the past. He has not politically organized nor intellectually defined a new consensus. When he leaves office in January 1961, the foreign policies and the domestic policies of the past generation will be about where he found them in 1953. No national problem, whether it be education, housing, urban revitalization, agriculture, or inflation, will have advanced importantly toward solution, nor its dimensions significantly altered. The Eisenhower era is the time of the great postponement."[2]

Revisionist scholars, however, have significantly altered the image of the Eisenhower presidency. They have contested Eisenhower's image as a political amateur, a ceremonial leader who delegated away too much of his power, and a weak president who accomplished little. By contrast, the new perspective, based on access to a wealth of new archival information, emphasizes his political skills, his personal (if often disguised or hidden) leadership, and his significant accomplishments.[3] The revisionist literature has demonstrated that Eisenhower was politically more astute than his critics believed. His projected image of being nonpolitical and above politics allowed him to pursue his political goals behind the scenes without eroding his popularity. This was a different model of presidential leadership from Franklin Roosevelt's, but it served Eisenhower's conservative purposes during the 1950s. In Fred Green-stein's words, "commentators usually associate activism with efforts to effect major innovations (usually liberal) in public policy. Eisenhower sought, at least in domestic policy, to restrain policy change, but he was active in doing so. He worked hard, considering it his responsibility to shape public policy, and followed through on his initiatives."[4] The literature stresses that he had a political philosophy to guide his administration, that he worked hard to achieve his political objectives, and that he was successful in avoiding the two greatest dangers feared in the 1950s — war and depression. What revision-ists have not explained is why no subsequent president or presidential can-didate has sought to emulate Eisenhower in the way aspiring politicians have sometimes evoked the memories of Roosevelt, Truman, and Kennedy. Even Republican presidents are likely to cite Roosevelt, Truman, and Kennedy rather than Eisenhower.

Still, there remain significant gaps in the revisionist literature on the Eisen-hower presidency. One of these gaps, and the focus of this study, is Eisen-hower's macroeconomic policymaking. This subject has been relatively ne-glected because "most revisionists have . . . agreed with the traditional view that Eisenhower was not especially interested in domestic policy unless it was directly related to national security and defense. His real interest, they con-clude, and the area where he showed the most talent as a leader and decision maker, was in foreign policy."[5] The negative evaluations in the 1950s and early 1960s were based on the noneconomic language used by Eisenhower and his first secretary of the Treasury, George Humphrey; the exhortations of a young and vigorous John F. Kennedy in 1960 to get the country moving again, which implied that it had been stagnant during the 1950s; and the fact that the gross national product (GNP) in the United States during the 1950s grew more slowly than the GNP in the Soviet Union, Western Europe, and Japan. Nevertheless, just as evaluations of Eisenhower's foreign policy have been changed by subsequent events, judgments of Eisenhower's economic policies should be more positively reevaluated — especially those formulated during his first term. In foreign policy, he ended the Korean War and avoided other wars; in economic policy, he avoided both high inflation and high unemployment, while achieving moderate levels of growth and only incremen-tal increases in the national debt. In this book I argue that, especially in light of the problems of economic growth, unemployment, inflation, and budget deficits over the past thirty years, Eisenhower's performance as "the manager of prosperity" merits a much higher regard than it has previously received.

THE PRESIDENT AS MANAGER OF PROSPERITY

The economy has strategic political significance probably second in importance only to issues of national security. The condition of the economy influences how voters and politicians view the performance of the president. The Keynesian notion that the economy can be managed by intelligent and compassionate policymakers so as to avoid the ravages of unemployment and inflation helped to spread the belief that uncaring policymakers are responsible when these maladies occur. Citizens expect the president and advisers to have the wisdom to protect their lifestyles from economic threats, and all presidential candidates claim to have that wisdom. Presidents certainly take credit when there is prosperity during their time in office; thus it takes political skill to avoid the blame when inflation or unemployment occur. Moreover, given the high expectations of the American public toward continuous prosperity and the nature of cyclical trends within the United States economy, economic conditions will never be perfect. Even during good times there will be negative trends—perhaps in a geographical region or a particular sector of the economy—that certain members of congress, pressure groups, bureaucrats, and economic advisers will argue should be reversed through the use of different policy instruments.

Before the Great Depression of the 1930s the president's economic role was limited to supporting programs that attacked specific problems, such as antitrust activities or regulating the banks. The president's economic role grew because of the widespread pain caused by the Depression, which led in 1932 to the electoral defeat of Herbert Hoover and the Republican party and the electoral victory of Franklin Roosevelt and the Democratic party. Although Roosevelt's New Deal never cured the Depression—World War II did that—the fact that his administration was perceived by a majority of the electorate as being more compassionate and more willing than the Republicans to use the powers of the federal government to turn the economy around had been proved to be an immense electoral advantage. The president's new role was institutionalized by the passage of the Employment Act of 1946, which explicitly acknowledged the federal government's macroeconomic responsibilities. Clinton Rossiter, a leading student of the presidency, defined this expanded role of the president as "manager of prosperity,"[6] which simply means that the American people expect the president to manage the economy in such a way as to maintain prosperity. And, since the president just happens to be the easiest person to blame for the problems that are easiest to see (and are among the hardest to solve), the performance of this role quickly became a measure of his success. If he failed at it, he would be replaced.

The Employment Act directed the federal government—with the cooperation of industry, agriculture, labor, and state and local governments, and in ways that would promote free competitive enterprise—to employ "all its plans, functions, and resources . . . to promote maximum employment, production, and purchasing power." The wording acknowledged that the U.S. economy was no longer solely a private concern; the federal government was now a partner in managing the economy. The nineteenth-century liberal idea of laissez faire, which held that the government should stay out of the economy and merely play the role of umpire to ensure fair competition, was giving way to the twentieth-century liberal belief, inspired by John Maynard Keynes, that government had to intervene to correct market problems by manipulating aggregate demand to prevent unemployment and inflation. Government had a public responsibility to insure that the business cycle did not cause economic misery. Implicit within the Employment Act is the Keynesian notion that the private market economy will not automatically correct itself and that governmental intervention will sometimes be needed.

The Employment Act did not specify when or how the federal government should intervene. According to Walter Heller, President Kennedy's chairman of the Council of Economic Advisers (CEA), the mandate from the Employment Act "generally evolved into the four dimensional objectives of full employment, high growth, price stability, and balance-of-payments equilibrium."[7] Because of liberal-conservative divisions within the Congress that enacted the Employment Act, there was a tension within the law between the ideas of government intervention and of reliance on free markets to manage the economy.[8] That tension continues to exist and to affect policy debates. Erwin Hargrove and Samuel Morley stress that "since 1946 liberals have been comfortable with the idea of selective government interventions in economic markets, and conservatives, while not rejecting that responsibility, have been more disposed to leave things alone in the belief that government intervention leads to market inefficiency, budget deficits, and inflation. These same tensions between intervention and caution exist within the discipline of economics."[9] And they existed within the Eisenhower administration.

Besides establishing national economic goals, the Employment Act also created new machinery to help attain them—the Council of Economic Advisers in the Executive Office of the President and the Joint Economic Committee in the Congress. The CEA is composed of a three-person board aided by a professional staff of about fifteen economists. The CEA serves one client—the president. It helps the president play the role of manager of prosperity by (1) preparing the president's annual Economic Report to the Congress each January; (2) forecasting economic trends; (3) assessing departmental proposals; and (4) advocating and defending the president's economic policies before Congress (the Joint Economic Committee), interest groups, and the public. Hargrove and Morley point out that "the mission of the CEA . . . coincides with the responsibilities of the president more closely than that of any other unit of government. The president is clearly responsible for maintaining high levels of employment and price stability. . . . The

CEA is his principal adviser in this task. The Treasury and the Bureau of the Budget share that responsibility, but their official responsibilities are more specific and limiting. Thus, the CEA's substantive mission coincides with presidential political accountability."[10] Whether the CEA takes advantage of this strategic position to be a major influence on economic policy depends on the relationship its chair is able to develop with the president and on the success of various other advisers who are competing to influence the president's economic decisions.

The CEA is only one of the agencies involved in macroeconomic policymaking, the other three being the Treasury Department, the Office of Management and Budget (OMB), and the Federal Reserve Board (FRB). While sharing responsibilities in this policy area, each institution has its own institutional perspective and emphasis. The CEA focuses upon forecasting the trends of the private economy and recommending what the federal government can do in its fiscal and monetary policies to promote a healthier economy. It will often be most sensitive to the unemployment rate. The Treasury is mainly concerned with taxes, managing the national debt, and the balance of payments. The secretary of the Treasury has cabinet-level status and is usually the administration's chief economic spokesperson. The Office of Management and Budget (before 1970 it was called the Bureau of the Budget (BOB)) concentrates on controlling federal expenditures and balancing the budget. An effective budget director will inevitably be referred to as the "Abominable No Man," because he will turn down so many requests for budget increases by different agencies. The Federal Reserve Board, an independent regulatory agency, is keenly sensitive to managing monetary policy in a way that will avoid inflation and balance of payments difficulties. The combination of different institutional perspectives and different advisers picking up varying signals from a complex economy means that the president will often receive conflicting advice concerning whether or when the federal government should intervene or what it should do. And whatever the president might decide is needed in terms of taxes or expenditures (fiscal policy), a majority of Congress must be persuaded to support the proposed policies — a difficult and time-consuming process.

For all presidents since the end of World War II, prosperity has been a necessary but precarious condition, a situation that can be rapidly threatened by either unemployment or inflation. A dynamic economy operating in a constantly changing world economy can deteriorate quickly, leaving the president in an exposed and vulnerable position. For the president, macroeconomic policymaking is an area of constant concern, a policy area that provides a torrential flow of information but relatively few decisions to make. There is constant monitoring of different components of the economy by the Departments of Treasury, Commerce, and Labor, the Office of Management and Budget, and the Federal Reserve Board. This avalanche of information is filtered and interpreted by the CEA in an effort to help the president make the few macroeconomic decisions that must be made each year. Prosperity cannot be commanded by presidential authority; it must be induced by well-timed fiscal and monetary moves. Many economists stress that maintaining prosperity requires policy flexibility. The liberal Walter Heller suggests that managing prosperity is a "full-time job" that, on the one hand, "calls for a willingness to change priorities among multiple economic objectives, to respond to secular shifts in the strength or composition of demand, to adjust policy to the growing exposure of the economy to international economic forces. On the other, it calls for readiness to shift policy from expansion to restriction and back again in response to the changing strength of private demand and changing size of public budgets."[11] The more conservative Neil Jacoby, a member of Eisenhower's CEA, writes, "Both history and theory demonstrate that if the United States economy is to attain optimal performance, government must be capable of making rapid changes in the variables that control aggregate demand and employment. They are the money supply, the federal spending rate, and tax payments."[12]

THE BUREAUCRATIC POLITICS APPROACH

The most effective way to examine Eisenhower's performance as manager of prosperity is to use a modified form of what is called the bureaucratic politics approach. This approach is largely based on the work of Graham Allison in *Essence of Decision*. Allison attempted to develop a model (or paradigm) that could be used to explain foreign policy. He viewed policies as outcomes that were not simply decided by a single decision maker because they represented best (most rational) choices, but were rather processes of accommodation between major advisers—reflecting personal and organizational interests—and the president. Allison attempted to construct policy-making patterns based on "the answers to four interrelated questions: Who plays? What determines each player's stand? What determines each player's relative influence? How does the game combine players' stands, influence, and moves to yield governmental decisions and actions?"[13] Policies are understood neither as choices nor as outputs, but as the *resultant* of various bargaining games among the principal players in the national government. Most resultants (policies) emerge from bargaining games among players who see different faces of an issue (political, economic, military, personal, symbolic, and so on) and who frequently disagree on the actions they prefer. Bargaining becomes a necessity because the top officials share power and often differ in what they see and what should be done about it. Thus, the players in Allison's approach "act in terms of no consistent sets of strategic objectives but rather according to various conceptions of national, organizational, and personal goals"; they "make government decisions not by a single, rational choice but by the *pulling and hauling* that is politics."[14] This milieu compels most policies to result from a political process—not a process of command.

Allison's approach has been criticized for underestimating the role of the president. It seems obvious that in many decision-making situations the president is more than just one of the "players"; he can be the dominant player. While Allison claims that players' stands on issues are frequently determined by their bureaucratic ties as captured in the dictum "where you stand is determined by where you sit," Dan Caldwell counters with "where you stand depends upon where the President stands. Indeed, the President determines whether his advisers are allowed to continue serving him."[15] Similarly, Stephen Krasner emphasizes that "the most important 'action channel' in government is the President's ear. The President has a major role in determining who whispers into it. . . . The ability of bureaucracies to independently establish policies is a function of Presidential attention. Presidential attention is a function of Presidential values. The Chief Executive involves himself in those areas which he determines to be important."[16] Hence, as one can see in chapter 2 and throughout this book, Eisenhower believed that managing prosperity was an extremely important presidential role, and so he was an attentive and active player in this policy area. Thus, in our modification of the bureaucratic politics approach, we pay considerable attention to President Eisenhower's economic values and activities.

Allison's approach has also been criticized for lack of attention to the external environment of decision making. According to I. M. Destler, officials, and especially the president, "must . . . consider each policy game not entirely on its own terms, but also for its relationship to other games."[17] To be understood, policies cannot be considered in artificial isolation from one another. For the president, another game of great importance is the political contest with the opposition party. Eisenhower's policy response to the 1953–54 recession was certainly influenced by Democratic party accusations that he was another Herbert Hoover. The United States is a pluralist democracy with an opposition party always ready to attack administration policy and a free press anxious to publicize divisions within the government. After policy is decided, it must be explained and defended. To be successfully implemented, it must often be successfully explained both to the general public and to specialized interest groups. Officials and the public must have faith that the policy will work. Optimism that a policy *will* work will give that policy more precious time to succeed. This is especially true in economic policymaking in a capitalist system in which business confidence is such an important variable. Hence it is necessary to modify Allison's approach by analyzing in chapter 3 the political context of Eisenhower's economic policymaking during the 1950s.

The bureaucratic politics approach has been applied mainly to national security policies, but by focusing on Eisenhower's performance in the role of manager of prosperity, it can be profitably used to explain his economic policymaking. Macroeconomic decision making inevitably involves the interaction among several officials. Few, if any, decisions can be implemented under the authority of any one official. This multiplies the number of agreements which must be negotiated across agency lines by lateral bureaucratic compromises, or by "escalation" up to the president. Thus, macroeconomic policymaking is a complicated game for high political stakes played by a small number of top officials involved in a constant struggle to gain optimum influence with the president. The president, more than likely, will not be a policy expert in this subject and so will be highly dependent upon the quality of advice received. In this policy area, the president can be an important, or even dominant player, but with authority sometimes weakened through lack of expertise, corresponding dependence on advisers, and the sharing of power with the independent policymakers in Congress and on the Federal Reserve Board.

The evidence needed to explain policy according to the requirements of the bureaucratic politics aproach is considerable, which helps to explain why Allison's study is more praised than replicated, but it can be satisfied by the data available at the Eisenhower Library in Abilene, Kansas. In dealing with economic policy, scholars do not run into the problem of restricted data because of national security considerations. Instead they have access to the key participants through their diaries, memos, letters, speeches, reports, press conferences, congressional testimony, and oral histories. Unfortunately, there are still some gaps in our understanding, but for the most part we can define the roles of, and interactions among, the president, the secretary of the Treasury, the chair of the CEA, the director of the Bureau of the Budget, and several other political advisers (such as Vice-President Nixon). Very little data is available on the chair of the Federal Reserve Board. Nevertheless, the data available will allow us to explain the general patterns of President Eisenhower's fiscal and monetary policies during the 1950s and deal more specifically with certain key issues, such as the recessions of 1953–54 and 1957–58 and the political battles over the FY 1958 budget.

Finally, Eisenhower's style of decision making is particularly compatible with the bureaucratic politics approach. As demonstrated in chapter 2, Eisenhower believed in formal staff procedures to discuss policy issues. Excellent records were kept of cabinet, National Security Council, and private meetings with the president which allows us to observe what different participants were thinking and proposing. The picture painted by Allison's model concerning how policy is made and the actual way (not the caricature of Eisenhower's critics) policy was decided within the Eisenhower administration are quite similar. Eisenhower even describes policymaking in expressions that duplicate the essence of the bureaucratic politics approach. For example, in a letter to Arthur Burns concerning a proposal for a tax cut, Eisenhower lamented, "One difficulty that occurs to me instantly is that caused by the laborious and tortuous channels that must be pursued in Washington in the process of translating any good idea into action that even remotely resembles the original thought. Even if, in unusual circumstances, the proposal and the result should be identical, yet they always involve time-consuming argument and pulling and hauling that erodes the psychological effect sought in the original plan."[18] There was "pulling and hauling" within the Eisenhower administration because of the personal and policy differences postulated by Allison's approach. This is true even for Eisenhower, whose critics complained that he surrounded himself with advisers sharing a conservative mindset and dedicated to preventing painful choices from burdening an aging and ill president. Thus, the record of macroeconomic policymaking in the Eisenhower administration is marked by conflicts among advisers in dealing with sluggish economic growth, recessions, taxes, budgets, and monetary policy. Indeed, that is the story of this book. Fortunately, the bureaucratic politics approach is designed to explain such policy situations.

CONCLUSION

President Eisenhower's economic policies have been a neglected subject that deserves to be evaluated. The general inherited a relatively new and expanding role that Clinton Rossiter labels "manager of prosperity." For the president, managing economic prosperity has become a political necessity, constantly threatened by inflation and unemployment. This study will demonstrate that Eisenhower played the role of "manager of prosperity" in a modern, conservative manner. Eisenhower's economic policies will be examined according to the lines of inquiry suggested by Graham Allison. This book makes two modifications in Allison's approach. First, critics of the bureaucratic politics approach have shown that when interested in and attentive toward a particular policy, the president will be a major, if not dominant player, in that game. This study will demonstrate that Eisenhower was interested in, attentive to, and a major player in economic policymaking. Second, in chapter 3, the political and economic contexts of policymaking during the 1950s will be analyzed. Policy outcomes are influenced by the political context in which decisions are made. Players' recommendations and choices are swayed by concerns with political feasibility. In brief, the bureaucratic politics approach, aided by the data sources available at the Eisenhower Library, will allow us to understand who participated in economic policymaking, what their values were, what they advocated, and what the resulting decisions were.

In subsequent chapters the following arguments are made. The major players who advised Eisenhower on macroeconomic policy are analyzed in chapter 2. I stress that Eisenhower was better served in the first term than in the second. In the first term, Eisenhower was trying to reconcile economic conservatism with welfare liberalism, which made the administration a very difficult target for the Democrats. In the second administration, Eisenhower became more conservative because of his commitment to balanced budgets and his fear of inflation. The economic and political context that influenced economic policymaking from 1952 to 1960 is described in chapter 3. I stress that as the decade progressed, the Democrats and the public held the Eisenhower administration to ever higher standards of performance. Eisenhower's prodigious efforts to provide balanced budgets each year and how he was able to achieve three balanced budgets during his eight years in office are examined in chapter 4. In addition, by reexamining Richard Neustadt's case study of the battle over the FY 1958 budget, I show why this was a clarifying experience for Eisenhower and why he became more rigidly conservative because of it. In chapter 5, I will review Eisenhower's policies to control inflation and to reverse the negative balance of payments the United States experienced in the late 1950s, arguing that the combined efforts of the Eisenhower presidency and the Federal Reserve Board were fairly effective in restraining price increases but that the president and the Republican party received few political rewards for these efforts. The Eisenhower administration's responses to the recessions of 1953–54 and 1957–58 are compared in chapter 6. I argue that the policy responses to the first recession were more politically astute than the reactions to the second. The final chapter delineates how our portrait of Eisenhower differs from the intellectuals' view in the 1950s and from the revisionists' perspective in the past decade. In this book Eisenhower appears as more of a conservative political activist than his contemporaries thought he was. And, in contrast to the revisionists' view, this study argues that Eisenhower's style of political leadership was less effective in the second term than in the first because of the president's increasingly rigid moral conservatism. The president of the first half of the 1950s was more in harmony with public opinion than the embittered, pessimistic, and aging man of the second half of the decade.

2

Economic Philosophy and Administration in the Eisenhower Presidency

Each presidential administration has its own view of the economy. Given the nature of the ever-changing U.S. economy in an ever-changing world economy, each administration also faces new economic conditions. These will usually require new policies; they may, or may not, demand a new philosophy. The political significance of macroeconomic policymaking creates pressures to construct a philosophy to guide and justify policy choices. The absence of such a philosophy implies that an administration is guided solely by political expediency; such "ad hockery" is costly since it indicates a lack of expertise in performing one of the institutionalized roles of the presidency — managing prosperity. However, no administration can be expected to adhere rigidly to its economic philosophy; every administration is likely to violate its philosophy at least occasionally because of political exigencies.

The economic philosophy of the Eisenhower administration was primarily a function of the interaction between the president and the officials who headed the Treasury Department, the Bureau of the Budget, and the Council of Economic Advisers. The president was not an expert in these policy areas; he was highly dependent on the expertise of these officials, relying on their abilities to explain the problems of taxes, balance of payments, budgets, economic forecasting, business cycles, and economic trends.

In addition to forging a philosophy, policymakers also have to create administrative procedures to assure that policy-relevant information and a feasible range of options reach the president for decision making. To conserve time and resources, the number of proposed options will always be limited by political feasibility and compatibility with the president's ideology.

MAJOR PLAYERS

President Eisenhower

President Eisenhower was the most significant player in determining his administration's macroeconomic policy. Of the major participants this chapter deals with, he was the only one in office during the entire period (1953–1961). The evidence in this and subsequent chapters will demonstrate that he was constantly attentive and often assertive in this policy area. This certainly does not mean that Eisenhower dominated this policy area in the way, for instance, that he controlled defense policy. The general recognized his lack of expertise and experience in economic policymaking and attempted to learn from those he felt had greater knowledge. The federal bureaucracy, especially the newly created (1953) Department of Health, Education, and Welfare (HEW), sometimes moved in a direction contrary to the president's philosophy. Eisenhower was also confronted with a Congress controlled by the opposition Democratic party for six of his eight years, a legislature which was trying to push policy, sometimes successfully, in a more liberal direction than the president wanted. Eisenhower may have been the most significant player in influencing economic policy, but, as one would expect from the bureaucratic politics approach, there were a number of outcomes he opposed. Indeed, this intensely competitive man ended the 1950s with growing feelings of frustration and pessimism because the nation seemed to be headed in a more liberal direction, a movement that his personal opposition apparently had only postponed. The victorious general of World War II yearned for a greater personal impact than he had been able to make.

At the beginning of his presidency, Eisenhower's critics claimed that he had no political experience and that he would have to rely on his beliefs, which were rooted in his hometown of Abilene, Kansas. Born in Denison, Texas, on October 14, 1890, "Ike" was raised in Abilene, the third of seven sons born to David Eisenhower, a creamery mechanic, and his wife, Ida, a religious pacifist. Despite his West Point education, his long, prestigious military career, and his tenure as president of Columbia University, Eisenhower's critics asserted that he had succeeded in outgrowing the antiquated beliefs of Abilene only in the national security policy area. In the domestic policy field he was still hindered by the hopelessly out-of-date attitudes of small-town America.

In reality, however, Eisenhower had evolved a fairly sophisticated philosophy that was often camouflaged by folksy rhetoric. Robert Griffith suggests that "it was from the military itself . . . that Eisenhower absorbed the principal elements of his education: a respect for the efficiencies of organization, a contempt for politics and politicians, a distrust of popular democracy and of the masses whose 'class fears and prejudices are easily aroused,' and, finally, a strong commitment to duty and to the ideal of disinterested public service."[1] Eisenhower's experiences in preparing the army budget under Gen. Douglas MacArthur in the early 1930s, in attending the Army Industrial College, in working on the army's plan for war mobilization early in World War II, in directing the Normandy invasion, and in heading the NATO alliance, which included many war-torn nations whose contributions were largely determined by their economic rehabilitation, all contributed to the development of his political and economic ideas.[2] While it was true that in early 1952 Eisenhower was unfamiliar with electoral politics, he had engaged in the politics of the military, the budget, international alliances, and foreign policy for many years. Only those with a narrow view of politics could have asserted that Eisenhower was politically inexperienced before he defeated Senator Robert Taft for the Republican nomination.

Eisenhower's philosophy was one of the major influences that motivated him to enter politics. Because of his contempt for partisan politics, he could justify entering the political arena only by his commitment to public duty and by his philosophy. He believed that the Democratic party was increasingly dominated by politicians and pressure groups "committed to centralized power and prosperity-by-inflation, and that the leftward drift, if continued, would fatally wound the nation in its contest with Communist power. Another [belief] was the equally strong conviction that the Republican Party, in consequence of its twenty years in opposition, was in danger of degenerating into baffled, sterile negativeness. The extreme right wing was about to grasp the party; the schism between it and the moderate elements and, even more, the community of political independents, was widening; and in Eisenhower's judgment only a Republican of moderate views could hope to repair the party breach and re-establish Republican conservatism in contemporary thought."[3] In brief, Eisenhower's philosophy provided him with an extensive political agenda which included stopping the leftward drift of public policies by defeating the Democratic party; rebuilding a moderately conservative Republican party to majority status; moving toward a balanced budget; establishing that prosperity is not dependent on bureaucratic centralization and inflation; establishing that prosperity is dependent on cooperation among government, business, and labor; and preparing the United States for a long struggle with the Soviet Union, in which the outcome would be determined more by economics than by the military.

Many of Eisenhower's ideas were expressed in popular form during the 1952 campaign. General Eisenhower blamed Democratic policies for producing inflation and denounced the "whole-hog theory" of government which introduced "the alien philosophy that our national destiny lies in the supremacy of government over all." During the campaign he regularly used a presawed length of wood which he dramatically broke to represent the decline in buying power of the dollar since 1945. He promised that his new policies would clean up "the mess in Washington," end corruption and bureaucratic waste, balance the budget, and reduce taxes. While attacking the expensive evils of "big government," Eisenhower repeatedly assured the electorate that he fully supported the extension of social security benefits and unemployment insurance as "a sound investment in a sounder America."[4] Eisenhower was like most candidates in promising many good things without clarifying the relative priority he placed on each pledge. He accepted the New Deal concept of president as manager of prosperity but imbued it with a Cold War perspective. Eisenhower responded to Democratic charges that the election of a Republican president would bring about a depression by stating:

> Never again shall we allow a depression in the United States. The Soviet communism is looking for one great victory. That victory is the economic collapse of our country. . . . So I pledge you this. If the finest brains, the finest hearts, that we can mobilize in Washington can foresee the signs of any recession, . . . the full power of private industry, of municipal, of state government, of the Federal Government will be mobilized to see that this does not happen. I cannot pledge you more than that.[5]

He certainly could. What would the finest brains and hearts do to prevent a recession?

After becoming president, Eisenhower designated the domestic economy as a priority area, second only to foreign affairs.[6] Sherman Adams, his top administrative assistant, wrote, "Eisenhower was more deeply concerned with economics than most people realized. He once told the Cabinet that if he was able to do nothing as President except balance the budget he would feel that his time in the White House had been well-spent. . . . Eisenhower was firmly convinced that the country's economic prosperity was as important to its security as planes and weapons."[7] Eisenhower defined his own role in a letter written to his brother Milton during the 1953–54 recession: "Maintenance of prosperity is one field of governmental concern that interests me mightily and one on which I have talked incessantly to associates, advisors, and assistants ever since last January. In these days I am sure that government has to be the principal coordinator and, in many cases, the actual operator for the many things that the approach of depression would demand."[8] Toward the end of his eight-year presidency, Eisenhower again wrote Milton concerning his interest in economic affairs: "I have the feeling that the subject of the American economy, like that of foreign affairs, should flavor every single talk that is delivered formally or informally by one in my position. These two subjects cannot be separated from each other."[9] In short, Eisenhower was attentive to economic policymaking because he thought it was vital.

Eisenhower's ideology has been the subject of dispute among scholars. In his attempt to differentiate his administration from reactionary conservatism and from the liberalism of his two Democratic predecessors, Roosevelt and Truman, Eisenhower variously described his policies as being guided by "dynamic conservatism," "progressive moderation," and "moderate progressivism." From a public relations point of view, none of these terms was successful. No label stuck. In his first term Eisenhower claimed that he was conservative in economic matters and liberal in human affairs. By the second term he was more likely to identify himself as basically conservative. Eric Goldman believes that the president "was . . . generally non-ideological. Eisenhower tended to look for an *ad hoc* solution to a given situation and was willing to listen sympathetically to quite contrasting points of view."[10] Richard Rovere, political journalist for the *New Yorker*, suggests that Eisenhower "was as conservative as the situation would allow him to be."[11] Stephen Ambrose, Eisenhower's major biographer, claims that the president's "liberalism . . . was usually closely connected with national security. He wanted better educational opportunities for Americans, for example, not so much for their own sake as for creating the scientists and technologists who could keep America ahead in the arms race. . . . When there was no direct Cold War connection on a domestic issue, Eisenhower's liberalism faded."[12] Fred Greenstein, a political scientist and leading revisionist, stresses that Eisenhower was an "issue oriented political leader" whose beliefs had a "profound impact" on his presidency. "Clear beliefs and policy positions founded on them are powerful instruments for leadership, since the leader who possesses them is better able to set priorities, communicate a public stance and delegate specifics to associates by giving them clear guidelines for making detailed decisions."[13] Greenstein also argues that Eisenhower compromised more on his domestic policy principles than on his foreign ploicy beliefs. Elmo Richardson handles the inconsistencies of Eisenhower's policies and philosophy with a subtle argument:

> Eisenhower's flexibility was fixed on a rigid base. His defense of principles in which his countrymen believed took the form of merely holding fast to those principles. If his rhetorical definition of the nation's interest sounded nebulous, he himself recognized it precisely in each issue, each problem, each crisis. But personal certitudes proved to be uncertain in application. His belief in the separation of governmental powers could not by itself provide a base for effective domestic programs.[14]

To use a contemporary phrase, Eisenhower was a "conviction politician." He did not merely want to be president; he wanted to further the ideas he so strongly held. As president, Eisenhower proposed that public policy be guided by what he called "the middle way." On January 16, 1953, Eisenhower said, "There is, in our affairs at home, a middle way between untrammeled freedom of the individual and the demands for the welfare of the whole nation. This way must avoid government by bureaucracy as carefully as it avoids neglect of the helpless."[15] The historian Robert Griffith claims that the concept of the middle way was not just a political platitude, but that it represented Eisenhower's attempt to resolve the chronic tensions of modern America. Griffith explains that "the term defined not only a political position — between capital and labor, between entrepreneurial liberalism and socialism, between the Republican Right and the Democratic Left — but also a series of programmatic commitments and a style of leadership."[16] What was unusual was that Eisenhower was thoroughly committed to a philosophy of moderation.

Eisenhower's set of beliefs is labeled "the corporate commonwealth" by Griffith. This commonwealth was designed to restore the social harmony that had been eroded by the Depression, Roosevelt's New Deal, and Truman's Fair Deal. It called for "the leadership of public-spirited and professionally skilled managers such as himself, who could exercise the disinterested judgment necessary to avoid calamities such as war or depression and achieve long-range goals such as peace and high productivity. The task of such leadership was to quell the passion of the masses, to encourage self-discipline on the part of business, labor and agriculture, and to promote the pursuit of long-term enlightened self-interest rather than immediate gain."[17] Short-term perspectives, emphasized by greedy leaders of interest groups, demagogic politicians, and self-serving bureaucrats, inevitably lead to class conflict, contentious party politics, and wasteful public policies. In Eisenhower's eyes, the kind of partisan strife that plagued the Truman period would fatally weaken the U.S. morally and economically in the struggle against the Soviet Union. Eisenhower wanted to depoliticize national politics by emphasizing consensus over conflict, persuasion over coercion, decentralization over centralization, and competitive markets over state controls. He wanted to appear "above politics" by encouraging restraint, working behind the scenes, delegating authority, and avoiding personality attacks (the conflict with Joseph McCarthy is illustrative). By defusing dangerous issues, Eisenhower would maximize his own room to maneuver while minimizing the opportunities for demagogic politicians.

This style of executive leadership was designed to prevent political disputes from becoming heated and, therefore irrational. It was a part of Eisenhower's philosophy to believe that many of the normal processes of "politics" did not result in good policy. "Politics" was a word he almost always used pejoratively to explain the selfish actions of politicians and pressure groups. He believed that many members of congress were solely interested in seeking votes, which was detrimental to the public interest.[18] It was an important element in Eisenhower's self-image that he was not engaging in "politics" but was always acting as a soldier or statesman doing his duty in the service of the national interest. Eisenhower was particularly disturbed that so many people were susceptible to the demagogic promises of politicians. In his view, the New Deal and the Fair Deal had created an atmosphere in which increasing numbers of people and interest groups were encouraged to focus their efforts on getting the federal government, and especially the president, to solve their problems instead of resolving them privately or at the local level. Within his first year in the White House, Eisenhower complained to his son John, "In this job it is not the work that kills you off, it is the incidentals — including the incidental of serving as a crying towel for everyone in the country who has a grievance of any kind. In our country all grievances these days are directed against the government."[19] Eisenhower considered this trend one of the most dangerous legacies of Franklin D. Roosevelt and one that he was determined to change.

Eisenhower's two favorite presidents were George Washington and Abraham Lincoln because "each of them moved relentlessly toward one goal: the founding of the nation in the case of Washington and preservation of the union in the case of Lincoln."[20] Thus, Eisenhower set for himself comparatively few strategic objectives. In stark contrast to Roosevelt's perspective on the role of the presidency, Eisenhower told the American people, "We have instituted what amounts to a revolution in Federal Government. . . . We have been finding things it can stop doing rather than new things for it to do."[21] Eisenhower accepted the idea that the president was responsible for managing prosperity but he proposed to perform this role in a conservative rather than a liberal manner. This meant more reliance on private competitive markets and less reliance on public interventions in the economy. Eisenhower's economic philosophy was nicely summarized by Arthur Larson, a major Republican spokesman during the 1950s: "The inherent incentives, drives and energies of private enterprises should be released and encouraged, as the proved motive force of our economy; but at the same time there should be just enough government activity (and no more) to avoid extreme tendencies in the business cycle, to protect the public against harmful practices, and to ensure adequate protections against the human hazards of a risk economy."[22] Eisenhower saw as proper government activity the improvement of such programs as unemployment insurance, social security, housing subsidies, bank deposit insurance, and securities regulation, since he believed that these established policies were essential to his strategic economic goal.

As is true of most conservatives, Eisenhower feared inflation more than unemployment. During his presidency, and especially in his second term, he was more willing to act — and endure the resulting political heat — to combat inflation than unemployment. He felt that infrequent, wisely selected, and well-timed governmental interventions in the economy could moderate economic fluctuations and provide for steadier growth. For example, Eisenhower believed that tax reductions, especially those designed to encourage investments, should be used to stimulate economic growth. And he always claimed that if a recession threatened to become a depression, he would support major public works projects to prevent unemployment. But he rejected the notion espoused by liberal Democrats and many Keynesian economists that more public intervention to manipulate aggregate demand would improve the economy and possibly eliminate the negative consequences of the business cycle. Eisenhower felt that only prudent intervention would have positive results; too much intervention in the quest for perfection would be counterproductive. In support of this conservative procedure, Larson quotes Gabriel Hauge, Eisenhower's assistant for economic affairs, who used to say that "the government should attempt to influence the economic weather and not try to ration raindrops."[23]

It was Eisenhower's fear that if intervention went much beyond what he was willing to engage in, the government would become the dominant factor in the economy and the very nature of our economic and political system would be changed — for the worse. Politicians could not operate a capitalist economy, nor could American democracy survive government's becoming the dominant factor in the economy. The government's taking a larger role would inevitably make the country's economy and the role of its citizens smaller. That is, if the government tried to regulate the economy too much, it would not only be counterproductive for the economy, it would also eventually be fatal for democracy.

Eisenhower's philosophy was more flexible and resulted in more politically successful policies in his first term than in his second. It is hard to guess whether Eisenhower's increasingly rigid conservatism (in domestic policy) was due to his illnesses, his age, his growing frustration with the job of being president, or other factors. A disillusioned Republican liberal, Emmet John Hughes, explains this phenomenon: "The progress of his presidency brought a more and more heavily conservative accent to Eisenhower's policies and pronouncements. But this was not a matter of slow acquiescence to new political pressures; it meant a gradual reaffirmation of old political persuasions."[24] Larson suggests that Eisenhower's transformation took place in 1957 in response to the political battles over the FY 1958 budget.[25] The analysis of budgetary politics of this time in chapter 4 supports Larson's view.

In Eisenhower's first term, his administration attempted to reconcile welfare liberalism with economic conservatism. But in the second term budgetary concerns and fears of inflation induced the chief executive to side decisively with economic conservatives. His obsession with balancing the budget caused Eisenhower to dig in his heels against the rising pressures for liberal reforms. Such inflexibility made the Eisenhower administration a stationary target and allowed the Democrats to put the president on the defensive, especially in the disastrous (for the Republicans) 1958 congressional elections.

By training, Eisenhower disliked politics and favored duty. He increasingly viewed most attempts at reform as reflecting selfish, partisan, demagogic, and bureaucratic interests. Obviously, since every reform proposal was at least partially motivated by selfish interests, this always provided the president with the justification to try to prevent it. Seldom, if ever, did he concede altruistic motives to the proponents of new federal legislation designed to confront the growing problems of the 1950s. The president's increasing self-righteousness about his own attitudes and cynicism about the motivations of others made compromise very difficult. Eisenhower felt it his duty to oppose many of these reform efforts, which he often condemned as promoting "paternalism and socialism."[26] Thus, in his second term, Eisenhower's beliefs placed him in the politically unsustainable position of a nay-sayer.

A word of caution here: We should not believe that Eisenhower the man, or his beliefs, can be neatly summarized. Most scholars who have studied Eisenhower have discovered that he was more complex than they first believed. To explain the inconsistencies of his behavior, writers have been forced to rely on contradiction. Thus, Greenstein contrasts the public and private images of Eisenhower: "As a thinker, the public saw a folksy, common sense replica of the man on the street. The confidential records show a man with extraordinary capacities for detached, orderly examination of problems and personalities. In public he seemed to be removed from the political arena. But the inner Eisenhower reasoned about political contingencies with greater rigor and readiness than many political professionals and drew on a long-standing acquaintance with the labyrinths of national and international governance."[27] Richardson makes the point that one major source of Eisenhower's popularity was that he provided the nation with "a conflicting set of contradictions: a soldier of peace, a plain-spoken intellect, a manager of power who advocated harmony and equity."[28] In brief, one must paint Eisenhower with subtlety. He was a complex man motivated by complex ideas, occupying an office subject to numerous conflicting pressures.

George Humphrey

Following the recommendation of G. Lucius D. Clay, President Eisenhower named George M. Humphrey, whom the president hardly knew, to be the fifty-fifth secretary of the Treasury. *Time* magazine, reflecting its Republican bias, was pleased with the selection: "By all readable portents he will be the first in a generation to restore Treasury to its function of high policymaking — by fiscal leadership — not by bureaucratic control of business."[29] George Humphrey was a self-made millionaire who had been president of the Mark A. Hanna Company, a steel conglomerate based in Cleveland. As a traditional conservative, Humphrey supported Robert Taft until Eisenhower won the Republican nomination. He was then named chairman of the finance com-

*George Humphrey arriving for a cabinet meeting at Camp David, December 9, 1955.
(Courtesy Dwight D. Eisenhower Library/U.S. Navy.)*

mittee of the Republican party during the campaign and was rewarded for his good work by being chosen as secretary of the Treasury.

The persuasive skill of Humphrey is illustrated by the fact that despite having supported Taft and not knowing Eisenhower personally in 1952, the secretary rapidly became a chief adviser and close friend of the president. Stephen Ambrose notes that Eisenhower "liked Humphrey enormously. Indeed, Humphrey was the only man in the Cabinet — save Dulles — with whom Eisenhower established a warm and close personal relationship. They were almost exactly the same age [62], had the same horror of deficit financing, and shared a love for hunting and fishing."[30] Describing Humphrey in his diary, Eisenhower wrote, "He is a sound business type, possessed of a splendid personality, and truly interested in the welfare of the United States. . . . He is almost a direct opposite of the caricatured businessman that so often appears in the columns of the 'liberal' press. He is persuasive in his presentations and usually has his facts well in hand."[31] The secretary was invited to a number of Eisenhower's stag dinners, and the president spent several vacations at Humphrey's plantation (renamed Humphrey's farm by the White House media experts) in Georgia. In December 1955, when there was still doubt about whether Eisenhower would run for a second term because of his heart attack, Ike suggested to Jim Hagerty, his press secretary, that Humphrey would make a good Republican presidential candidate in 1956.[32] This was not a politically realistic proposal, but it was reflective of the president's great respect for Humphrey. For Humphrey's sixty-sixth birthday in 1956, the president sent him a greeting: "I value exceedingly our association, both official and personal."[33] When Humphrey left the administration in July 1957 to return to the Mark Hanna Company, Eisenhower wrote his departing friend, "I shall regret your absence from our weekly Cabinet and National Security meetings and, of course, at those informal conferences where I have been accustomed not only to see you, but to lean upon your wisdom and experience, and integrity."[34] Even after leaving the administration, Humphrey remained the president's friend and adviser.

Early in Eisenhower's first term, Humphrey established himself as a major adviser. It became widely known that the president turned to Humphrey for counsel in economic and domestic matters as frequently as he turned to John Foster Dulles on foreign policy issues. Humphrey presented himself as a successful, vigorous, practical businessman whose mind was uncluttered with either complexities or doubts and who knew the simple truths in a very complex world. Humphrey had the ability to condense complicated ideas into workaday metaphors, a skill the president appreciated. For Humphrey the good life was dependent upon living within your income, a dictum that he believed should be followed by Treasury secretaries and managers of households. Hughes portrays Humphrey's style: "Vigorously and bluntly, he enlivened almost every Cabinet session with little polemics on checking deficits, spoken as ardently as Dulles' exhortations on checking Communists. And Humphrey at times almost seemed to view the deficits as the more menacing of the two enemies."[35] Perhaps the best description of Humphrey in decision-making situations was provided by Larson:

> Humphrey was probably the most effective official I have ever encountered, in the sense that, somehow or other he always seemed to get his way in a group. Just to observe his performance in a committee meeting was worth a year at Harvard Business School. To begin with, he was always totally prepared, with facts and figures all in place ready to be used at the right moment. He never said much early in a meeting. He radiated confidence and good humor. . . . With unerring instinct, he would wait until everyone else had had his say and until the meeting was on the verge of dissolving in confusion, and then he would say, 'Why don't we try this?' Quietly he would unfold a well-worked-out line of action, and the exhausted participants would gratefully seize upon the course that Humphrey knew all along would prevail.[36]

Humphrey's style and influence with the president engendered conflict within the administration. Steve Neal points out that the president's younger brother and intimate adviser, Milton, "had never been an admirer of the treasury secretary, whom he considered too rigid and unyielding in policy matters and 'much too certain of his infallibility.' The reflective Milton and the nonintellectual Humphrey were opposites. . . . Milton and Humphrey were to clash more than once, yet their differences did little to harm their respective positions with Ike."[37] Neil Jacoby, a member of the CEA from 1953 to 1955, also found dealing with Humphrey difficult. Jacoby, a professor of economics, complained that Humphrey was self-assured to the point of arrogance. Humphrey felt his sound, practical view had been sanctified by his business success; professors were theorists and dreamers who did not understand the realities of the world because they had never met the obligations of a payroll. Jacoby considered Humphrey to be an "economic illiterate" who had not learned anything from the Keynesian revolution: "Humphrey's view was that he had become Secretary of the Treasury to pursue a 'sound' fiscal policy, by which he meant keep the Federal budget in balance, 'come hell or high water.' . . . He would pound the table and raise his voice. I remember on one occasion his remarking that he'd run a big business and he wasn't going to have professors tell him how to run the treasury of the United States. This was a tip-off on a certain streak of anti-intellectualism that he had."[38] This attitude, reinforced by partisan concerns that there were too many Democrats in the Treasury Department, caused Humphrey to remove many policy-oriented economists from departmental ranks. Such behavior weakened the creative capability of the Treasury to respond to the recession of 1953–54 and provided an opportunity for Arthur Burns and the CEA to establish their policy credentials.

Nevertheless, in terms of economic policy, George Humphrey considered himself to be *the* expert adviser and conservative conscience within the administration. Humphrey was a traditional conservative who believed his own rhetoric and who expressed himself in clichés widely heard and revered in corporate board rooms. The secretary believed that inflation was "theft" caused by budget deficits that should be avoided "like the plague."[39] He advised the cabinet that the United States could not have full employment without war and that the administration should not be afraid of the "trickle down" theory. Humphrey explained his support of corporate tax cuts to the congressional Joint Committee on the Economic Report: "The goose that lays the golden egg is production. . . . If you haven't got a payroll, you haven't got consumers."[40] And, of course, Humphrey's most famous cliché was put forward in January 1957 when the secretary claimed that unless Congress found some way to cut Eisenhower's proposed 1958 budget, the United States would suffer a depression that "would curl your hair." With his publicized portrait of President Coolidge's secretary of the Treasury, Andrew Mellon, hanging in his office, Humphrey was a very reassuring figure for the business community.

For Humphrey both the political system and the economy were fragile. He frequently referred to Lenin's alleged quote on the collapse of capitalism coming from the "debauching" of the currency. Humphrey once told the columnist Joseph Alsop that "two more years of Truman would have landed this country in communism."[41] Humphrey believed that since 1933 the United States had been treading "a dangerous path" by following "unhealthy policies that induced inflation, depreciated our currency, and threatened to exhaust our credit." History demonstrated, at least to Humphrey, that if such policies were continued, inflation would soar out of control, resulting in the "utter collapse" of the nation.[42] The only remedy was to reverse course and establish a sound currency by reducing expenditures and balancing the budget.

Still, Humphrey was not what would today be called a supply-sider. As an economic conservative, he advocated that expenditures should be cut first before reducing taxes. He understood that major reductions in federal expenditures could be achieved only if the military budget was significantly decreased. High military expenditures not only prevented a balanced budget, they also promoted inflation by putting money into the domestic spending stream and not providing enough goods for consumers to buy. Humphrey was sure that military and government expenditures could be slashed if the Eisenhower administration would apply the cost-cutting techniques of successful businesspeople. Nevertheless, he was deeply concerned that the United States was going to have to provide jobs for at least one million new workers per year over the next decade or two. Each one of those jobs was going to require fifteen to twenty thousand dollars worth of capital. Thus, he felt strongly that the tax structure the administration had inherited from twenty years of Democratic rule would eventually be lethal for the economy because it was too high, it increased the cost of living, and it threatened to destroy the vital incentives to work, to save, and to invest.

Humphrey believed that high federal expenditures could be justified only during a national emergency. He complained that one of the dangerous legacies of the New Deal—people seeking solutions for their local problems through national intervention rather than local efforts—kept federal taxes and expenditures too high: "I think that in this country we must basically insist that the Federal Government's activities be more restricted and that we do not try to solve every local problem by running to Washington."[43] He opposed welfare state liberals by asserting that "as our economy produces more it does not mean that the Government must spend more, continually increasing the paternalism of Government. Just the opposite is true. The more we have the better able more of us should be to do for ourselves and be less and less dependent upon the Government."[44]

Humphrey was a vigorous advocate of cutting expenditures and taxes, balancing the budget, removing controls of prices and wages, stabilizing the value of the dollar, and maintaining business confidence. Hidden behind all

President Eisenhower, Treasury Secretary Robert Anderson, and Undersecretary Douglas Dillon, November 28, 1960. (Courtesy Dwight D. Eisenhower Library/National Park Service.)

of Humphrey's self-confidence and blustering clichés was his view that both the economy and the political system were fragile. But no Eisenhower adviser was more sure of himself; no one expressed ideas more forcefully in cabinet and National Security Council meetings.

Robert B. Anderson

In July 1957, Robert B. Anderson replaced George Humphrey as secretary of the Treasury. Anderson was born in Burleson, Texas, on June 4, 1910, the son of a cotton and dairy farmer. In 1932 he was elected to the Texas legislature on the same day he received his law degree from the University of Texas. He later served as Texas tax commissioner, taught law at the University of Texas, and was general counsel of the W. T. Waggoner estate, a land, cattle, and oil empire that sprawled over five hundred thousand acres in six Texas counties. Eisenhower appointed Anderson secretary of the navy in 1953, deputy defense secretary in 1954, and then, after a two-year break during which Anderson returned to the private sector as the president of a Canadian mining company, secretary of the Treasury.

General Eisenhower first met Anderson in January 1951, in Washington, D.C., when President Truman and his Treasury Department were having a well-publicized squabble with the Federal Reserve Board over the sale and price of U.S. bonds. When Eisenhower told his friend Chief Justice Fred Vinson that he did not understand this conflict, Vinson suggested that they call up Robert Anderson, who happened to be visiting Washington, and ask him to brief Eisenhower on the dispute. Vinson telephoned Anderson, and the Texan came to Eisenhower's hotel suite.[45] Eisenhower was impressed with Anderson's ability to explain this arcane subject in simple language, an ability that Eisenhower believed too few policy experts had. Thus, although strikingly different from Humphrey, Eisenhower developed a great respect for the tall, intelligent, religious, soft-spoken Texan.

Anderson continued to impress the president. As secretary of the navy, in 1953 Anderson desegregated the naval installations in the southern ports of Norfolk and Charleston quietly and effectively, thereby earning Eisenhower's "intense admiration."[46] On December 8, 1954, Eisenhower wrote to his lifelong friend from Abilene, "Swede" Hazlett, that Anderson "is just about the ablest man that I know anywhere. He would make a splendid President of the United States, and do hope that he can be sufficiently publicized as a young, vigorous Republican so that he will come to the attention of Republican groups in every state in the union."[47] In his own diary, Eisenhower recorded that Anderson "is one of the most capable men I know. My confidence in him is such that at the moment I feel that nothing could give me greater satisfaction than to believe that next January 20, I could turn over this office to his hands. His capacity is unlimited and his dedication to this country is complete."[48] At the end of Eisenhower's second term, the president wrote to Anderson that "I shall never be able to tell you of the depth of my gratitude for your readiness to return three and one-half years ago to governmental service as secretary of the treasury. Your sound grasp of fiscal, financial and general governmental problems ha[s] made you a real stalwart in this Administration and invaluable to me."[49] Eisenhower undoubtedly would have been shocked to learn that in June 1987 Anderson was sentenced by a federal district judge to a month in jail, five months' house arrest, and five years' probation for evading income taxes and operating an illegal offshore bank. Robert Anderson died in August 1989.

There was no issue of Anderson's integrity in July 1957 when Anderson took over the Treasury Department and became Eisenhower's chief economic adviser and spokesman. Within a few months, at Eisenhower's request, he was tutoring the president in monetary policy.[50] Anderson's economic views were as conservative as Humphrey's, but he was considered more knowledgeable in economics, easier to work with, and politically more skillful in dealing with Congress—Anderson was a personal friend of his fellow Texans and members of Congress, Sam Rayburn and Lyndon B. Johnson. He was less prone than Humphrey to predict dire consequences for the economic and political systems if his policy proposals were not followed. More importantly, the president acknowledged that his and the secretary's views regarding the budget and inflation were "nearly the same."[51] Anderson believed that the United States should have budget surpluses in times of prosperity and automatic budget deficits in times of recession. He was very concerned that the post–World War II period demonstrated that it was easier to achieve a deficit in a recession than a surplus in a boom and that growing recognition of this fact was encouraging a general expectation of inflation—an "inflationary psychology." The result was accumulating budget deficits that were causing further inflation. This problem was exacerbated by a hostile Congress, which prevented Anderson from attaining both the tax cuts and expenditure pruning he was advocating. Thus, Democratic control of Congress inhibited the Eisenhower administration from using fiscal policy to fight inflation through budget surpluses. Inevitably, the administration turned to monetary policy. According to Anderson, "achievement of a net Federal surplus over the business cycle as a whole would significantly ease the task confronting the monetary authorities and, in addition, would reduce the extent to which we may be forced to rely on monetary policy as a stabilization device. In my judgement, the lack of adequate [budget] surpluses in the prosperous years following the Second World War, which has resulted in a more than $30 billion increase in the public debt since the end of war financing, has meant that monetary policy has been called upon to bear more than its proper share of the burden in promoting sustainable economic growth."[52]

Anderson also believed that expanding deficits were decreasing the ability of the Treasury Department to manage the debt and fight inflation. The secretary considered inflation the major economic problem confronting the Eisenhower administration because it was the "enemy of growth" that threatened business confidence. During the recession of 1957–58, Anderson was a conservative influence on Eisenhower, arguing that the administration ought not to overreact in trying to reduce the unemployment rate because the more dangerous and lasting effect might be increasing deficits.[53] Following the recession, which produced a budget deficit of over $12 billion in FY 1959, Anderson was a strong proponent of immediately balancing the budget for FY 1960. This effort was successful in producing a small budget surplus in FY 1960, but it also brought about a sluggish economy that may have fatally damaged Nixon's campaign against Kennedy. Whatever the merits of Anderson's economic advice, it did not bring political success in either the 1958 or 1960 elections.

Finally, Anderson provided Eisenhower with a new justification for being conservative. He felt that conservative economic policy was necessary for the United States to meet its international responsibility since the dollar was used as a reserve currency by the major trading nations. Increasing difficulties in balance of payments meant that the United States was failing to meet this international obligation. Since 1953, foreign holdings of U.S. currency had exceeded U.S. gold stocks required for conversion from dollars to gold — and the gap was growing larger. If inflation continued it would lead to declining exports and an eventual loss of confidence in the dollar. Foreign governments would then cash in their dollars for gold, which would disrupt world trade. Anderson stressed that in becoming the "world's banker" since the end of World War II, the United States had an obligation to maintain confidence in the dollar. A lack of domestic discipline would have negative international consequences.[54] Anderson appealed to Eisenhower's powerful sense of duty as a world leader to conduct conservative domestic fiscal and monetary policies. Taking such a world view usually placed Eisenhower in opposition to conservative Republican thinking (for example, in his support of foreign aid), but, in this case, Anderson's arguments for sound economic policies to meet international obligations and to restore confidence in the dollar reinforced the conservative trend in Eisenhower's thinking in the second term. Anderson was not as self-confident as George Humphrey, or as brilliant as Arthur Burns, but no one was better at knowing how to appeal to Eisenhower's sense of duty.

The Bureau of the Budget

The Bureau of the Budget was created in 1921 by the Budget and Accounting Act and was originally located in the Treasury Department. In 1939, following the recommendations of the Brownlow Committee, the BOB was moved to the newly created Executive Office of the President (EOP) and became the first staff agency created to serve the institutional needs of the chief executive. The director of the BOB did not require senatorial confirmation. By the early 1950s its chief functions were (1) to prepare and administer the annual budget; (2) to serve as the president's legislative clearing house (i.e., to make sure that all legislative proposals from the executive branch were in accordance with the president's program); and (3) to serve as the president's organization and methods staff. The BOB staff (about two hundred and fifty professionals, with one hundred having doctorates) was characterized by technical competence and experience (at both the federal and state levels) in dealing with the problems of budgeting, accounting, administrative theory, and personnel administration. With the exception of the director and the deputy director, no political criteria were used in the recruitment of the staff; they were selected because of their professional skills. Moreover, Robert Merriam, an Eisenhower appointee to the bureau, pointed out that "from the very instant a young man joins the Bureau, he's instilled in the history of the presidency and the role of the BOB in helping the president, whoever he may be, whatever his views on politics may be."[55]

However, following the election of Eisenhower in 1952 the question arose as to whether the BOB could serve the interests of a Republican chief executive. President Truman and his budget director, Fred Lawton, were committed to preserving the nonpartisan integrity of the bureau. Soon after the 1952 election, President Truman suggested that President-elect Eisenhower send a representative to the BOB and observe the final decisions concerning the submission in January 1953 of the FY 1954 budget. Eisenhower responded by naming Joseph Dodge as his representative. General Eisenhower had met Dodge in Germany, where Dodge had successfully managed the fiscal affairs of the United States occupation. Although Dodge was critical of the policy decisions of the Truman administration, which he felt had led to a massive deficit, he was impressed by the technical competence of the BOB staff. He believed that the staff was qualified and willing to implement the budgetary philosophy of President Eisenhower and he saw no need for a partisan purge.[56]

Because the federal budget had soared from less than $4 billion in 1932 to over $80 billion in 1953, Eisenhower wanted the BOB to serve as his instrument for constraining spending trends. This role was emphasized by his choice of budget directors. The president's first two directors, Joseph Dodge (January 22, 1953, to April 15, 1954) and Rowland Hughes (April 16, 1954, to April 1, 1956), were bankers; Percival Brundage (April 2, 1956, to March 17, 1958) and Maurice Stans (March 18, 1958, to January 20, 1961) were accountants. The principal goal of the budget director was to help Eisenhower achieve his objective of providing for a strong national defense position and an adequate domestic policy within the constraints of an annual balanced budget, except in years of national emergency. Summarizing the budget director's role, Larry Berman writes, "Between 1953–1960 a budget director's task was to balance the numbers. They were technicians responsible for advising the President how government could be run for less money. Unlike their predecessors in the Roosevelt and Truman administrations, they were not public administrators, and, unlike their immediate successors in the Kennedy and Johnson administrations, they were not policy-oriented economists."[57] Their guiding principle was to make costs a dominant issue in decision making: otherwise expenses would multiply. Eisenhower's budget directors believed, perhaps naively, that if costs were a constant concern in administration councils, savings would multiply.[58]

In Eisenhower's presidency, the budget director was an important member of the team. Dodge was the second official Eisenhower selected for his administration (the first was John Foster Dulles), and the president, for the first time in history, elevated the budget director to cabinet status and made him a member of the National Security Council. Throughout his presidency, Eisenhower met regularly with his budget director and frequently supported him in the inevitable struggles that took place when cabinet secretaries objected to BOB cuts for their departments.[59] Eisenhower was particularly

Percival Brundage being sworn in as director of the Bureau of the Budget by Justice Harold V. Burton, April 2, 1956, with Eisenhower, former director Rowland Hughes (right), and Mrs. Brundage attending. (Courtesy Dwight D. Eisenhower Library/National Park Service.)

fond of Dodge, who achieved the most success in reducing expenditures, and Stans, who fulfilled a "mission impossible" by reversing the $12 billion deficit in FY 1959 to a small surplus in FY 1960.

Eisenhower was deeply committed to balancing the budget because he believed that excessive federal expenditures and deficits inevitably led to inflation. The government was under constant pressure, in both good and bad times, to provide more benefits and services than the public and politicians were willing to finance. Whereas proponents of new programs within the departments and the Congress tended to overestimate their benefits and underestimate their costs, the BOB stressed that it possessed the neutral competence to advise the president on how to fulfill his responsibility to keep aggregate costs down by casting a skeptical, penny-pinching eye on all new proposals. Each of the budget directors tried to enhance his bureaucratic power in constraining the budgetary demands of other cabinet secretaries by appealing to Eisenhower's conservative belief that deficits cause inflation. For example, Brundage warned Eisenhower in a May 1956 memo that the early successes of the administration to cut expenditures in 1953 and 1954

Official portrait of Joseph Dodge, director of the Bureau of the Budget.
(Courtesy Dwight D. Eisenhower Library.)

had been reversed; budget expenditures had increased since 1955 along with inflationary pressures. "These trends raise some basic questions. Are we currently moving contrary to the Administration's fundamental philosophy so as to foreshadow long-run economic dangers? As the Federal Government has taken on new and enlarged activities in dealing with national problems, has it allowed itself to interfere in some things which the people can individually (or through local groups or governments) do well enough for themselves? Have we gone too far in advocating or accepting desirable objectives which are leading to large and continued increases in spending?"[60] Similarly, Stans later argued that "the idea that a little inflation is good for us is a dangerous delusion. America dare not become so intoxicated by the tasty stimulant of inflationary expansion that it loses sight of the essential importance of financial integrity. A bit of inflation works out to be an installment on a lot of inflation."[61]

This narrow focus of balancing the budget did cause some dissension within the BOB; some of its members resented using costs as the sole criterion for decision making. These dissidents felt that such thinking condemned the bureau to a negative role and prevented it from being a constructive player in the formulation of reform legislation.[62] Nevertheless, such single-minded devotion to the narrow course by each of the budget directors did succeed in helping the Eisenhower presidency achieve three balanced budgets and led to its proposing balanced budgets for FY 1961 and FY 1962 (which were subsequently unbalanced by the Kennedy administration).

Arthur F. Burns

During Eisenhower's first term, George Humphrey's major rival in the making of economic policy was forty-eight-year-old Professor Arthur F. Burns. Burns was born in Stanislau, Austria, in 1904 and immigrated to the United States with his family when he was ten. He was a brilliant student, graduating Phi Beta Kappa from Columbia University in 1925 and receiving a Ph.D. in economics in 1934. In 1930, while studying for his Ph.D. and teaching economics at Rutgers, Burns attracted the attention of Professor Wesley C. Mitchell, an eminent American economist of the period and the founder of the National Bureau of Economic Research. He asked Burns to join the bureau and the two of them coauthored a major study of the business cycle. Burns succeeded Mitchell as director of research at the bureau in 1945 and continued in that role until Eisenhower chose him to be chairman of the CEA.

One of the reasons for Burns's selection was that he was recognized as a leading expert on the business cycle. The response to the selection was generally favorable, although *Fortune* magazine suggested two potential problems: "Perhaps the only serious question to be raised about the fitness of the Burns appointment is whether this scholar of the business cycle is enough of an operator to bring his advice to bear in the right places and at the right times. There might be a question, too, whether Burns' scientific caution, blending with the administration's political caution, might in fact create a political risk: that the new administration, by comparison with its predecessors, may seem to offer too little in the way of government influence on the course of economic affairs."[63] Neither one of these problems materialized.

Arthur Burns being sworn in by Frank K. Sanderson, White House administrative officer, as chairman of the Council of Economic Advisers, with President Eisenhower looking on. (Courtesy Dwight D. Eisenhower Library/National Park Service.)

Burns served as chairman of the CEA until December 1956, when he resigned for personal reasons. In his letter of resignation to Eisenhower, Burns wrote, "By giving the Council of Economic Advisers every possible encouragement and opportunity to bring economic knowledge to bear on the Nation's problems, you have honored and enlarged the scope of the economist's profession."[64] In Eisenhower's farewell to Burns before a cabinet meeting, the president praised his "honesty, accuracy, and sometime uncanny ability of prophecy."[65] Burns returned to the National Bureau of Economic Research, but he continued to advise the president through a series of letters. Subsequently he served as a White House counselor to President Nixon, as chairman of the FRB, and as ambassador to West Germany under President Reagan. Burns died in 1987.

During his confirmation hearings, Burns described his advisory role as nonpolitical. Puffing on his ever-present pipe, he promised to give the president his best professional judgment concerning the economy and then remain "eternally quiet."[66] The CEA would also prepare the annual Economic Report mandated by the Employment Act. In short, Burns originally viewed his role in terms of researching, analyzing, and recommending certain courses of action, based on professional, objective economic criteria. Burns later admitted that his original role expectations were unrealistic: "I thought that the Council would be engaged to a significant degree in long-term research on the needs of economic policy, and that we would be devoting little time to short-run economic problems. But all that collapsed. A recession got under way in 1953, and we had to mobilize all the energy we could muster in developing plans for limiting the recession. Soon after that, a threat of inflation came along."[67] As he became a major economic policy adviser to the president, Burns's role became increasingly political.

Eisenhower obviously liked Burns and found him a valuable member of his "team." In his memoir he described Burns as "one of the most brilliant economists in the United States."[68] By 1953, Burns was not only briefing the president, he was also instructing the cabinet. At the president's invitation, Burns would make a full presentation to the cabinet whenever there was danger of unemployment or inflation. Sherman Adams said that Burns's "adeptness in drawing out of the situation the points of the economic compass, . . . and his ability to sense the turn of events, made him an extremely valuable adviser, and Eisenhower . . . came to the conclusion that the Cabinet ought to have some schooling in the business of economics. . . . Burns made analyses of such things as audits and inventories and the various indices that economists use to measure the forces at play in the economy, and drew from these indices conclusions which he expressed in very understandable terms to the Cabinet." Indeed, Adams suggests that Burns was sometimes more influential than Humphrey.[69]

Burns became influential because he had the kind of expertise that Eisenhower needed and could give explanations that Eisenhower understood. He had also forged powerful White House allies in Gabriel Hauge and Sherman Adams, which assured his regular access to Eisenhower. Moreover, the president genuinely liked Burns, and, by bestowing praise upon the professor in an administration dominated by big businessmen, he increased Burns's policy influence. The president often read Burns's speeches and he reviewed the Economic Report each year. In early January 1955, when Humphrey attacked a draft of Burns's Economic Report as "socialistic," Eisenhower read the report and sent the following in a memo to Burns: "I have every conviction that it is going to be a magnificent document — even if some of our radical liberals will unquestionably call it a reactionary treatise, while the real reactionaries will call it a 'blueprint for socialism.' All of which probably proves that you are just about right."[70] On a more personal level, Eisenhower gave Burns portraits he had painted of Presidents Washington and Lincoln. On receiving the Washington portrait, Burns wrote to his boss: "This portrait, as well as the one you did of Lincoln last year, will help my children . . . to appreciate the three greatest Presidents of our beloved country."[71] *Fortune* need not have worried about Burns; he knew how to operate within the administration.

Burns and the CEA did have trouble operating with George Humphrey. While their conflicts were hidden during the first term, years later Burns admitted that there had been "serious clashes" with Humphrey. Burns felt that Humphrey did not understand countercyclical theory. In January 1955 he was told by his ally Gabriel Hauge that Humphrey was leading a cabal against Burns and his 1955 Economic Report. Burns later commented, "After this episode was over, I made no effort to conceal my feelings toward Humphrey. He had been so brutal in condemning the report. He didn't make one specific criticism, besides calling it socialistic. I really doubt that he had even read it."[72]

Despite this conflict, Burns was able to play a major policy role in the first Eisenhower administration because his economic philosophy was compatible with the president's policy goals. Burns wanted to reconcile welfare liberalism with economic conservatism. He understood that modern governments, with their huge powers to tax and spend, could no longer play a passive, nineteenth-century liberal role. As a result of the Depression, the New Deal, and the Employment Act of 1946, the issue was no longer whether to intervene but when and how to intervene. As a student of business cycles, he recognized that ups and downs were inevitable characteristics of a capitalist economy and that governments would employ their fiscal and monetary powers to moderate economic fluctuations. For Burns the policy dilemma was how to use governmental intervention without making government the dominant factor in the economy. Burns shared Eisenhower's fear that if the federal government became the dominant factor, our political traditions of freedom would be violated and the entrepreneurial spirit that is so vital for innovative private enterprise would be destroyed. Finally, Burns shared Eisenhower's Cold War perspective. In 1957, Burns wrote, "We have learned that in the course of a depression many men lose faith in themselves, and that some lose faith even in our economic and political institutions. We have learned that economic progress is a powerful weapon in the ideological struggle that of late has been stirring man's minds in distant lands, and that the continuance of property is our best answer to the Marxist prophecy of crisis and collapse of free economics."[73] Such thinking supported Eisenhower's view that managing prosperity was a component of national security policy.

Much of Burns's philosophy was derived from his studies of the Depression. Before 1929 the conventional wisdom of orthodox economics had been that periodic depressions were the price of progress in that they eliminated inefficient enterprises and encouraged labor to work harder. However, as the Depression continued, intelligent observers noted that efficient businesses were suffering bankruptcies, hard-working laborers were losing their jobs, and usually reasonable people were becoming desperate enough to be attracted to extreme solutions. They began to feel that the national government would have to develop the means to prevent such a catastrophe from happening again.

Burns believed that Hoover had waited too long to counteract the recession; early actions, when there were still significant levels of business confidence, might have been more effective.[74] When Hoover did act, he increased taxes in a vain attempt to balance the budget, which only accelerated the spiraling contraction of demand. Many of Roosevelt's policies had the effect of weakening the business confidence essential for economic recovery. Roosevelt's programs and his partisan hostility toward business caused many investors to fear that countercyclical policies would result in permanent governmental domination and the reduction in the profitability of investment. In Burns's words, "By spreading fear that the tax system was increasingly being used to redistribute income and to punish success, they weakened the incentives to invest and to innovate. In retrospect, there can be little doubt that the fiscal policies of the 1930's, which combined onerous taxation with sharply increased spending and borrowing, disrupted the confidence of many people in the country's economic future and thus reduced the effectiveness of the constructive measures taken at the time to lay a foundation for economic recovery and to speed its course."[75]

By supporting the need for the government to moderate economic fluctuations, Burns performed the contradictory feats of accepting several of Keynes's basic ideas while becoming known as a critic of the British economist. Burns accepted the Keynesian perspective that the economy would not automatically stabilize itself and that the government could and should intervene to promote stability. Indeed, government had a continuous responsibility to be "prepared to take preventive as well as remedial action."[76] He agreed with the Keynesian prescription of expenditure increases and tax reductions to prevent a recession and their policy opposites to inhibit inflation. But Burns was also critical of Keynesian doctrine because, in Herbert Stein's words, "he found it too simple and mechanical as an explanation of the economic process. It assumed as constant too many relationships that were variable, and whose variation would upset predictions based on Keynesian reasoning."[77] This meant Burns was very skeptical about the ability of economists to forecast accurately, and inaccurate forecasting was likely to cause economists to recommend policies that if implemented, would be counterproductive. Being more cautious than the more activist Keynesians, Burns did not believe that government could effectively prevent minor economic declines. (In the 1960s he was a vigorous opponent of Walter Heller's concept of "fine-tuning.") At their outset, such declines would trigger the automatic stabilizers: Revenue from personal and corporate taxes would decline, unemployment compensation would increase, and expenditures for farm price supports would rise. Conversely, inflation would automatically trigger the opposite responses, thus restricting aggregate demand. Only when the data indicated that economic conditions were worsening would Burns recommend more discretionary and activist policies—increasing the money supply, cutting taxes, and financing public works projects.

Burns, more than most Keynesians, believed in the early effectiveness of such monetary policies to combat recessions. While many Keynesians argued that expanding the money supply in the early stages of a recession would be ineffective because it was analogous "to pushing on a string," Burns felt that monetary policy could be usefully employed against an economic decline if it were used in a timely fashion: "It is not enough that the monetary authorities increase the availability and reduce the cost of credit during the declining phase of a business cycle. If such action is to be used with maximum effectiveness, it must come when the level of business and consumer confidence is high. This condition is more likely to prevail in the early than in an advanced stage of a business contraction, and it is most likely to prevail when the government is attentive to the need for maintaining policies that protect and strengthen economic incentives."[78] To fight inflation, Burns was also more willing to employ a tight money policy (pulling on the string) than the Keynesians were. In brief, Burns considered monetary policy to be more flexible and effective than the Keynesians did.

Burns conceptualized the high-employment economy of the United States as moving along a narrow road. On one side lay the danger of inflation; on the other, the danger of unemployment. Competitive markets do not automatically keep the economy on the narrow road. To avoid inflation or recession, the government must constantly monitor and occasionally intervene to moderate economic movements before they acquire momentum. The business confidence that generates prosperity can balloon into the overconfidence that launches speculative booms. The increase in unemployment can degenerate into a spiraling contraction. According to Burns, "In a high-level economy like ours, neither the threat of inflation nor the threat of recession can ever be very distant. We live in a world in which economic changes, both domestic and foreign, are continuous and many. If our economy is to advance firmly on the narrow road that separates recession from inflation, the Federal Government must pursue monetary, fiscal and housekeeping policies with skill and circumspection."[79] To stay on this narrow road of prosperity, Burns cautioned policymakers to make sure their occasional economic intervention did not threaten business confidence. Here, he agreed with Humphrey's belief that business confidence was a vital subjective stimulant necessary for economic growth. But, whereas Humphrey generally believed that business confidence should be maintained by the government's promising not to interfere in the economy, Burns postulated that "the Federal Government generates confidence when it restrains tendencies toward recession or inflation, and does this by relying largely on indirect means influencing private behavior rather than by direct controls over people, industries, and markets."[80] For Burns, the attraction of maintaining business confidence was that it could serve as an ideologically appealing alternative for major countercyclical interventions. Democrats and Keynesians frequently preferred more activist policies to promote economic growth and to counteract either recession or inflation. They would rely more on the accuracy of their forecasting model, rely less on the automatic stabilizers, and intervene earlier with discretionary changes in fiscal policy to steer the economy toward full employment.

Burns stressed that the United States had learned how to prevent another Great Depression but that it was still subject to the fluctuations of the business cycle. No country or economist had unlocked the key to promoting stable, permanent economic growth. He felt it was unrealistic for the public to expect perfection and that it was demagogic for Democratic party leaders to promise it. There would continue to be occasional periods of rising unemployment or price inflation. To demand frequent and massive interventions, as sometimes advocated by the more activist Keynesians and by liberal leaders such as Senator Paul Douglas or Walter Reuther, would cause more instability than stability.

Burns suggested that macroeconomic policies should be prompt, gradual, and flexible. Experience taught him that fiscal policy was less flexible than monetary policy for keeping the economy on the narrow road between inflation and recession. At the first warning signs of inflation or recession, the government should prepare a set of Keynesian-inspired countermeasures in case the automatic stabilizers prove inadequate. If the negative trends continue, relatively mild countercyclical policies should be initiated. Since we live in a rapidly changing economic world, no preconceived set of fiscal and monetary measures will work effectively in all circumstances; each threat to the economy requires its own creative response. If action is postponed too long, even strong and costly policies (massive tax cuts, expensive public works projects) may prove insufficient. Timing is essential. The policies should also be gradual and flexible because economics is not yet an exact science, and policymakers cannot be sure of the consequences of their actions. Immediate results cannot be expected. The propensity of a complex economy to emit mixed signals limits the accuracy of forecasting trends. Policymakers need to be able to shift gears quickly from fighting unemployment to fighting inflation. According to Jacoby, Burns's colleague on the CEA, "Economic analysis provides clues to trends and prospects; but so much remains unknown about the behavior of man, individually and socially, that our vision of the future is restricted. We can see our hands before our faces, but not much farther than that. All honest prognoses of the future of the economy must be labelled 'tentative and subject to revision.'"[81] Democrats interpreted this lack of faith in forecasting as reflecting Republican complacency—that is, a reluctance to use Keynesian tools to improve the performance of the economy due to satisfaction with the status quo. It should also be noted that there is a contradiction between Burns's advocacy of prompt responses to the dangers of either inflation and recession and his skepticism regarding the accuracy of economic forecasting.

From left to right, Sherman Adams, Raymond Saulnier, and Arthur Burns. Saulnier is about to replace Burns as chairman of the Council of Economic Advisers, December 3, 1956. (Courtesy Dwight D. Eisenhower Library/National Park Service.)

Raymond J. Saulnier

Arthur Burns resigned the chairmanship of the CEA on December 1, 1956, and was immediately replaced by Raymond J. Saulnier. Saulnier was born in 1909 in Hamilton, Massachusetts, graduated from Middlebury College in Vermont, and received his Ph.D. in economics from Columbia. As a young economist he was a colleague of Burns's at the National Bureau of Economic Research, where Saulnier became the director of the bureau's financial research program. He was a nationally recognized expert on mortgage finance and, during the Truman administration, was an adviser to the Department of Agriculture on farm credit. When Burns went to Washington, D.C., in 1953, he hired Saulnier as a special consultant to the CEA. Saulnier became a member of the council in 1955, replacing Neil Jacoby. In December 1956, Eisenhower accepted Burns's advice and appointed Saulnier as the chairman of the CEA.

The new chairman was never able to establish as close a relationship with the President as Burns had had. He suffered the disadvantage of assuming an advisory position in an administration that had been in power for four years and was set in its ways. Although Saulnier fulfilled all the formal roles of Burns, Eisenhower never acknowledged his chairman as an indispensable source of expertise. The chairman did attend all cabinet meetings, participated in meetings with congressional leaders, briefed the president on possible economic questions for press conferences, assisted in speech preparation, and advised the president on whether to sign or veto legislative bills, but he did not have the weekly scheduled meetings with the president that Burns had had. Still, he had good relations with White House assistant Gabriel Hauge and his replacement, Donald Paarlberg; in addition, he worked well with George Humphrey and even better with Humphrey's successor, Robert Anderson. According to Hargrove and Morley, "Like Burns, Saulnier also maintained that the Council must take a 'professional' stance above politics, but he was not as insistent on maintaining his confidential advisory relationship with the President when called to testify before Congress. Saulnier did not insist on testifying in executive session and was willing to allow the release of transcripts of CEA testimony."[82] Thus, while Saulnier carried on most of the advisory functions that Burns had performed, what was missing were the demonstrations of respect, praise, and affection that Eisenhower had bestowed upon Burns. Simply put, Saulnier was less of an inside player than Burns had been.

Philosophically, Saulnier was more conservative than Burns. In his book, Saulnier stresses his commitment to a competitive market-oriented economy because it provides "maximum opportunities for self-directed personal development."[83] Saulnier asserts that "only orthodoxy is viable in finance. We may be unorthodox without too much danger and possibly to our benefit in the style in which we have our houses built, in the music we prefer, and in dozens of other things that are important to each of us, in our fashion; but in finance we are orthodox or we are lost. . . . We must understand price stability as a condition prerequisite to the attainment of vigorous and sustainable economic growth, not merely as a desirable accompaniment to it. It is not an objective of economic policy competitive with the objective of vigorous and sustainable growth; it is a condition that makes that kind of growth possible." Therefore, "anti-inflation is the first imperative of economic policy. No other policy will work." Inflation, he asserts, should be controlled by a restrictive monetary policy and balanced budgets. In the late 1950s monetary policy could not have been employed to promote a higher rate of economic growth because of the large and continuing deficit in the balance of payments. He writes that future economic growth could best be encouraged by lowering income taxes on upper-income individuals and corporations so as to encourage higher rates of investment.

Saulnier defined himself as a parochialist and a pluralist: "I believe in things coming from the bottom up instead of from the top down. I'm concerned about centralization and, accordingly, I have trouble . . . with the problem of coordination of policy in a decentralized policymaking apparatus — decentralized in the sense that you've got the Fed over here, the Treasury under the White House, and the Congress up here. I don't want to be understood as advocating centralization of all that, because that would go against my democratic grain. You resolve this problem by establishing good working relations among these centers of influence."[84] This cautious perspective led Saulnier to oppose the more activist Keynesians who claimed they could rationally manipulate aggregate demand to insure more rapid economic growth: "I feel we should have more respect for what we don't know about this whole process. I'm not against tuning the economy—because I'm an activist in that—but don't try to persuade me that the Chairman of the CEA or the Chairman of the Federal Reserve Board or the President or the Secretary of the Treasury or all of them in concert have got a set of levers they can operate— and that they can make the economy do what they want. They can't."[85] Thus, Saulnier was not likely to be innovative in advising the president on how to reinvigorate the economy.

When Saulnier became chairman of the CEA in December 1956, the consumer price index was rising 3.5 percent a year, a figure that was considered frightening during the 1950s. Saulnier believed that his major function was to advise the president on how to reduce that inflation rate. He opposed the view that "a little inflation is a good thing," although he realistically accepted the idea that zero inflation was an impossibility. When pressed, he defined success in fighting inflation as preventing price increases of more than 1.5 percent a year.[86] A higher rate of inflation, he felt, would begin to feed off itself, creating an inflationary psychology that would lead to serious imbalances in the economy. Saulnier urged that all elements of economic policy be employed to combat inflation—that is, the budget should be balanced, the FRB should restrict the money supply, and the federal government should use its moral suasion to restore a balance between labor costs (which were rising disproportionately) and labor productivity.

Saulnier's single-mindedness on fighting inflation did not serve Eisenhower's political interests during the second term. It helped put the administration on the defensive against Democratic accusations of being more interested in money than in solving people's problems. A president needs a chair of the CEA who will offer flexible advice concerning what economic objectives can best be achieved under prevailing conditions, especially since such advice is not likely to come from the more bureaucratic and tradition-bound Treasury Department and the BOB. Arthur Burns provided Eisenhower with such advice. However, even if Saulnier had offered politically more appealing recommendations to Eisenhower that would have allowed the administration to regain the economy as a positive issue, it is possible that the increasingly conservative president would have rejected it.

Eisenhower's Economic Advisory System

Organizational concerns were an integral part of Eisenhower's political philosophy. He believed in organization and teamwork more than in individual heroism. Unlike John F. Kennedy, Eisenhower had never experienced combat; his career successes were based on his organizational skills. In at least one sense it could be argued that he was a more "modern" president than his younger successor because he understood the organizational requirements of the office—namely, that "presidential capacity depends in part on staff capabilities. To govern outside the White House, presidents must accept the challenge of organizational governance within the White House."[87]

Eisenhower was particularly interested in economic policy, but he recognized that he was not as knowledgeable in this area as he was in national security. Hence, he was more dependent on his economic advisers than on his national security advisers. In administrative matters, the secretary of the Treasury was given greater leeway than the secretary of defense. Eisenhower expected his economic advisers to teach him about such subjects as the business cycle, debt management, and monetary policy, as well as to make policy recommendations. Eisenhower was an unusual executive in that he was personally secure enough to admit to his underlings that he did not understand a particular subject and would like to have it explained. It is significant that several of Eisenhower's economic advisers—including George Humphrey, Arthur Burns, Gabriel Hauge, and Robert Anderson—performed this tutorial function and became his friends.

Eisenhower's economic advisory system was created and evolved in a manner that was compatible with his customary administrative practices. Each economic adviser had specific formal responsibilities, but each was expected to interact extensively with other officials in a variety of committee assignments. For Eisenhower, effective policymaking was most likely to result from the interaction of officials who were accustomed to working with each other. Teamwork was essential because major problems tended to cut across jurisdictional lines. In response to such major problems, the president would frequently set up a new committee charged with the formal responsibility of studying a specific problem and making specific policy recommendations.

When Eisenhower became president, he appointed Gabriel Hauge as one of his special assistants, a title that was later made more accurate by a change to special assistant for economic affairs. Hauge received his Ph.D. in economics from Harvard in 1947, and later joined General Eisenhower's campaign staff (on the recommendation of Thomas Dewey) as a researcher and speechwriter. In the White House, Hauge worked under Sherman Adams, enjoyed a great deal of access to Eisenhower, and continued to write speeches for the president. He advised Eisenhower on federal appointments to the Federal Reserve and recommended Arthur Burns for the chairmanship of the CEA. Hauge was also responsible for reviewing the economic aspects of proposed legislation as well as any foreign trade questions concerning tariffs, the control of which had been transferred in 1934 from the Congress to the president. Hauge and Burns worked out a division of labor whereby the special assistant was responsible mainly for microeconomic policies and the chairman was responsible primarily for macroeconomic policies. In 1958, Hauge resigned to take a position with a banking firm in New York City and was replaced by Donald Paarlberg, a Ph.D. in agricultural economics from Cornell who had been working under the secretary of agriculture, Ezra Benson.

In terms of macroeconomic policymaking, Eisenhower's major advisers were the secretary of the Treasury, the chair of the CEA, and the director of the BOB. Of these three positions, the least institutionalized in 1953 was the chair of the CEA. The CEA had been created by the Employment Act of 1946. Its first chairman, Edwin Nourse, had not been able to get along with Truman because he believed that being a professional economist precluded providing political support for the president; he was forced to resign in 1949. Its second chairman, Leon Keyserling, had alienated Congress because he was considered too partisan. Consequently, in 1952 Congress severely cut the budget for the CEA for FY 1953, anticipating that its funds would be exhausted by March 1953. Shortly after the 1952 election, Hauge recommended the continuance of the CEA in a memo to the president-elect:

> The continuing task of thinking up ways and means for keeping our economy a stable, expanding one falls rightly on your CEA. This Council . . . needs a complete housecleaning. . . . It is my opinion that the Council, given new Leadership, can become an indispensable economic headquarters staff for the immense task of focusing study and planning in the field of economic stability.[88]

In March 1953, Eisenhower appointed Arthur Burns as an economic adviser and asked him to investigate the situation and report back with a definite set of recommendations concerning the economic advisory function. The president indicated that he would prefer to have Burns as his sole economic adviser rather than a council of three economists, but he wanted Burns's considered judgment: "But I must warn you, I don't want a long report, because I don't know how to read." Burns quotes himself as replying, "'Mr. President, since you don't know how to read and I don't know how to write, the chances are that we may be able to get along.' That was the beginning of an extraordinary personal as well as professional friendship."[89]

During the spring of 1953, Burns demonstrated highly proficient political skills by consulting such administration officials as Nelson Rockefeller, Herbert Brownell, and Joseph Dodge and such congressional figures as Senators Robert Taft and Paul Douglas so that there would be no major opposition to his proposals. The two arguments of Burns were: "First, that the President definitely needed economic advice on a continual basis and on a professional level. Second, that a deliberative body would serve the President better than a single economic adviser."[90] Therefore, Burns recommended that the council be maintained as a professional group of economists operating in the Executive Office of the President rather than there being a single macroeconomic adviser operating as a part of the more politicized White House staff. In conformity with one of the Hoover Commission recommendations, Burns also proposed that the chair be granted administrative control of the council and its staff. The position of vice-chair of the CEA would be eliminated. To avoid the public squabbling that had occurred among the three council members in the Truman administration, communication from the CEA to the president would be channeled through the chair. With the endorsement of Hauge, Eisenhower accepted these proposals and easily pushed them through Congress. In August 1953, the CEA resumed its activities with Burns as chair. It had received a full year's appropriation from Congress and almost an entirely new staff hired by Burns. In addition, Eisenhower promptly nominated the chairman's recommendations for the council's two other positions: Neil Jacoby and Walter W. Stewart. Thus, within a few months, Burns had helped to save the CEA and to make it a major contender in the formation of economic policies within the administration.

By late spring 1953, Burns was not only briefing the president, he was also instructing the cabinet. At the president's invitation, Burns would make a full presentation to the cabinet whenever there was danger of unemployment or inflation. At a cabinet meeting on March 12, 1954, Eisenhower said, "Dr. Burns ought to come in at every Cabinet Meeting to summarize developments and keep us alert. He should be the Ghost of Banquo so we can't forget."[91] Until Eisenhower's heart attack in September 1955, Hauge and Burns also met privately with the president for a half hour each Monday morning at 11 A.M. Although these meetings were not their only contact with Eisenhower, they allowed Burns to brief the president on current economic trends and to broaden his understandings of economic problems.

But this did not mean that Eisenhower relied solely on Burns and the CEA for economic advice. The president was also meeting regularly with the secretary of the Treasury and the director of the Bureau of the Budget. George Humphrey tried to monopolize the role of tax adviser to the president, but was not successful.[92] Moreover, Bryce Harlow, a top White House aide, claimed that because of Eisenhower's commitment to balancing the budget, the director of the BOB was "tremendously influential" throughout the 1950s.[93]

In December 1956, Raymond Saulnier replaced Arthur Burns as chairman of the CEA. Although Saulnier never developed as close a relationship to Eisenhower as Burns had had, over the next four years Saulnier met regularly with the president at least once every two weeks, with sessions lasting about half an hour. In addition, according to Saulnier, "If I wanted to see him, I would ask my secretary to see if the president would have some time. And I never asked for time without getting it within a day or two, and if it were an emergency, you'd simply say it was that, and you would walk across the street and be there."[94] However, it is significant (in terms of who was most likely to influence the president) that when Eisenhower needed tutoring about monetary policy early in his second term, he turned to Robert Anderson instead of Saulnier.[95]

Saulnier describes two types of meetings with the president. The first type would concern a policy problem that might require an executive decision. Present at such a meeting would be the president, Saulnier, either Sherman Adams or Wilton Persons (Adams's assistant, who replaced Adams as chief of staff in 1958) or a member of their staff, and, if it was a tax proposal, a representative from the Treasury Department. Saulnier would normally meet along with Eisenhower in the second type of meeting — designed to keep the president informed about the business cycle or trends in unemployment. Both Burns and Saulnier were comparatively free to inform the president on any aspects of the economy they thought he should be advised about. Eisenhower preferred that these reports on the economy be direct and oral. According to Saulnier, the president would ask for specific recommendations and require that these recommendations be defended but would not probe to see the extent of agreement — or disagreement — among economists over a particular issue.[96]

Both Burns and Saulnier understood that "government is a continuous conversation, a never-ending conversation with your peers."[97] Both chairmen believed that in such conversations, their bargaining advantage was their professional expertise. Whenever there was a disagreement over the condition of the economy, they could cite the appropriate theory, refer to the proper historical analogy, and, most importantly, "trot out the numbers." Burns described his role in the Eisenhower administration:

During 1953–1956 . . . the Chairman of the Council had weekly scheduled meetings with the President. . . . He had full access to the President at other times and he used it when necessary. He represented the Council at weekly Cabinet meetings, made frequent reports on current and emerging policy requirements, and participated actively in Cabinet debates on economic matters. He served as Chairman of various Cabinet committees and used the opportunity to advance the Council's programs. He worked closely with the Secretary of the Treasury and the Chairman of the Federal Reserve Board. He and his Council colleagues spent a good part of practically every day striving for a consensus on policy issues with representatives of the various departments and agencies. The Council thus fought tirelessly within the Executive establishment for the policies that it deemed needed and proper.[98]

To facilitate systematic links with the other parts of government, Burns had suggested and Eisenhower had accepted that the Advisory Board on Economic Growth and Stability (ABEGS) be created. In 1954, Eisenhower by executive order created ABEGS with Burns as its chair. ABEGS was composed of undersecretary-level officers of eight (later expanded to ten) federal agencies most directly involved in the economy (i.e., the Departments of Treasury, State, Commerce, Labor, Agriculture, and Health, Education, and Welfare, and the Housing and Home Financing Agency, along with the CEA, the BOB, and the FRB). ABEGS met about once every two weeks. Burns viewed ABEGS as a forum where the policies and perspectives of each agency could be explained and coordinated in order to achieve as much compatibility as possible in line with the administration's overall economic strategy. Given the nature of bureaucratic politics, in which each agency strives to achieve its own objectives, this goal of coordination proved very difficult to achieve. The council, which saw itself as a planning agency whose major purpose was to advise the president on how to insure economic prosperity, had a very broad mandate that inevitably caused turf fights with more narrowly focused agencies. For example, in 1954 when the council was encouraging other agencies to accelerate public works expenditures to fight the recession, the BOB was still striving to fulfill its objective of holding down executive branch expenditures in order to balance the budget.[99] Similarly, the Treasury Department believed that it alone should determine how to handle the expanding public debt and resisted efforts by the council to coordinate this policy in conformity with the administration's prevailing macroeconomic strategy.[100]

The Eisenhower administration also saw the need for coordination at the highest levels of fiscal and monetary policies. This required the interaction and cooperation of the president, the secretary of the Treasury, the director of the BOB, the chair of the CEA, and the chair of the FRB. In October 1957, following a suggestion by the secretary of the Treasury, Robert Anderson, Eisenhower initiated a series of private, informal meetings with these four advisers (tentatively called the "Little Four"). A memorandum from the first conference stated: "The President suggested that the group meet regularly; regularity should minimize public comment. The President said the meetings could be in his office, at 1:00 PM over lunch, or at 6:00 PM with refreshments. He concurred in Secretary Anderson's suggestion of bi-weekly meetings and asked the Secretary to arrange them."[101] These meetings became one of the most important forms of interagency communication and cooperation established during the 1950s and proved useful in negotiating the administration's antirecession policy in 1957–58. They at least insured that the FRB knew the administration's view of economic prospects and what needed to be done and probably the reverse as well.[102] These informal meetings were eventually institutionalized during the Kennedy years as the Troika (minus the chair of the FRB) and the Quadriad (including the chair of the FRB).

CONCLUSION

Each of these major players in economic policy in the Eisenhower administration brought a supply of intellectual capital to the job that influenced recommendations and decisions. The "constant conversation" among the president, the Treasury secretary, the chair of the CEA, the director of the BOB, and the chair of the FRB resulted in the Eisenhower presidency's assuming a conservative role in managing the country's prosperity. The very size and importance of government in terms of taxes, public expenditures, and regulation of the money supply meant that it could no longer be a neutral factor within the economy; the issue, therefore, was how to make it a positive force. Just as an administration requires a strategic doctrine to steer its defense policy, so does it need an economic philosophy to direct its fiscal and monetary policies. That economic perspective became more conservative during Eisenhower's second term. In the first term, Eisenhower, influenced by Arthur Burns, tried to reconcile economic conservatism with welfare liberalism. In the second term, Eisenhower became more conservative because of his fears of inflation and unbalanced budgets and because of the pressure for new programs from the Democrat-controlled Congress. Moreover, Robert Anderson pulled Eisenhower in a more conservative direction by appealing to his sense of international responsibility and by emphasizing that it was vital to maintain the stability of the dollar because the dollar was used as a reserve currency by the major trading nations. The lack of innovative economic advice from Saulnier and the CEA during the second term left the administration overly dominated by the orthodox, conservative policies of the Treasury Department, the BOB, and the FRB. This put the administration in a politically vulnerable position for which the Republicans paid the price in the 1958 and 1960 elections.

3

The Political Economy
of the 1950s

Whenever economic advice is formulated, received, and acted upon, it is influenced by a set of political and economic factors from the external environment. A policy history that restricts itself to information directly connected with the formulation of that particular policy is likely to distort how policy decisions are actually made. Lower level bureaucrats may make decisions based on narrow grounds, but top officials, operating in a more generalized atmosphere, are subject to a wide array of pressures. This is especially true for the president, who functions in the most highly politicized office in the nation. The president and his policymakers are likely to select options that promise to provide positive responses to more than one problem.[1] That is, since any presidentially decided policy is evaluated in terms of its political feasibility, a policy choice may be selected because it also answers a political demand of the moment, such as one that calls for the president to look decisive, or to appear compassionate, or to assuage a wing of the president's party.

To understand economic policymaking during the Eisenhower administration, one must understand the 1950s. This chapter is *not* an attempt to write a history of that decade; rather it is an effort to point out the external factors that influenced the mindsets and the decisions of the administration's policymakers. Today the decade of the 1950s appears tranquil because of the greater turbulence of the decades surrounding it, but it was a period that included such international conflicts as Korea, French Indochina, Guatemala, Quemoy and Matsu, the Soviet invasion of Hungary, the Suez crisis, Lebanon, Berlin, Cuba, and the increasing threat of a nuclear war between the United States and the Soviet Union. Domestically, the decade was characterized by growing racial conflict, McCarthyism, three recessions, and rapid demographic and technological changes. A *New York Times* editorial published in June 1957 and aimed at the expanding number of college graduates captures the contrasting moods of the decade: "Our graduates are certainly not coming out into a static society. On the contrary, they are probably entering one of the most exciting periods in all the world's history, and one of the most challenging. That this is a time of peril has been repeated almost endlessly. It is also a time of magnificent opportunity."[2]

AN ECONOMIC OVERVIEW OF THE 1950s

The 1950s were characterized by a high rate of population growth, which peaked in the mid-1950s. From 1950 to 1960 the population increased from 158 million to 180 million. The general fertility rate peaked in 1957 at 122.7 births per 1,000 women in the 15 to 44 age group; in the year 4,322,000 babies were born (in 1986, the general fertility rate was about half that rate, or 64.9). An even more interesting contrast to the late 1980s is that during the 1950s the average family size was larger for middle- and upper-income strata than for lower-income groups. The economic significance of this baby boom, according to Harold Vatter, "endowed the 1950s with the consumption, production, and public-service patterns of a children's influx."[3] For example, Ronald Lora points out that "total school enrollment, virtually unchanged for twenty years, in the 1950s expanded by 13 million pupils. . . . Enrollment in kindergarten and grades one through eight, stable in the 1940s, jumped by more than 10 million in the 1950s."[4]

Much of this population growth was concentrated in the standard metropolitan statistical areas (SMSAs) — central cities with their surrounding suburban areas of fifty thousand or more. The total population grew by about 18 percent between 1950 and 1960, while the population of the SMSAs expanded by 24 percent. The population of the central cities increased by about 8 percent during the decade, while the population in the suburban areas surrounding the central cities soared by 47 percent. By the end of the 1950s, "suburbanites already outnumbered city dwellers, and were stretching their lead daily, for the suburban growth was forty times that of cities."[5] Suburbanization was destined to have enormous consequences for the economy and the politics of the United States.

A suburban America represented a more middle-class society, a more consumer-oriented economy, and a more mobile and less community-oriented life style. The majority of Americans now owned their own homes, which were increasingly filled with consumer goods bought from the nearby shopping centers. Between 1950 and 1960 the number of households with television sets rose from 9 percent to 87 percent. Television quickly became the major channel through which advertisers enticed viewers to buy consumer goods and politicians communicated with voters. Equally important was the automobile. According to William O'Neill, "In 1945 there had been 25 million automobile registrations; in 1960 there were 2.5 [times] as many. By then nearly one-fifth of suburban families had two cars and two out of every three workers in the United States were commuting by car to their places of employment."[6] The boundless wants of the American consumer, combined with those of the defense industry, depleted domestic resources at a prodigious rate, and the United States was forced to begin importing monumental amounts of goods from overseas.

One of the major themes of the 1950s was that while conditions generally improved, consumers were encouraged to want even more, both for themselves and for their children (even for their pets!). Whereas in the 1940s many people had been afraid of the possible recurrence of a depression and would have been content with assurances that the economy would provide them with a steady job necessary to finance a house and a car, by the 1950s citizens desired far more. People now wanted to move up to a better home as their incomes escalated; they wanted a second car, a second television set, a second phone, a second vacation, and so on. Faced with having to pay a mortgage and monthly installment payments on several durable consumer goods, and preparing to send their sons and daughters to college, Americans relied more and more on successful governmental management of the economy. The good life would collapse if there was recession and jobs were lost or if there was inflation and credit became tight. Thus, improvement in the standard of living multiplied the pressure on the federal government to ensure the continuance of mass employment, mass production, mass consumption, mass education, and the availability of mass credit.

In retrospect, members of the Eisenhower administration believed that they had successfully responded to these pressures. In his memoirs, Eisenhower boasts that during his term in office the GNP rose about $100 billion (in constant prices) or nearly 25 percent, to well over $400 billion. This economic growth was not fueled by inflation. While the 1939 dollar was worth 52 cents in January 1953, the 1953 dollar had lost only about 5½ cents of its value by 1961. Eisenhower concluded that "looking back from 1960, we could see that in those intervening years the achievement of a widespread prosperity and the repulse of an insidious inflation had helped to bring a chance for the good life to more Americans than ever before."[7]

By the end of the 1950s, however, the Eisenhower economic growth record was being challenged. While poverty was reduced during the 1950s, the Eisenhower growth record was marred by three recessions (1953–54, 1957–58, and 1960–61), and the real GNP increased at an average annual increment of 2.9 percent, notably below the 4.7 percent annual increment for the period 1921–1929 and the 3.72 percent per year estimated for the period 1879–1919. Moreover, partly because of the Korean War, the economic growth rate for the first half of the decade was considerably faster (4.7 percent) than for the second half (2.25 percent). According to Vatter, "If the annual growth rates of GNP in the first half of the decade are extrapolated and viewed as the poten-

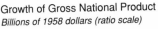

Figure 3.1   The Goals of National Economic Policy, 1952-60

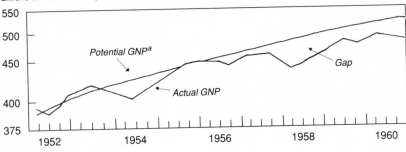

Growth of Gross National Product
Billions of 1958 dollars (ratio scale)

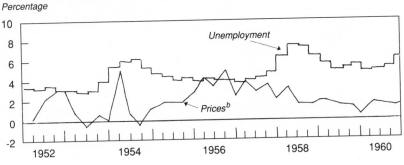

Unemployment and Prices
Percentage

Source: G. L. Bach, *Making Monetary and Fiscal Policy* (Washington, D.C.:
Brookings Institution, 1971), 104. The data used in the figures are seasonally
adjusted quarterly totals at annual rates.
[a] Trend line of 3.5 percent through middle of 1955 to fourth quarter of 1960.
[b] Percentage change in GNP price deflator at annual rates.

tial growth rate applicable to the last half of the decade, the data reveal a
substantial and continuous gap between potential and actual GNP from the
beginning of 1956 through 1961."[8] (See Figure 3.1.) By the end of the 1950s
the Democrats and many Keynesian economists were blaming Eisenhower
for blocking the potential growth possibilities of the economy because of the
president's obsession with balancing the budget and tightening the money
supply in order to prevent inflation. Hence, the dilemma of the Eisenhower
administration was that economic growth came to be viewed as the best
available solution to a number of problems just as the growth rate was slowing down.

A sluggish growth rate meant a slowly rising unemployment rate. The
post–World War II era had avoided the massive unemployment rates, ranging

from 15 to 25 percent of the civilian labor force, that had occurred between 1931 and 1940. The average unemployment rate for the 1950s was 4.6 percent, or about 3.2 million people unemployed. The lowest unemployment rate was achieved during the Korean War, but thereafter the rate crept upward. Fortunately, the postwar recessions were brief; there were eleven months of contraction in 1948–49 (under Truman), thirteen in 1953–54, eight in 1957–58, and ten in 1960–61. But as Figure 3.1 illustrates, the recoveries during the 1950s failed to reduce the unemployment rate to the levels achieved in earlier recoveries. The average unemployment rates during the three recovery periods ascended from 3.0 percent (1951–53), to 4.2 percent (1955–57), to 5.3 percent (1959–60). Vatter stresses that "this pattern of ever higher unemployment rates as the economy proceeded through its recession and recovery sequences during the decade was one of the more disturbing aspects of the economic history of the times."[9] This issue became more salient as the unemployment rate reached 7.6 percent in 1958, was succeeded by a short, sluggish recovery, followed by a rising unemployment rate in 1960, which seriously wounded the Nixon campaign.

Finally, the Eisenhower administration considered the slowly rising prices during the 1950s a far more ominous trend than did Democratic critics. Although consumer prices edged up at a rate of only 1.4 percent a year from 1952 to 1960, the president and his economic advisers were deeply disturbed that inflationary pressures had not been overcome by three recessions. They also felt that rising prices were hindering economic competition with the nations of Western Europe and Asia, causing an alarming drain on U.S. gold supplies. To combat inflation, the Eisenhower administration generally supported the FRB's policy of tightening the money supply and, in addition, proudly produced balanced budgets in FY 1956, FY 1957, and FY 1960. The significance of this latter feat is demonstrated by the fact that the United States has produced only seven balanced budgets since the end of World War II.

THE COLD WAR

The most important contextual factor that influenced public policy during the 1950s was the Cold War, a unique international situation in which there was neither peace nor war between the United States and the Soviet Union but instead a condition of chronic tension between the two superpowers, each of whom had the nuclear power to destroy the other. A shooting war was avoided (barely) by deterrence based on the balance of terror; cooperation was inhibited by mutual hostility. Both sides spent enormous sums of money on increasingly sophisticated and deadly weapons. The two nations' economies were competing in what was mutually viewed as a long-term struggle to sustain military power and to appeal to the hearts and minds of the newly emerging Third World nations. The Cold War became institutionalized during the 1950s; its presence was felt and acted upon by policymakers. Eisenhower explained this Cold War context to a friend: "It is scarcely an exaggeration to say that every domestic problem of any moment must, before it can be properly solved, be examined critically against the background of our international situation."[10]

The pervasiveness of the Cold War perspective inevitably influenced a number of policy areas. The conflict with the Soviet Union was used to justify the expansion of presidential power, the increase in military expenditures, and the taxes needed to finance national security. In the 1990s it is easy to forget that under the influence of the Cold War, it was primarily Democratic liberals who pressured Eisenhower to spend a lot more on defense throughout the 1950s. That pressure multiplied after the Soviet launch of Sputnik on October 4, 1957. For many Americans, Sputnik symbolized that the United States was no longer protected by two vast oceans and technological superiority. Soviet technological success induced the United States to engage in educational reforms, such as the passage of the 1958 National Defense Education Act. School systems became part of the war against communism. In brief, during an era frequently characterized by political stalement, a profitable strategy for a policy entrepreneur was to point out how a particular reform (the interstate highway system, civil rights, the space program) would promote the national interest of the United States in its deadly struggle with the Soviet Union.

The Cold War added a national security component to macroeconomic policy. The death of Stalin, the rise of Khrushchev, and the end of the Korean War suggested that conflict with communism and the Soviet Union would probably not be settled by a shooting war; the most likely forecast was a long competitive struggle. In such a protracted conflict, the "winner" would probably be determined by economic capabilities. For the Eisenhower administration that meant growth with stability brought about by balanced budgets and monetary discipline, whereas, for many liberal Democrats, that meant unleashing the full potential of the economy through the use of discretionary Keynesian policies. When it was announced in 1958 that the Soviet Union's economic growth rate had become roughly twice that of the United States, the Democrats were able to put the Eisenhower administration on the political defensive.[11] In short, Cold War tensions did not reduce the partisanship of domestic politics, although Eisenhower did change the context of party politics during the 1950s. It is to that subject we now turn.

THE PARTISAN CONTEXT

Eisenhower's Popularity

In the political struggle between the Democratic and Republican parties during the 1950s, the dominant factor was Eisenhower's personal popularity. Since the end of World War II, both parties had wooed Eisenhower because his broad-based appeal made him an ideal presidential candidate.[12] Because of his World War II record, Eisenhower did not have to prove his leadership skills or his goodness. The American people liked Ike before, during, and after his two terms as president. Eisenhower averaged 64 percent approval in Gallup's monthly polls measuring how Americans evaluate the president's performance, a rate that still exceeds the rates of all post–World War II presidents except Kennedy.[13] Only in 1958, due to the recession and reaction to the Sputnik launch, did Eisenhower's monthly popularity dip below 50 percent. When Eisenhower left office in January 1961, he still had the support of 60 percent of the electorate.

Eisenhower's personal appeal, which cut across partisan and philosophical lines, posed great difficulties for his Democratic opponents. Gary Reichard points out that "evidently voters could (and did) see whatever they wanted to see in Eisenhower Republicanism at the time: in a Gallup Poll of 1955, 65 percent of those who called themselves liberals conceived of the president as a liberal, while 61 percent of those identifying themselves as conservatives thought he was a conservative."[14] Few people hated Eisenhower; even his Democratic adversaries liked him. Given such attitudes, it was difficult to mobilize voters against Eisenhower.

Eisenhower was also more popular than his political party. Until Eisenhower's 1952 victory, the Republican party had been out of power since 1932, and it was still the minority party in terms of party identification of the American electorate. In the 1952 elections, Ike ran ahead of most Republican members of congress because he attracted the votes of some Democrats and many independents. It was clear that Eisenhower put the Republican party in power and not the reverse. In Nixon's words, "The Republican Party is not strong enough to elect a President. We have to have a presidential candidate strong enough to get the Republican Party elected."[15] After Eisenhower's heart attack in September 1955, when there was intense speculation whether he would be able to run again, Richard Rovere wrote, "Everyone . . . is persuaded that the Republican cause would be hopeless without the President; the public opinion polls all seem to show that just about any Democrat could beat just about any Republican except Eisenhower, who can beat anyone anywhere."[16]

Eisenhower's popularity was based on his ability to convince the public that he possessed integrity and competence and that he acted "as a patriotic moral leader eager to preserve traditional standards of decency and common sense even when coping with the most controversial issues."[17] It was reinforced by the performance of the Eisenhower presidency, which generally provided peace and prosperity. And it was maintained by a leadership style that was suited to the 1950s. After the highly politicized presidencies of Franklin Roosevelt and Harry Truman, the American people were receptive to a president who generated less partisan heat. Eisenhower's commitment to social harmony was contingent upon a style of executive leadership that emphasized restraint, moderation, and delegation of authority. This style of leadership not only was compatible with the less partisan, more consensual mood of the 1950s, it actually fostered that sentiment. The Eisenhower administration helped to defuse (but not necessarily solve) many of the divisive issues of the period. Although Eisenhower's 1952 campaign shouted about a "crusade," once the general became president, he soon became a symbol of conciliation. The people not only liked Ike, they trusted his judgment.

Because Eisenhower played the role of president differently than his two predecessors had played it, his political skills were largely unrecognized during the 1950s. Over the past twenty years, however, revisionist scholars have successfully challenged the notion that Eisenhower was a political amateur.[18] Eisenhower was an effective politician who liked to think of himself as acting "above politics." From this lofty position he often controlled the morally high ground against his political opponents. He was able to convince himself and many of the voters that his decisions were motivated not by personal or partisan concerns, but by the public interest. For much of the public, to act politically is to act in a partisan, selfish manner, while to act nonpolitically is to act in a public-spirited way. In the public's eye, so much of Truman's behavior reeked of political calculation, but Eisenhower's conduct appeared to be that of a folksy war hero from the Midwest applying common sense to a difficult job that he had accepted out of a sense of duty rather than for pleasure. This image was carefully cultivated by the president and his advisers.

Eisenhower's style of leadership made him a very difficult target for the Democrats. He deflected much criticism by employing an administrative style that emphasized the delegation of authority to staff and line officials. By effective leadership he did not mean heroic leadership; for Eisenhower, leadership meant insuring that individual officials and complex organizations would pull together as a team. At his first presidential press conference in February 1953, Eisenhower explained, "Now look, this idea that all wisdom is in the President, in me, that's baloney. . . . I don't believe this government was set up to be operated by any one acting alone; no one has a monopoly on the truth. . . . We must work together."[19] Teamwork was essential because, as the president readily admitted, he was not—and could not become—an expert in all the policy areas in which he was expected to make decisions.

Hence, in Eisenhower's administrative system, each staff and cabinet official was expected to solve the problems within the area of delegated authority and within the limits of established policy. These procedures allowed Eisenhower to share the credit for successful policies and to diffuse the political heat for unpopular policies. Thus, a whole series of officials, ranging from John Foster Dulles in foreign affairs to Sherman Adams in domestic political affairs to George Humphrey in economic policy to Ezra Benson in agricultural policy, served as lightning rods for the administration. This allowed Eisenhower to emphasize his unifying role of chief of state, hoard his personal popularity, and avoid partisan strife. The cost of this administrative style was that it sometimes made him look like an out-of-touch executive dominated by cabinet officials and staff members.

Electoral Politics of the 1950s

Table 3.1 summarizes the electoral results of the 1950s. The figures demonstrate that Eisenhower was consistently more popular than the Republican party. Eisenhower won two landslide presidential elections because he was able to attract Democratic and independent votes while holding the (minority) Republican vote, but he was not able to weaken the partisan loyalty of a plurality of voters to the Democratic party. Voters who identified themselves as Democrats continued to outnumber those who labeled themselves Republicans by a ratio of three to two. In the words of several electoral experts, "The tide toward Eisenhower was a transient one which was registered in votes rather than in shifts of underlying party loyalty. Democrats who had voted for Eisenhower in 1952 and 1956 went on considering themselves Democrats, voting Democratic in off-year elections and even in some measure voting Democratic at lower levels after a presidential vote for Eisenhower. . . . He drew personal votes but failed to convert his Democratic admirers to his party."[20] This failure would prove costly to Eisenhower.

In 1952 Eisenhower received over 55 percent of the vote, winning thirty nine of the forty eight states. Adlai Stevenson, a popular candidate, received three million more votes than President Truman had won in 1948, but the governor of Illinois carried the electoral college votes of only eight southern states and West Virginia. Although Eisenhower received almost twelve million more votes than Thomas Dewey had in 1948, the Republican party was able to attain only a slight plurality of the vote in the congressional elections, picking up twenty-two seats in the House and one in the Senate. This gave the Republicans tiny majorities in the 83d Congress (1953–54).

In the 1952 presidential election, the Democratic slogan was "You Never Had It So Good." Democratic literature compared the massive unemployment that plagued the nation under the last Republican president, Herbert Hoover, with the current unemployment rate of 2.4 percent. In an election

Table 3.1 Results of National Elections, 1948–1960

Election Year	Presidential elections			House elections			Senate elections
	Democratic % of Total Vote (no. of votes)	Republican % of Total Vote (no. of votes)	Electoral College	Democratic % of Total Vote	Republican % of Total Vote	Net Gain in Seats	Net Gain in Seats
1948	49.5 (24,105,587)	45.1 (21,970,017)	303–189	51.6	45.4	75D	9D
1950				48.9	48.9	28R	5R
1952	44.1 (27,314,649)	55.1 (33,936,137)	89–442	49.2	49.3	22R	1R
1954				52.1	47.0	19D	2D
1956	42.0 (26,030,172)	57.4 (35,585,245)	73–457	50.7	48.7	2D	1D
1958				55.5	43.6	49D	15D
1960	49.8 (34,221,344)	49.5 (34,106,671)	303–219	54.5	44.8	22R	2R

Source: Stephen J. Wayne, *The Road to the White House*, 3d ed. (New York: St. Martin's Press, 1988), 301–302; Norman J. Ornstein, Thomas E. Mann, and Michael J. Mallin, *Vital Statistics on Congress* (Washington, D.C.: Congressional Quarterly, 1987), 47–49.

eve broadcast, President Truman summarized the Democratic party strategy by warning, "This election may decide whether we shall go ahead and expand prosperity here at home or slide into a depression."[21] In brief, the Democratic party's argument was that a Republican presidency would repeat the mistakes of the business-dominated administrations of the 1920s and end the prosperity the Democrats were producing.

The chief Republican slogan was that after twenty years of Democratic rule, "It's Time for a Change." In the Republican advertisements, Eisenhower talked about high taxes, the rising costs of living, corruption in the Truman administration, communism, and Korea. To counter Democratic charges, Eisenhower gave stronger and stronger pledges during the campaign that he would not undo the progressive policies of the New Deal and would use the full power of the federal government to avoid a depression. *Time* magazine, in its analysis of the election results, stressed that Eisenhower won, not because of the economic issues, but because "never has a people looked so critically at a superficially successful present and voted so overwhelmingly for a more solidly based future."[22]

In the 1954 congressional elections the Republicans lost control of both the House and the Senate. The Democrats picked up nineteen seats in the House, which gave them a majority of 232 to 203, and one seat in the Senate, which gave them a majority of 48 to 47. These shifts were frustrating for Eisenhower because during the campaign he traveled about twenty thousand miles campaigning for Republican candidates, delivering 204 speeches in 95 cities.[23] Eisenhower overcame his scruples against campaigning for congressional candidates "to prevent an Old Guard take-over," which he feared would soon end Republican influence.[24]

Because of the 1953–54 recession, Eisenhower recognized that he and his party were vulnerable on the economic issue. By election time the unemployment rate, while declining, was still about 5 percent, which the Democrats claimed was a scandal. An October campaign memo by Nixon warned Republicans that the Democrats "can always *outpromise* us on economic issues. Only our *performance* on economic issues can win for us, and performance may not take place in time to win for us on those issues by election day."[25] It did not.

In the 1956 election, the Democrats waged a somewhat different presidential campaign than in 1952. In the 1952 campaign the Democrats had predicted that the party of Herbert Hoover could not provide prosperity; in 1956 they charged that the prosperity that the Republicans had provided was unevenly distributed. Farmers and workers had not received their fair share. Stevenson stressed that Eisenhower had appointed too many big businessmen like George Humphrey to his cabinet to have a fair and compassionate administration. Although Stevenson claimed he was not antibusiness, he charged that Eisenhower had become overly dependent on his big business advisers, with their narrow, self-serving view of the national interest. They had cut taxes for the rich and turned over natural resources to private interests. In one of Stevenson's speeches he proclaimed, "We cannot understand — and we will not accept — turning the government over to men who work full time for the wrong people or a limited group of people."[26] However, it proved difficult to pin the label of tool of big business on the former General.

Still, Democratic party strategists were acutely aware that Eisenhower was far more popular than his party and even his policies. One of Stevenson's electoral strategies was to prevent Eisenhower from maintaining an unassailable position "above politics"; the Democratic goal was to identify Eisenhower with the Republican party and its policy positions. This strategy was impeded, first, by Senate Majority Leader Johnson's and House Speaker Rayburn's practice of seeking legislative compromises with Eisenhower, and, secondly, by the president's heart attack on September 23, 1955, and his surgery for ileitis on June 8, 1956, which made such partisan attacks appear unseemly. The Democrats' target then became Nixon, who was far less popular than Eisenhower. Democratic speeches and advertisements stressed that a part-time Eisenhower meant a full-time Nixon. Often implicitly, but sometimes explicitly as in Stevenson's election eve speech, the Democrats warned that Eisenhower might die and that Nixon could become president. To counter this argument, all Eisenhower had to do was campaign vigorously and look healthy, which he did.[27]

As the incumbent, Eisenhower ran under the most ideal conditions imaginable. There was peace, prosperity, and progress. The mild recession of 1953–54, forgotten by voters, had been followed by the unprecedented prosperity of 1955, which spilled over into 1956. With suburban homes, automobiles, television sets, and clothing selling at record rates, there was little dissatisfaction for the Democrats to mobilize.

Two of Stevenson's campaign staff later reflected on their frustration in confronting the insurmountable obstacle of Eisenhower's popularity. Kenneth Davis wrote, "Awesome to all, gratifying to most, dismaying to the few who believed that a complacent and ill-informed America drifted in a dangerous world was this renewed evidence of Eisenhower's tremendous appeal to the average citizen. His popularity seemed to tower like a rock above the political seas. Every adverse argument, every citation of adverse evidence, seemed to break futilely against it."[28] Similarly, John Bartlow Martin complained that "the most maddening thing about the 1956 campaign was Eisenhower's apparently indestructible popularity. . . . He was almost totally above the battle, unreachable. Moreover, people did not seem to identify him with failures of his administration, and while they might not like things his administration had done, they did not hold him responsible. . . . Eisenhower was, above all, the man of peace, and no matter how often Stevenson declared that neither party wanted war, the Democrats remained in the public mind the war party."[29] Thus, the startling events of late October 1956 just before the election—the Suez Crisis and the Soviet invasion of Hungary—only reinforced most voters' attitudes that in this dangerous world, they preferred Eisenhower at the helm.

Eisenhower won over 57 percent of the vote in 1956, carrying forty-one states with an electoral college vote of 457, and receiving over nine million more votes than Adlai Stevenson. However, the personal nature of Eisenhower's victory was revealed by the fact that the Republicans lost two House seats and one Senate seat in the congressional elections. Thus, Eisenhower became the first president since Zachary Taylor in 1848 to be elected without his party's winning a majority in at least one house of Congress. A University of Michigan electoral study concludes that the president's victory "was accomplished by an even larger proportion of ticket-splitting by Democrats and Independents than was observed in 1952. Three out of four of these people who voted for Mr. Eisenhower rejected the party whose ticket he headed."[30]

Unfortunately for the Republicans, conditions were not ideal to regain ground in the 1958 congressional elections. The nation was still suffering the effects of the 1957–58 recession; of the forty-nine House districts in which incumbent Republicans lost their seats, thirty-eight districts still had substantial unemployment.[31] In addition, a major scandal erupted in the administration when it was discovered that Sherman Adams, Eisenhower's chief of staff, had used his influence to benefit Bernard Goldfine (a New England businessman) and had received special gifts in return. The scandal was uncovered by the Democrats in the late spring of 1958. It festered over the summer, and Adams was forced to resign in September. Finally, Eisenhower was often on the defensive for what most Democrats and even some Republicans (like Nixon and Rockefeller) believed was an inadequate response to the launch of Sputnik in October 1957.

Thus, the Democrats picked up forty-nine seats in the 1958 House of Representative elections and controlled that body by a margin of 282 to 153, the largest Democratic majority since 1936. Republican House defeats were heaviest in the Midwest, where twenty-three seats were lost, and in the East, where twenty seats were lost. In the Senate, the Democrats added fifteen seats, the largest shift of seats from one party to another in that chamber's history. When the Senate convened in January 1959, the Democrats controlled it by a margin of sixty-four to thirty-four. The 1958 senatorial elections were significant because they weakened the power of southern Democrats. Whereas in the previous decade there had been approximately an equal number of southern Democratic and northern Democratic senators, after 1958 there were twenty-four Democrats from the South and forty from the North and West. In brief, the southern conservative Democrats with whom Eisenhower could make deals were losing influence to the northern liberal

Democrats. These northern Democrats would increasingly put Eisenhower on the defensive, and one of them, Senator John F. Kennedy, would be elected president in 1960.

In January 1961, Kennedy, the youngest man ever elected president, replaced Eisenhower, the oldest man (until Reagan) ever to occupy the White House. The catchphrase of Kennedy's campaign was "I think we can do better." Actually, the United States was doing well, but Kennedy, astutely appealing to the optimistic "can do" spirit of the American people, loudly proclaimed that the previous decade's accomplishments could be significantly improved upon. Kennedy's claim that new leadership was needed "to get the country moving again" implied that under the "old" leadership, the nation was stagnating. The 1950s, according to the Democrats, had been a period of the "great postponement." Problems, such as inadequate economic growth, racial tensions, poverty, the missile gap, and the Soviet challenge in the Third World, which had been avoided, could have been solved if they had been confronted by a more vigorous leadership. Eisenhower's pride in avoiding the depression many had feared was interpreted as complacency by the youthful Kennedy. The senator simply — and unrealistically — promised to do "more" on virtually every issue. In essence, the Kennedy campaign was the culmination of an effort by the Democrats to subject the Eisenhower administration to ever higher standards of performance.

The Republican Party

Adlai Stevenson liked to picture the Republican party as a two-headed elephant. One head was the Old Guard, the frustrated conservative supporters of Senator Taft, who, after Taft's death in 1953, gradually became followers of Senator Barry Goldwater. The other consisted of the more moderate "Modern Republicans" who supported Eisenhower. The Republicans had been out-of-power for twenty years; that lack of governing experience meant there were many in the party, especially in the Old Guard, who had little sense of what could actually be accomplished by a new Republican president. One of Eisenhower's political goals was to reinvigorate the Republican party so that it could successfully compete against the Democrats without being dependent upon his personal popularity. As Eisenhower wrote to his friend, British Prime Minister Churchill, "If I could devote myself exclusively to a political job, I'd like to take on the one reorganizing and revitalizing the Party."[32] One measure of the president's interest was the fact that party affairs were on the agenda for at least 37 out of the 239 cabinet meetings held during the Eisenhower presidency.[33]

Eisenhower took a gradualist approach in promoting his conception of the Republican party. Despite Eisenhower's 1952 campaign rhetoric about heading a crusade, once in power, he emphasized incremental policy change. The president understood that public opinion supported many New Deal programs and that any Old Guard attempt to dismantle them would have negative electoral consequences. As Eisenhower tried to explain to the most conservative of his brothers, Edgar, "Should any political party attempt to abolish social security, unemployment insurance, and eliminate labor laws and farm programs, you would not hear of that party again in our political history."[34] Eisenhower hoped that by reconciling liberal humanitarian policies with fiscal conservatism, he could broaden the electoral base of the Republican party, thus depriving the Democrats of their hold on the "common man." He also wanted to attract younger men to the party—(Eisenhower's views toward women were not progressive)—who would modernize its structure and policy perspective. Greenstein concludes that "in the interest of building a stable Republican majority, he was prepared to moderate his fundamental conservatism. Voicing political sentiments that were more liberal than his private credo made sense to him in domestic policy."[35] As suggested in chapter 2, Greenstein's conclusion is more accurate in describing Eisenhower's behavior in the first term than in the second.

Eisenhower understood that as president his main function was to govern and that he would need Democratic support to govern successfully. In June 1953, he wrote a friend, "As of today, every measure that we deem essential to the progress and welfare of America normally requires Democratic support in varying degrees."[36] Such support became even more vital when the Democrats gained control of both houses of Congress after the 1954 election. The president often expressed his affection for southern Democrats, who he believed were more intelligent and responsible than members of the conservative wing of his own party. In private conversations, Eisenhower labeled those of his party's right wing as "the most ignorant people living in the United States."[37] He condemned Goldwater "for trying to parlay woeful ignorance into political popularity."[38] Sometimes Eisenhower fantasized that it would be easier to govern if he could create a third party by merging southern Democrats and Modern Republicans.[39]

Eisenhower never created a third party and never succeeded in making Modern Republicanism the dominant force within his party. Some moderate Republicans, like Senator Jacob Javits and Emmet Hughes, criticized the president for not providing more dynamic leadership. They particularly disapproved of Eisenhower's increasing conservatism in his second term, which was brought about by his concern with balancing the budget. In Javits's words, "Among people like myself there was the hope that he would turn out to be interested in the party enough . . . to bring it to a more progressive stance and therefore to give it greater status as the alternative in the two party system. And I would say in that regard our hopes were never realized. But the President had these instincts . . . except that he found it very difficult to distinguish between economy in government and the things that government had to do in order to answer many of the problems of the people."[40] A more rigidly conservative Eisenhower handicapped moderate Republicans from competing successfully with the increasingly liberal Democrats. The Democrats could promise to do more by spending more in the policy areas of health, education, and defense.

While some moderate Republicans expressed disappointment in Eisenhower's presidency, many members of the Old Guard turned bitter, condemning Eisenhower for defeating Taft, betraying Joseph McCarthy, accommodating the New Deal, and continuing Truman's containment policy. According to James Sundquist, conservatives "abhorred 'me-tooism.' Their goal for federal policy was retrenchment — in the size of government, its budget, its debt, its impact on private enterprise, and its tax rate."[41] For good measure, they also demanded an end to negotiations with the Soviet Union and the immediate liberation of Eastern Europe. Perhaps the most scathing criticism of the president came from William Buckley, the editor of the *National Review.* Buckley was outraged that the Republican party had disavowed Taft, a man of principle, for Eisenhower, a man of "ideological toothlessness." In Buckley's mind Eisenhower simply did not understand the twin threats of communism and liberalism. Taft was forsaken because Republican delegates were seduced by Madison Avenue propaganda machines like *Time* magazine that proclaimed that only Eisenhower's popularity could lead the Republican party back to power. Buckley conceded that Eisenhower was popular, but, echoing liberal complaints about Eisenhower's leadership, he stressed that "personal charm . . . cannot move vast political landscapes." In Buckley's inimitable prose,

What the New Republicans needed was a great political shapelessness, an infinite ideological plasticity which, on approaching the great unresolved political problems that have arisen out of the growth of Communism and the omnipotent State, could be relied upon to ooze its way over these problems, without . . . friction. The Eisenhower approach was designed not to solve problems, but to refuse, essentially, to recognize that problems exist.[42]

In brief, conservative Republicans criticized Eisenhower's leadership style for blurring the conflicts between Democrats and Republicans, a political stance which also frustrated liberal Democrats.

The Democratic Party

Leaders of the Democratic party believed that Eisenhower's popularity was blocking their mission to complete the "unfinished business" of the New and Fair Deals. For Democrats, who considered themselves political professionals, it was humiliating to be defeated by someone who claimed to be a political amateur. During the 1950s two sectors of the Democratic party evolved conflicting strategies in dealing with the president. A moderate congressional group, led by Senator Lyndon B. Johnson and Speaker Sam Rayburn, stressed cooperation with Eisenhower in order to establish a record of legislative achievement. The more liberal, activist wing of the party, led by Adlai Stevenson and including many Democratic members of Congress, emphasized confrontation with Eisenhower in order to sharpen the issue differences between the two parties. Both sets of Democrats tried to successfully perform a very sensitive task: criticize effectively an aging war hero and popular president presiding over a period of perceived peace and prosperity.

One safe way to attack Eisenhower was to criticize his administrative style. Attributing many of Truman's problems to sloppy staff work, Eisenhower was determined to develop a highly specialized and efficient staff system. However, the Democrats accused him of overorganizing the White House and underusing the political power of the office. Organization was viewed as an enemy of innovation, creativity, and the fulfillment of the president's political responsibilities. The Democrats charged that the increases in the White House staff were not designed to help the president but to replace him. This was particularly true of Sherman Adams's role as assistant to the president. In reality, Adams served as the first White House chief of staff. In creating such an administrative position, Eisenhower was accused of distancing himself from information, conflict, and options. Critics saw the president as shielded rather than informed by his staff.[43] Attacking Eisenhower's decision-making style drew attention in a politically acceptable manner to his military background, age, and declining health. In Elmo Richardson's words, "Eisenhower's view of the executive branch as 'a great organizational body' and his emphasis on teamwork as the basis of leadership convinced some Americans that he was unable to realize the heroic potential of the presidency."[44]

The Democrats claimed that Eisenhower's leadership was comforting rather than challenging—"the bland leading the bland." By appeasing the Old Guard, Eisenhower was preventing himself from leading a progressive charge—he was blowing an "uncertain trumpet." Democrats repeated jokes about the Eisenhower doll—"wind it up and it does nothing for eight years." Instead of being blamed for a chaotic mess, the Eisenhower administration was criticized for complacency, an accusation that indirectly supported the contention that Eisenhower's staff system generally performed well. Because the administration was rarely in disarray, the opposition was forced to argue that the apparent surface calm hid festering problems that would be more difficult to solve in the future.

Eisenhower's leadership style and the improving conditions of the 1950s forced the Democrats to grope for issues and campaign themes. Stevenson demonstrated the Democratic dilemma when he wrote a friend in 1955, "I think we realize that mediocrity, materialism, social indifference and repulsive showmanship cannot be forever disguised by wholesome smiles, golf clubs, and a Bible firmly clutched beneath the right arm if seldom read; and somehow I feel that ways and means must be found to get at these imperfectly preceived realities and incomprehensible language by means that touch masses. It will be hard, if not impossible, . . . with prosperity, peace and a contented press."[45]

The major Democratic charge was that Eisenhower's administration was dominated by one interest—big business. Democrats felt they were more capable of governing fairly because they represented a wider array of interests. Stevenson was careful to state that he and the Democrats were not anti-big business; they simply believed that the public interest required that a broader range of Americans be taken into account. Democrats labeled the members of Eisenhower's first cabinet as eight millionaires and a plumber and accused the president of surrounding himself with "Big Dealers." The business orientation of the Eisenhower administration was blamed for tail fins on cars, the Edsel, frivolous luxury consumption, the decline in the quality of television shows, and cheating on TV game shows, as well as lack of national purpose. Stevenson's speechwriters tried to show that

it was the business community that determined the nation's fiscal policy, which in turn affected national defense, which in turn influenced the bluff-and-backdown diplomacy. It was the business community's hostility to public power, its primary commitment to personal monetary profit, that determined the Administration's view of the T.V.A. as creeping socialism, incited the give-away (as Democrats called it) of natural resources in the public domain, and caused the government to make haste very slowly indeed in the development of atomic energy for productive uses. It was the business community's faith in the automatic beneficence of a free market . . . that determined the Administration's apparent indifference to the plight of the family sized farm. It was the business community's awareness that its concepts of government would prove vastly unpopular, if frankly stated, that determined the duplicity of the Administration's public relations—its substitution of vague slogans for clear ideas, its constant effort to manipulate rather than inform public opinion—and it was the business community's domination of the means of mass communications that made this duplicity effective.[46]

On the other hand, the pragmatic Senator Johnson and Speaker Rayburn advocated that congressional Democrats play the role of the loyal opposition—in Parmet's words, "three parts loyal and only one part opposition."[47] Their strategy was to encourage and to cooperate with the progressive part of Eisenhower's policies, ultimately giving the president more than he asked for. This required all of the legislative skills of Johnson and Rayburn, who met regularly with Eisenhower and had to decipher how far the Democrats could push without provoking the president's veto, which was usually lethal — between 1953 and 1960 Eisenhower used his veto 181 times and was overridden by Congress only twice. The congressional leaders' strategy was complicated by the fact that liberal Democrats preferred to provoke Eisenhower's use of the veto in order to sharpen the contrast between the two parties. Johnson and Rayburn preferred achievements. According to one of the majority leader's aides, "In Johnson's eyes, it was the continual pushing of issues without bringing anything to achievement that had toppled the Truman Administration. He was convinced that the Democrats needed to demonstrate responsible accomplishment in order to return to power."[48]

Johnson and Rayburn felt vindicated after the 1956 elections when the Democrats retained majorities in both the House and the Senate while Adlai Stevenson suffered a crushing defeat. Stevenson and his liberal supporters interpreted the situation differently, believing that a distinctive, attractive party program could not be established during a presidential campaign. In Sundquist's words, "The attacks on the Republicans had to be made, and the programs had to be assembled and presented to the public, day by day and week by week in the long years between presidential elections — and the only place where that could be done was on Capitol Hill. Failure to achieve those objectives was the direct consequence of the Johnson-Rayburn approach to legislative leadership. . . . The 'responsible' compromises which were the pride of the congressional leaders might be necessary to get bills passed but they blurred the image of the Democratic Party."[49] The way to weaken Eisenhower was to challenge him more aggressively. The mechanism created to do that was the Democratic Advisory Council (DAC).

The DAC, created by the Executive Committee of the Democratic National Committee on November 27, 1956, was a committee authorized to proclaim party policy in the periods between the national party conventions. Some of its original members were Adlai Stevenson, President Truman, Averell Harriman, and Eleanor Roosevelt. Johnson and Rayburn refused to join the DAC because they viewed it (correctly) as competing with their legislative leadership. Senators Estes Kefauver and Hubert Humphrey joined immediately, and John Kennedy and Stuart Symington were members by 1959. Eventually, the DAC had over thirty members, including most of the Democratic candidates for the 1960 presidential nomination with the exception of Lyndon Johnson. Six auxiliary committees were also created to advise the DAC on a variety of subjects, such as foreign policy and economic policy. The Harvard economist John Kenneth Galbraith headed the economic advisory group. Galbraith penned the famous line that Eisenhower's budget policies resulted in the United States' living in a condition of "private opulence and public squalor."[50]

The DAC subjected Eisenhower to greater demands and criticisms. It also reflected a countertrend to complacency, articulated by Stevenson as a new willingness "to feel strongly, to be impatient, to want mightily to see that things are done better."[51] The Democrats responded to and encouraged this change of mood. Because of the general prosperity, the Democrats began to structure their programs to narrower social groups and geographical areas.

As the demands for the government to do more in both domestic and foreign affairs grew, the best solution seemed to be economic growth. Rapid and sustained economic growth would reduce the unemployment rate and provide the tax revenues to finance more defense and social expenditures. The economic policy group of the DAC stressed that the Eisenhower administration was retarding economic growth through its stodgy concern with balancing the budget and false fears of inflation. Liberals advocated that the United States ought to be pursuing a more aggressive form of Keynesianism, labeled the "New Economics," which called for a more active manipulation of aggregate demand by fiscal and monetary policies to reach the full employment potential of the economy. Under Eisenhower, according to Walter Heller, "Policy thinking had been centered more on minimizing the fluctuations of the business cycle than on realizing the economy's great and growing potential."[52] Kenneth Davis summarizes the DAC economic reports: "The Federal budget . . . ought to be purposefully used as an instrument of economic growth. Instead, under Eisenhower, it was being used to stunt growth and prevent adequate spending for imperative needs in the public sector of the economy. As a result, the nation had been kept in recession half the time since 1953 and its growth rate had been held to less than half what it should have been."[53] Thus, by 1958 Democratic liberals viewed Eisenhower's avoidance of a deep recession and his countercyclical economic policies as a minimal fulfillment of the president's role as manager of prosperity. The challenge was to perform the prosperity role in terms of the latest scientific advances in the New Economics.

Eisenhower's emphasis on combating inflation by balancing the budget was viewed by the Democrats as a misplaced priority that benefited bankers and businesspeople at the expense of workers and farmers. Democratic politicians countered Eisenhower's rhetoric about the necessity of a "sound dollar" with their own concern for "sound people." For liberal Democrats rising unemployment and the slower rate of economic growth in comparison with the Soviet Union and U.S. industrialized trading partners were more significant and dangerous than creeping socialism or creeping inflation. Hence, the more militantly conservative "New Eisenhower" that emerged in 1957–58 was placed in a far more vulnerable and defensive position than the earlier, more moderate Eisenhower. As one of Stevenson's aides gleefully noted, "The New Eisenhower, colliding head-on with the new economics, became increasingly identified in the public mind with one side of a basic issue, and the less popular side at that."[54] Eisenhower's position ceded to the liberal Democrats a monopoly in proposing legislation to deal with the most pressing problems of the late 1950s. The New Eisenhower seemed to have no vision beyond balancing the budget — an inadequate political posture at the end of the decade.

CONCLUSION

In spite of three recessions, the economy generally prospered during the 1950s. One of the decade's developments was that as economic conditions improved, Americans, rather than being satisfied, were encouraged to want more. The major dilemma for the Eisenhower economic policymakers was that as economic growth came to be seen as the best response to a number of problems, the growth rate began to slow down.

In 1952 the Democrats opposed the Republicans' using blunt instruments. Raising the specter of Herbert Hoover, the Democrats claimed that the Republicans were dominated by big business and would inevitably lead the country into another depression. When this did not happen, the Democrats shifted their attack to stress that Eisenhower was not providing rapid enough economic growth to match the country's cold war adversary, the Soviet Union, or economic competitors in Western Europe and Japan. Moreover, the Democrats charged that the Eisenhower prosperity was not providing social justice. When the Eisenhower administration defended itself by citing pertinent economic statistics, it was accused of being complacent and materialistic, consumer-oriented rather than people-oriented. By the late 1950s the Democrats were claiming that by using the New Economics, they could produce a faster and fairer prosperity.

As the 1950s progressed, the Democrats held the Eisenhower administration to ever higher standards of performance. To bring about full employment, they advocated maximal rather than moderate rates of economic growth. After 1956, Eisenhower grew less effective in responding to this criticism. His growing conservatism and concern for balancing the budget caused more confrontations with the increasingly powerful Democratic majorities in Congress and lessened his ability to promote the interests of moderate Republicans. The president's budget priorities contributed to a logjam of legislative bills and to the feeling that he was blocking progress. By the late 1950s, elections and public-opinion polls demonstrated that while Americans continued to "like Ike," they also favored programs that the president opposed. Senator Kennedy capitalized on this frustration by emphasizing that he could get the country moving again through vigorous leadership and by fulfilling the heroic potential of the presidency. Thus, at the end of the decade, the aging Eisenhower was still personally popular, but his ideas were increasingly viewed as old-fashioned. One of those "old-fashioned" ideas was balancing the budget, the principal focus of the next chapter.

4

The Battle over the Budget

One of Eisenhower's "old fashioned ideas" was that unless there was a war or a recession, the United States should have a balanced budget. Eisenhower's growing commitment to a balanced budget increasingly influenced politics and policy throughout the decade. Nothing belies the conventional image of Eisenhower as a passive president in domestic affairs as much as his vigorous efforts to bring about three balanced budgets during his time in office. Democrats complained that budget policy was the tail that wagged the dog, but for Eisenhower it *was* the dog. He saw budget policy as a strategically important measure of the discipline necessary to maintain the democratic way of life. Eisenhower generally did not view budget policy as a discretionary instrument that could be used as advocated by the proponents of "new economics" to manipulate aggregate demand.

EISENHOWER'S BUDGETARY GOALS

The Eisenhower administration inherited a budget crisis from the Truman presidency. Although Harry Truman was as fiscally conservative as his successor and had produced three balanced budgets during his seven years in office, the Korean War, beginning in June 1950, had forced the Truman administration to accept massive increases in the defense budget. Truman's defense budget had soared from $12.2 billion in FY 1951 to $46.3 billion for FY 1954. As the government changed hands in January 1953, national defense was consuming about 70 percent of the federal budget. President Truman's last budget, submitted to Congress in January 1953, estimated total revenues at $68.7 billion and total expenditures of $78.6 billion, leaving a deficit of $9.9 billion for the fiscal year running from July 1, 1953 to June 30, 1954. In 1953 the accumulated annual budget deficits from the Depression and especially from World War II and the Korean War added up to a national debt of $267 billion, dangerously close to the $275 billion statutory limit authorized by Congress.[1]

During the transition period, Eisenhower's future director of the Bureau of the Budget, Joseph Dodge, had met regularly with Frederick Lawton, Truman's director, concerning the presentation and submission of the FY 1954 budget. It was also Dodge's responsibility to explain the budgetary facts of life to Eisenhower's new and politically inexperienced cabinet at a pre-inaugural cabinet meeting at the Hotel Commodore on January 12, 1953. According to Dodge's estimates, during the two preceding years Congress had authorized, over and above the actual deficit, a prodigiously expensive rearmament effort which was not covered by current revenue. Since FY 1950, these "unfinanced authorizations" had totaled $81 billion. "This sum," according to Charles Murphy, "represented claims against current and future government income or borrowings and, given the acceleration of the military buildup, the peak weight of the claims was scheduled to fall during the first two years of the new Administration—that is, in fiscal 1954 and 1955."[2] Meanwhile, mandatory tax cuts were scheduled under existing legislation to take place in FY 1954 and FY 1955, which would reduce revenue by about $8 billion per year. Dodge likened the administration's financial plight "to that of a family with an accumulated debt four times bigger than its annual income, with never more money in the bank than it needed to cover one month's living expenses, facing a ten percent reduction in income and with current bills for C.O.D. purchases hanging over its head larger than a year's total income."[3] Dodge's discouraging message was that the Eisenhower administration would certainly not be able to balance the budget immediately and would have enormous difficulty achieving this goal during its first four years in office.

Eisenhower, however, was determined not to allow the "mess" he inherited from Truman to block him from achieving his budgetary goals. On October 2, 1952, in Peoria, Illinois, candidate Eisenhower had promised, "My goal, assuming the cold war gets no worse, is to cut Federal spending to something like $60 billion within four years. Such a cut would eliminate the deficit in the budget and would make way for a substantial tax reduction."[4] As president, Eisenhower informed the public that he was immediately imposing a new budget philosophy, though he realized it would take time for budget deficits to be transformed into a budget surplus.

Balancing the budget was a strategic goal of President Eisenhower. In July 1953, he wrote a friend, "I am committed to an Administration of economy, bordering on or approaching austerity."[5] Whereas the Democrats charged that the goal of balancing the budget reflected a lack of social vision, Eisenhower believed a balanced budget was a mathematical assurance that the public interest was being served frugally. When the budget was unbalanced because of unnecessary expenditures, narrow interests benefited at the expense of the public interest. Eisenhower accepted—privately, not publicly—the Keynesian concept of employing budget deficits to stimulate aggregate demand in order to offset a contraction in the economy, but he felt that generally the government should operate under the fiscal rule of annually balanced budgets. This discipline of matching revenues with expenditures was necessary for democracy because demagogic politicians were tempted to cater to the demands of the present set of voters at the expense of the next generation. In Eisenhower's view, a lack of fiscal discipline would inevitably lead to rampant inflation, regimentation, and the end of our democratic way of life.[6]

In his memoirs, Eisenhower writes, "The making of a federal budget imposes one of the most burdensome problems that confronts responsible officials. Seldom if ever will a government department recommend a reduction in current expenditures—the demand for more and more sums out of the federal Treasury is incessant and insatiable. Invariably the aggregate of these annual requests far exceeds the amounts projected in income."[7] Although he was involved in preparing the annual budget, it was an onerous chore for Eisenhower because of his ambivalence on the subject. He never completely escaped the pre–World War II belief that high federal expenditures could be justified only in a national emergency such as a depression or a war. His modern side accepted the need for liberal programs to satisfy human needs and for the inevitable evolution of modern weapons. As a candidate in 1952 he had promised both to balance the budget and to implement a number of progressive programs that would increase federal expenditures. In a memo to his first budget director in November 1953, Eisenhower explained, "I consider it a necessity for this Administration to announce broad and liberal objectives in certain fields that affect our whole country directly or indirectly, and which serve also to fix in the public mind the character of our political thinking. So in (a) slum clearance and public housing, (b) utilization of America's water resources, (c) extension of social security and old age benefits, I should like to put ourselves clearly on record as being forward-looking and concerned with the welfare of all our people."[8] During his first term, the end of the Korean War and economic prosperity allowed Eisenhower to avoid a hard choice between his conservative and liberal propensities. The president was confronted with far more difficult budget choices in his second term.

Early in his presidency Eisenhower believed that painful choices could be avoided because of waste and duplication in the federal bureaucracy resulting from twenty years of Democratic party rule. Placing economy-minded Republican businessmen in administrative positions would quickly reduce bloated bureaucracies. An indication of how much "fat" Eisenhower budget officials felt was in Truman's FY 1954 budget was contained in Dodge's instructions to each governmental agency to cut expenditures by at least 10 percent.[9]

Eisenhower also believed that his budgetary goals could be achieved by instituting a "subtraction process" to counter the "additive process" that had become entrenched under the Democrats. The additive process is a natural tendency in government whereby each year politicians and bureaucrats add new programs to respond to the national crises of the moment and incrementally increase the budgets for most old programs. In addition, very few old programs are ever eliminated because of alliances with political appointees, bureaucrats, pressure groups, and members of Congress designed to assure both continuance and annual increments in budget allocations.

A successful subtractive process would be dependent upon the effectiveness of the director of the BOB, Joseph Dodge, and the secretary of the Treasury, George Humphrey. To enhance their bureaucratic clout, in 1953 Eisenhower promoted Dodge to cabinet-level status and placed both Dodge and Humphrey on the National Security Council. With Eisenhower's encouragement, these two men forged an alliance "to take a hard look at everything" proposed by other officials. Their goal was to cut spending "to the bone" so that a balanced budget could be achieved soon, thus allowing the Republicans to pass tax cuts. In Dodge's words, "With the President's approval, George Humphrey and I established a principle: all departments and agencies were required to put a price tag on their individual programs and to rank them by priority. As higher priorities collected at the top, the lower ones were pushed toward the bottom and their urgency eliminated. The cuts always come out of the bottom. This is something you do all the time in business. But the subtractive process had all but disappeared in the government until we restored it."[10] In brief, Dodge and Humphrey were supposed to serve as constant spurs to reducing expenditures in a final skeptical screening of any new proposals coming before the cabinet or the NSC.

George Humphrey was a particularly active player in the budgetary battles during the first five years of the Eisenhower presidency. As the self-assured conservative conscience in the administration, he was constantly pressuring other officials to reduce budgets. At a cabinet meeting on May 22, 1953, he strongly urged the administration to set a target of a $60 billion budget for FY 1955 in order to allow a Republican tax reduction in 1954.[11] After the Eisenhower administration was able to cut $4.5 billion from Truman's FY 1954 budget, Humphrey announced in June 1953, "I personally am disappointed that we have not been able to make greater reductions in expenditures."[12] At a cabinet meeting on November 4, 1955, the Treasury secretary said that if the administration could not balance the year's budget by the following June "we ought to hang our heads and put our tails between our legs."[13] Even when the budget was balanced in FY 1956, the result of an enormous effort, Humphrey complained that the $60 billion goal had not yet been reached and expenditures and taxes were still too high. On September 7, 1956, Humphrey wrote a letter to Eisenhower lamenting that "we made a big step forward when we first arrived. For the last two years we have been going backwards . . . and I think it is essential that we change the trend. . . . I do not believe that we can control inflation and continue any reasonable stabilization in our cost of living unless we can reverse the present upward trend of Government military expenditures."[14]

Humphrey was convinced that taxes were too high, and he saw high taxes as a greater menace to the U.S. than communism: High taxes threatened both the democratic political system and economic system by impairing individual rights and liberties as well as incentives to save and invest. In June 1957 Humphrey told Senator Harry Byrd's Senate Finance Committee: "I have said ever since I have been here, and I cannot repeat it too strongly, that our present rates of taxation . . . are too high to be maintained over a period, and that we should shape our affairs to reduce those at the earliest possible moment."[15] Humphrey was so driven by this passion to cut taxes that he advised Eisenhower that curtailing taxes should *precede* the actual achievement of a balanced budget because balancing the budget could result from increased economic growth, which a tax reduction would stimulate.[16] But the president resisted this supply-side argument: "Beginning in June 1952 . . . I have always maintained one thing—that the annual federal deficit must be eliminated in order that tax reductions can begin. Reverse this order and you will *never* have tax reduction. . . . So I spend my life trying to cut expenditures, balance the budget, and then get at the *popular* business of lowering taxes."[17] As an authentic conservative, Eisenhower resisted the temptation of what later was called voodoo economics.

George Humphrey was involved in two of the major budgetary conflicts of the 1950s. At the legislative leaders' meeting in the cabinet room of the White House on April 30, 1953, Eisenhower outlined his budget for the coming fiscal year to the Republican congressional leaders. The president explained that he had cut $7 billion from the military budget and had reduced Truman's projected FY 1954 deficit from $9.9 billion to $4 billion. Instead of being pleased with these figures, Senator Robert Taft, the Republican majority leader, was appalled. As the leader of the Republican Old Guard, he had expected a Republican president to slice Truman's $80 billion budget to about $70 billion in FY 1954 and then to $60 billion in FY 1955. Such progress would allow the administration to slash taxes twelve to thirteen percent across the board and would help the Republicans to maintain control of Congress in the 1954 elections. When Taft heard that Eisenhower would not be able to balance the budget or cut taxes as soon as anticipated, the senator responded, according to Sherman Adams, "in the most explosive emotional outburst against the President that I saw in all my six years in the White House."[18] Sitting across the table from the president, Senator Taft proclaimed,

"I can't express the deepness of my disappointment at the program the administration presented today." Taft angrily accused Eisenhower of following the Truman road of fiscal irresponsibility, especially in the areas of the military and foreign aid. He ridiculed the Eisenhower budget cuts as "puny." He predicted that if the Republicans accepted this program, they would lose decisively in the 1954 elections. Finally, the senator said he could not support the Eisenhower budget program and would have to oppose it publicly. When Taft was finished there was a stunned silence in the cabinet room, and it was obvious that Eisenhower was barely controlling his temper. At this critical moment, Humphrey, a former supporter of Senator Taft, "fearing an explosion as he watched Eisenhower's face flush red," ventured into the debate in support of the president.[19] For half an hour Humphrey, joined by Dodge and Dulles, argued over the budget figures with Taft, which allowed Eisenhower to calm down and prepare a well-reasoned reponse to Taft's attack. Thus, Humphrey helped prevent a widening of the political cleavage between the Eisenhower and Taft Republicans.

All of Eisenhower's economic advisers agreed that the key to achieving the administration's budgetary goals was to reduce military expenditures. This meant that the crisis-inspired increase in defense expenditures instituted by President Truman in FY 1951 — when the defense budget was expanded from about $13 billion in FY 1950 to about $48 billion — would have to be reversed. Truman's defense policy was based on the recommendation contained in a National Security Council memorandum, NSC-68, adopted in 1950 in response to the fall of Nationalist China to Mao Tse-Tung and the shocking news that the Soviet Union had developed the atomic bomb in 1949 much sooner than the United States had expected. The authors of NSC-68 predicted that the period of maximum danger for the nation when Soviet leaders might believe they had built up the necessary military strength to defeat the United States, would occur in the years 1954 to 1955. NSC-68 argued that the long-term nature of the Cold War might require the United States to allocate up to 20 percent of its GNP to national security to maintain the military superiority necessary for rapid mobilization and to successfully resist Communist aggression anywhere in the world. With the Soviet Union possessing atomic weapons, it was no longer reasonable to believe that the United States could follow its traditional policy of mobilizing after hostilities were initiated — mobilization after a nuclear Pearl Harbor would be impossible.[20]

The last Truman budget, for FY 1954, requested more than $50 billion in new obligational authority (authorization to spend). That budget also expected expenditures of about $55 billion in FY 1954 for previously authorized military programs. Horrified by those figures, the Eisenhower administration cut about $10 billion from the new obligational authority for FY 1954, a 20 percent reduction that sliced the asking figure to about $39.5 billion. In its implementation of the 1954 defense program, the Eisenhower team reduced the year's actual outlay to about $46.5 billion, or 15 percent below the Truman estimate, for a net savings of $8.5 billion. Humphrey and Dodge hoped that by 1956, they could reduce and stabilize the military budget at about $30 billion per year.

Throughout the 1950s many Democrats and disgruntled military officers charged that Eisenhower's national security policy was determined by economic and budgetary considerations. This, of course, was Eisenhower's intent. Whereas some Democrats and military men argued that the United States ought to decide first what was necessary to protect the national security and then pay the cost, Eisenhower reasoned that a sustainable national security policy had to be tied to what the country's economy and government's budget could afford. Remembering the isolationism of the 1930s, which had left us woefully unprepared for World War II, Eisenhower was apprehensive that the public would reject internationalism if its responsibilities were viewed as too expensive. Thus, Eisenhower stressed that the United States should develop a defense strategy based on a defense budget that the government could maintain for the foreseeable future. Instead of rapidly rising defense spending designed to mobilize the country for what NSC-68 called the year of maximum danger (1954), the president planned for a national security policy supported by steady, adequate defense budgets designed to protect our vital interests over the "long haul." He rejected the idea that anyone could predict the "year of maximum danger" and insisted that "we're not in a moment of danger, we're in an age of danger," which Eisenhower predicted might last for another fifty years.[21]

Unlike many of his national security critics, Eisenhower understood that United States history was characterized by a fluctuating commitment (feast or famine) to financing the country's military. In the context of the Cold War, a steady, long-lasting commitment, not driven by periodic crises or temporary feelings of détente, was required. The strategic economic goal of the country should be to maintain its technological superiority over the Soviet Union without bankrupting the nation. As the president explained in his 1954 State of the Union address, "Our problem is to achieve adequate military strength within the limits of endurable strain upon our economy. To amass military power without regard to our economic capacity would be to defend ourselves against one kind of disaster by inviting another."[22]

According to Elmo Richardson, "Eisenhower, the professional soldier, was in many ways the least militaristic of any of the American presidents."[23] As a military man whose judgment and patriotism had been proven in World War II, Eisenhower was able to curtail the defense budget by advocating adequate instead of maximum military expenditures. With the experience of Pearl Harbor still so vivid in the minds of the military, and with the public and Congress frightened by the Soviet Union's earlier-than-expected ability to explode an atomic bomb in 1949, followed by the hydrogen bomb in 1953 and the launching of Sputnik into space in 1957, the pressure for larger defense budgets was enormous. But under the leadership of Eisenhower, the United States probably spent less for defense than it would have under any other president that could conceivably have been elected during the 1950s.

Eisenhower understood that higher defense expenditures did not necessarily mean more national security. Military costs were a necessary evil because one had to defend vital national interests, but military goods added nothing of value to the economy. Indeed, each bomber, aircraft carrier, and tank meant fewer homes, schools, and hospitals. Eisenhower emphasized that "once you spend a single dollar beyond adequacy, you are weakening yourself."[24] Overspending on defense was an unnecessary evil, a terrible waste, and one that Eisenhower tried desperately to prevent throughout his years in office.

To measure how much the United States could afford over the long haul for defense, Eisenhower talked about the Great Equation—"how to equate needed military strength with maximum economic strength." The president viewed national security as resting upon two pillars—military strength and a sound economy. He insisted that the nation must have all the military resources that realistic intelligence forecasts—not worst case scenarios—advocated. Eisenhower explained his thinking about the Great Equation in a letter to the secretary of defense that was publicly released:

> Defensive forces in America are maintained to defend a way of life. They must be adequate for this purpose but must not become such an intolerable burden as to occasion loss of civilian morale or the individual initiative on which, in a free country, depends the dynamic industrial effort which is the continuing foundation of our nation's security. . . . It is at this point that professional military competence and political statesmanship must join to form judgements as to the minimum defensive structure that should be supported by the nation. . . . to build excessively under the impulse of fear could, in the long run, defeat our purposes by damaging the growth of our economy and eventually forcing it into regimented controls.[25]

To balance the Great Equation, Eisenhower believed that no more than 10 percent of the GNP should be allocated to defense (unless there was a major threat to national security). To avoid waste, the president called for a dynamic equilibrium in defense expenditures: "Development of sound, long-term security requires that we design our forces so as to assure a steadily increasing efficiency, in step with scientific advances, but characterized by a stability that is not materially disturbed by every propaganda effort of unfriendly nations."[26] However, the president suggested that, *within* each year's defense budget ceiling, monthly outlays could be speeded up or slowed down in order to manipulate aggregate demand. As Eisenhower explained to Adm. Arthur Radford, chairman of the Joint Chiefs of Staff, "If we could take the same approach to military production that we do to public works . . . it would be very helpful. In other words, you put the heat on this production when we face an economic depression and take off the heat when the economy is going at full tilt."[27]

To fill the position of secretary of defense, Eisenhower turned mainly to businessmen such as Charles Wilson and Neil McElroy. Eisenhower had great respect for men who had run large corporations; he felt they could impose an efficiency on the Pentagon that would get more "bang from a buck." Thus, the task of the secretary of defense was to curtail defense costs rather than to make military policy—that role Eisenhower reserved for himself.

Charles Wilson was the president of General Motors from 1941 to 1953 before the president selected him to be his defense secretary. Eisenhower felt that the head of the nation's largest corporation could successfully manage the government's largest department. As the president noted in his diary on May 14, 1954, "In his field, he is a really competent man. He is careful and positive, and I have no positive doubt that, assisted by the team of civilian and military men he has selected, he will produce the maximum security for this country at minimum or near minimum cost."[28] Wilson implemented Eisenhower's policies by reducing the size of the standing army, developing new weapons systems, and instituting a cost-conscious approach to management. According to Wilson's biographer, "These policies often brought criticism from legislators and military leaders who charged that Wilson intended to 'wreck' this or that particular program. But Eisenhower had warned Wilson that he 'had to be willing to be the most unpopular man in government.'"[29] By 1957 the outspoken Wilson may have achieved that dubious distinction. He resigned shortly before the Soviets launched Sputnik in October 1957 and was replaced by Neil McElroy, the president of Proctor and Gamble. In December 1959 McElroy resigned and was replaced by Thomas Gates, the secretary of the navy, for the remainder of Eisenhower's second term.

Eisenhower's strategic views were summarized by Kinnard as follows: "To rely on deterrence and rule out preventive war; to stress the role of nuclear technology and to reduce reliance on United States conventional force; to place heavy reliance on allied land forces around the Soviet periphery; to stress economic strength, achieved especially through reduced defense budgets; and to be prepared to continue the struggle with the Soviet Union over decades."[30] The crucial point was that with both sides possessing nuclear weapons, deterring war was now more vital than attempting to win a war. The former general knew there would be no winner in a nuclear war. The death of Stalin, a completely new membership in the Joint Chiefs of Staff, and most importantly, the end of the Korean War, which made army reductions possible, gave impetus to Eisenhower's new defense strategy. In July 1953

Eisenhower presided over the first of several meetings designed to produce revisions in U.S. strategic thinking. By the end of that year, the media labeled the resulting defense policy the "New Look," a term that was then being used to describe a new style of women's clothing.

The New Look strategy was embodied in NSC-162/2, which was hammered out during the fall of 1953 and reflected the perspectives of Eisenhower, John Foster Dulles, George Humphrey, and Admiral Radford. In Samuel Huntington's words, "The establishment of a new economic-military balance, reconciling security needs, balanced budgets, and tax reduction, was the first key element of the New Look. The second was the maintenance of this balance over the 'long haul.'"[31] The evidence suggests that the adoption of the New Look was largely determined by Eisenhower's fiscal conservatism. The United States could not afford to fight in a series of limited wars like Korea. The United States could afford nuclear weapons because they were cheaper than maintaining a large standing army. Nuclear weapons would also be more effective in deterring aggression from the Soviet Union and Communist China because the United States simply could not match the size of the armies of these countries. Thus, the New Look was more than a defense strategy; it was a national policy that integrated the defense, fiscal, and political goals of the Eisenhower administration.

The New Look produced big savings in the defense budget but at the cost of much criticism. According to Ambrose, "At times it seemed that, except for Humphrey, Eisenhower was the only man in Washington who supported it. From 1955 onward, the Democrats would concentrate their criticisms of Eisenhower on his defense policy, charging that the President — and Humphrey — were allowing their Neanderthal fiscal views to endanger the security of the nation."[32] Outraged criticism also exploded from the army because it was targeted for the biggest cutbacks in both manpower and budget. Both army representatives on the Joint Chiefs of Staff, Gens. Matthew Ridgeway and Maxwell Taylor, resigned and authored scathing criticisms of the New Look.[33]

In the first few years of the 1950s the United States had the ability to destroy the Soviet Union without the fear that Moscow could successfully retaliate. This was no longer true after 1955. Both sides now had the capability of massive retaliation, which created a new condition aptly labeled the balance of terror. To avoid accelerating the already crushing burden of the arms race, the Eisenhower administration responded by developing the concept of "sufficient deterrence," which stressed that "deterrence rested not so much on the relative strategic strength of both sides as on their absolute ability to inflict unacceptable damage to each other."[34] The "New New Look" policy continued to emphasize the stabilization of military expenditures, but inevitably the defense budget expanded. There was great pressure to augment the United States' capability to fight limited wars because the effectiveness

Table 4.1   The Budgetary Record of the Eisenhower Administration (in billions of dollars)

Fiscal Year	Federal Budget	Predicted Surplus (Deficit)	Actual Expenditure	Actual Surplus (Deficit)	Over (Under) Expenditure
1953	84.6	(14.4)	74.1	(9.4)	(10.5)
1954	77.6	(9.9)	67.5	(3.1)	(10.1)
1955	65.4	(2.9)	64.4	(4.2)	(1.0)
1956	62.1	(2.4)	66.2	1.6	4.1
1957	64.6	0.4	69.0	1.6	4.4
1958	71.2	1.8	71.4	(2.8)	0.2
1959	73.6	0.5	80.3	(12.4)	6.7
1960	76.3	0.1	76.5	1.2	—
1961	79.1	4.2	81.5	(3.9)	2.4
1962	80.9	1.5	87.8	(6.4)	6.9

Source: Nelson W. Polsby, *Congress and the Presidency,* 4th ed., (Englewood Cliffs, N.J.: Prentice-Hall, 1986), 184.

of the U.S. nuclear threat to deter the Soviet Union from encouraging local aggression was now less credible. Would the United States risk massive retaliation by threatening or attacking the Soviet Union to prevent local aggression in the Middle East or Southeast Asia? Huntington summarizes the modification of the New Look by writing, "The balance of terror and the desire for economy necessarily yielded a strategy of sufficiency. . . . The New Look assumed superiority in strategic capabilities and inferiority in conventional forces. The New New Look assumed superiority in neither but adequacy in both."[35] Even the goal of adequacy would be terribly expensive to achieve.

BUDGETARY ACCOMPLISHMENTS

Through hard work, perseverance, and the courage to withstand considerable political heat, the Eisenhower administration achieved an impressive share of its budgetary goals. The Eisenhower team produced three balanced budgets in FY 1956, FY 1957, and FY 1960 (see Table 4.1). In addition, Eisenhower proposed balanced budgets for FY 1961 and FY 1962, but under the Kennedy administration both of these budgets ended up in the red. In contrast, the Eisenhower administration transformed the predicted deficits of President Truman's last two budgets (FY 1953 and FY 1954) and reduced spending by over $20 billion. Eisenhower demonstrated his intense commitment (his adversaries called it his obsession) to balancing the budget by transforming the largest peacetime deficit to that point — $12.4 billion in FY 1959, brought about by the recession — to a slight surplus in FY 1960. Balancing the budget in FY 1960, in spite of heavy Democratic majorities controlling both houses of Congress, may have been the most remarkable budget achievement in the history of the United States. It is hard to believe any other politician could have achieved it.

Much of Eisenhower's success in controlling federal expenditures was due to curtailing federal civilian employment. In eight years the Eisenhower administration reduced federal employment from 2,623,000 to 2,349,000, a decrease of 274,000. The overall cuts were achieved despite the necessity of increasing personnel in the Post Office and of staffing new and growing agencies such as the National Aeronautics and Space Administration and the Federal Aviation Agency.[36]

Eisenhower's budget policies also succeeded in making federal expenditures less dominant within the United States economy. In FY 1953, federal expenditures accounted for 21 percent of the GNP. Eisenhower's last proposed budget (FY 1962) called for expenditures of only 15 percent of the GNP. Measured in another way, in FY 1953 the cost of running the federal government amounted to $468 for each person in the United States. In FY 1962, despite the effect of inflation, budget expenditures per capita had been reduced to $437.[37] Similarly, Vatter talks of the "relative retardation of Federal welfarism" under Eisenhower. From the 1930s to the 1950s most United States welfare policies consisted of transfer payments in which the federal government collected taxes and then transferred benefits to entitled citizens. Among such programs were old-age and survivors insurance, unemployment insurance, and veterans benefits. According to Vatter, "The 1950s failed to reveal any noteworthy rise in the importance of Federal transfer payments as compared to the New Deal days. They accounted for about 4 percent of GNP in 1939 and 4.4 percent in 1960. If one adds Federal civilian expenditures to these, then the total of such Federal expenditures plus transfers equaled 7.4 percent of GNP in 1939 but only 6.0 percent in 1960."[38]

Eisenhower did not succeed in fulfilling his 1952 pledge to reduce and stabilize federal expenditures at around $60 billion. In FY 1955 his administration was able to lower expenditures to $64.4 billion, but thereafter federal costs crept upward incrementally. One of the goals of the subtractive process — the elimination of a number of federal programs — was not achieved. In FY 1959 and FY 1961, federal outlays broke the $80 billion mark. This inexorable annual budget increase caused Eisenhower much grief because he believed creeping budget increases fed creeping inflation. He had hoped that budget surpluses in years of prosperity would prevent inflation and lower the national debt.

Eisenhower was also terribly frustrated that he was unable to reduce the national debt. He had inherited a national debt of $266 billion, and he passed

Table 4.2   National Defense Spending, 1950–1960 (in billions of 1954 dollars)

Calendar Year	Total	Calendar Year	Total
1950	16.0	1956	37.0
1951	34.3	1957	38.4
1952	46.8	1958	38.0
1953	50.0	1959	37.7
1954	41.2	1960	35.8
1955	37.6		

Source: Samuel Huntington, *The Common Defense* (New York: Columbia University Press, 1961), 281. According to Huntington, "These figures are federal government purchases of goods and services for national defense. This category corresponds closely to the classification 'major national security' in the annual budget. The latter includes expenditures for the military programs of the Department of Defense, atomic energy, military assistance, stockpiling, and defense production."

on a debt of over $286 billion to President Kennedy. Since the GNP grew much faster than the debt throughout the 1950s, the ratio of the debt to the GNP was reduced from about 90 percent to about 60 percent in 1960. However, whereas the federal government was paying $6.5 billion in interest on its debt in FY 1954, by FY 1960 it had to pay $9.3 billion, or 12 percent of the administrative budget. The high interest charges were due to the Federal Reserve Board's use of monetary policy to tighten the money supply in order to fight inflation.

What success the Eisenhower administration had in fulfilling its budgetary goals was largely due to its ability to hold down defense expenditures. Tables 4.2, 4.3, and 4.4 reveal that the Eisenhower administration was able to stabilize defense outlays and to restrict the defense budget to about 10 percent of the GNP. When the budgetary totals are adjusted for inflation, as they are in Table 4.2, the president actually reduced defense expenditures from 69.2 percent of the federal budget to 59.1 percent.[39]

Defense outlays were stabilized mainly by reducing military personnel from approximately 3,513,000 in January 1953 to approximately 2,500,000 in December 1960, with about half of this decrease attributable to the termination of the Korean War. The New Look targeted the army for the most severe reductions in personnel and money. In 1954 army manpower was slashed 37.5 percent (600,000 personnel) from 1.6 million to one million; the navy and marines were cut 13 percent (130,000 personnel) from 920,000 to 870,000; and the air force was increased from 960,000 to 970,000.[40] Whereas the three branches of the military had each received about one-third of the military budget under Truman, under the New Look policy the army received 22 percent, the navy 29 percent, and the air force 47 percent. Under the New Look

Table 4.3   Gross National Product and National Defense Spending, 1950–1960 (in billions of dollars)

Calendar Year	Gross National Product	National Defense Spending	Percentage
1950	284.6	14.3	5.0
1951	329.0	33.9	10.3
1952	347.0	46.4	13.4
1953	365.4	49.3	13.5
1954	363.1	41.2	11.3
1955	397.5	39.1	9.8
1956	419.2	40.3	9.6
1957	442.8	44.4	10.0
1958	444.2	44.8	10.1
1959	482.1	46.0	9.5
1960	503.2	45.1	9.0

Source: Samuel Huntington, *The Common Defense* (New York: Columbia University Press, 1961), 282.

these proportions became relatively fixed. The cuts in military expenditures allowed the Eisenhower administration to support $7.4 billion in tax reductions in 1954, a subject discussed in chapter 6.

Despite these budget constraints, there were revolutionary innovations in weapons systems during this period. Propeller-driven B-36s were replaced by B-52 jets. In 1954 the Atlas, a liquid-fueled inter-continental ballistic missile (ICBM), was given top priority by the air force, becoming operational in the fall of 1959. In December 1958 two intermediate range ballistic missiles (IRBM), the air force's Thor and the army's Jupiter, became operational. By 1960, two nuclear Polaris submarines were available, each armed with sixteen solid-propellant long-range ballistic missiles. A second generation, solid-propellant ICBM, the Minuteman, was being developed and was scheduled for deployment in 1962. In response to the launch of Sputnik, the Eisenhower administration placed thirty-one satellites into orbit between January 1958 and January 1961. In brief, Eisenhower's commitment did not prevent the modernization of United States weaponry and the creation of the strategic triad—bombers, missiles, and Polaris submarines—that has successfully deterred nuclear war.[41]

Table 4.4   Total Budget Expenditures and Major National Security Expenditures, FY 1950–FY 1960 (in millions of dollars)

Fiscal Year	Total Expenditures	Major National Security Expenditures	Percentage
1950	39,606	13,009	32.8
1951	44,058	22,306	50.6
1952	65,408	43,976	67.2
1953	74,274	50,363	67.8
1954	67,772	46,904	69.2
1955	64,570	40,626	62.9
1956	66,540	40,641	61.1
1957	69,433	43,270	62.3
1958	71,936	44,142	61.4
1959	80,697	46,426	57.5
1960	77,233	45,627	59.1

Source: Samuel Huntington, *The Common Defense* (New York: Columbia University Press, 1961), 283.

EISENHOWER'S TECHNIQUES FOR TRYING TO ACHIEVE A BALANCED BUDGET

Eisenhower used a variety of techniques to impede the expansion of the federal budget. Not all of these methods were successful, but they clearly signaled that the president was committed to balancing the budget. Unlike most presidents, Eisenhower did not have a "soft spot" for, as examples, proposals to increase military expenditures or new social welfare programs. Eisenhower was unique in that he was uniformly tough on any type of proposal that would increase expenditures. The relative success Eisenhower had in achieving some of his budgetary goals was largely due to the fact that he generally applied downward pressure uniformly on all expenditures throughout his term in office.

From the beginning of his administration to the end, Eisenhower worked to reduce the number of governmental employees. On February 3, 1953, a White House directive instructed all agencies to review budgets for this purpose. Secretary of Defense Wilson ordered a freeze on civilian employment in the military. After a review in March 1953, Wilson ordered the firing of over thirty-nine thousand civilian personnel by May 31.[42] In May 1957, when the president learned that the Interior Department had recently added thirteen hundred employees, Eisenhower exploded at a cabinet meeting: "I don't think you're tough enough with your subordinates. . . . I'm interested in these [figures] because I want you to be. [You are] just not tough enough on restricting hirings. Nobody ever fires anyone. . . . I learned long ago that every boss,

Rowland Hughes being sworn in as director of the Bureau of the Budget, April 16, 1954, by Justice Harold V. Burton. Sherman Adams and Mrs. Hughes are in the background. (Courtesy Dwight D. Eisenhower Library/National Park Service.)

however small, has a stake in adding people because it brings him a higher grade!"[43] At a meeting in September 1959, Eisenhower approved a proposal from Budget Director Stans directing each agency to reduce employment by two percent.[44] Such efforts applied countervailing pressure from the top to the natural tendencies of the public bureaucracy to expand.

Eisenhower constantly exhorted his cabinet colleagues to balance the budget. Meetings with the president were filled with admonitions to cut costs. He advised each cabinet secretary to designate an assistant whose specialty would be to review with skepticism any increases in costs.[45] At a cabinet meeting shortly after the launching of Sputnik, the president exclaimed, "I'd like to know what's on the other side of the moon, but I won't pay to find out this year!"[46] At a meeting with Admiral Radford and Budget Director Hughes, the president stated that he wanted defense department expenditures reduced to a "spartan basis." In response to officers he had known all his life constantly asking for more money, the president declared, "I say the patriot today is the fellow who can do the job with less money."[47] Using this standard, to Eisenhower's increasing dismay, there were few patriots in the Pentagon, or in any other department.

Eisenhower's growing frustration was dramatically demonstrated in remarks he made to the cabinet meeting on November 27, 1959. In this harangue, the president explained, "I just want to make clear to my own conscience that I have made clear to each of you the thing that worries me most about our survival as a free nation." Western civilization's "true problem" was whether free government, confronted by the threat of the Soviet Union's growing economy, can "continue to exist, in view of the demands which are made upon free governments and on their free economies." The United States must meet the challenge of the Soviet Union "by keeping our economy absolutely healthy." This can be achieved by a strong, united executive leadership that resists the enticing entreaties of pressure groups and by getting "out of every unnecessary activity. We can refuse to do things too rapidly. . . . Suddenly we seem to have an hysterical approach—from health programs and welfare programs and grants to the states—to everything: to where we are going to 'cure it all' in two years, or five years—by putting in a lot of money." The nation is

approaching the limits of taxation and spending. . . . We must keep our expenses down and we must put our emphasis on productivity. . . . It is a mistake to keep temporizing with Congress. . . . We must not compromise $600 million proposals for $200 million proposals and feel that we have accomplished something, when we did not believe in the proposals in the first place. . . . If we do not pay as we go . . . we will have no recourse than to do what we desperately do not want to do: to desert liberty as we understand it. . . . If I have to show an unbalanced budget, if I have to show a trend of upward spending—then I am defeated. . . . We must remember: frugality, economy, simplicity with efficiency, I cannot tell you how deeply I believe this.[48]

If such heart-felt exhortations had been effective, Eisenhower would have produced eight balanced budgets instead of only three.

Eisenhower's final exhortation to control defense expenditures was contained in his farewell address of January 17, 1961. The aging president was deeply concerned that the "spenders" were about to control both the legislative and executive branches. He feared that the spending tide he had held back would be released by a new spending coalition whose expensive proposals would be legitimated by concern for national security and respect for science. Eisenhower warned his fellow citizens, "In the councils of government, we must guard against the acquisition of unwarranted influence, whether sought or unsought, by the military-industrial complex. The potential for the disastrous rise of misplaced power exists and will exist."[49] We can now see that the president's farewell address was a polished articulation — written by Malcolm Moos — of ideas Eisenhower had been forming throughout the decade. It is ironic that liberals in the following decades frequently quoted this speech in support of their arguments when Eisenhower's warning was specifically aimed at the liberals of the 1950s.

Another method used by Eisenhower to control expenditures was his attempt to develop decision-making rules and principles to guide budget allocations. For example, when dealing with whether government should take on a particular responsibility, Eisenhower would cite Abraham Lincoln: "The legitimate object of government is to do for a community of people whatever they need to have done, but can not do at all, or can not so well do, for themselves — in their separate and individual capacities. In all that the people can individually do as well for themselves, government ought not to interfere."[50] Not surprisingly, this principle proved ineffective in helping to decide whether the government should intervene to deal with a particular problem. It was even more difficult to develop a rule of thumb to determine whether a problem, such as education, health, or crime, was primarily a state or federal responsibility.

One early budgetary rule developed by Dodge and Eisenhower was for each agency head to differentiate between programs that were merely desirable and those that were necessary. The former were supposed to be cut, but, needless to say, bureaucrats had little difficulty in proving their programs necessities — especially when they were championed by members of Congress. Few programs were eliminated under this guideline.

An example of the president's thinking can be seen in a March 29, 1957, meeting with twelve scientists. Dr. I. I. Rabi complained to Eisenhower that the defense department was too narrowly focused on weapons research and was not adequately funding basic research that would have a wider application and be more economical in the long run. In response, according to Staff Secretary Goodpaster's notes, "The President said he had a question regarding this deduction — it is where, in a society like ours, responsibility should be placed for basic research. Where is the dividing line between the efforts that should fall to government and those that should fall to universities and to industry. He said he would be greatly helped by a set of simple yardsticks."[51] Such yardsticks were never developed. In some ways this search for decision-making rules that would both rationalize and reduce budget expenditures was as futile as the search for the Holy Grail. However, Eisenhower never stopped looking.

Using a variety of techniques, the president achieved some success in controlling the defense budget. The annual military budget was administered by the three service secretaries and by military comptrollers and had a target ceiling (somewhere between $35 billion and $40 billion), with fixed service allocations of the budgeted monies. As was mentioned earlier, Eisenhower struck down the parity of the three military services, which had been maintained by an approximate 1:1:1 division of the budget, by setting allocation figures of 47 percent for the air force, 29 percent for the navy, and 22 percent for the army. This decision magnified the already high interservice rivalries. Each service chief argued that the money allocated to the other two was sufficient to finance their missions, but the amount approved for his own branch was frighteningly inadequate. Eisenhower desperately wanted to change the Joint Chiefs of Staff to a corporate body that would publicly support his New Look strategic policy from the strife-torn body in which each chief represented and fought for his own branch's interests. But the chiefs blocked Eisenhower's efforts, arguing that this would politicize its members and inhibit each from offering his best professional advice. It enraged Eisenhower that each service chief's best advice always turned out to be so self-serving.

Eisenhower could not prevent the growing number of leaks and complaints from military officers who fervently believed that budgetary concerns were inhibiting an adequate response to the Soviet Union's growing military power. Nevertheless, Eisenhower largely controlled the output of the national security process by carefully selecting top military advisers, demanding public loyalty to the administration's New Look policy, suppressing interservice squabbles, and reorganizing the defense department in 1953 and 1958. Under Eisenhower's command, budgetary considerations largely determined strategic policy, not the other way around. In Kinnard's words, "There was no precise mix of forces or weaponry needed to carry out the Eisenhower strategy. The final force mix, which was expressed in terms of the defense budget, came about as a result of a political bargaining process dominated by the president. The outcome of this political bargaining, rather than a strategic policy paper, determined what strategic policy was to be pursued. . . . A political bargaining process over the defense budget determined not only the budget itself, but what kind of strategic policy [was] to be pursued."[52]

At the beginning of his administration Eisenhower tilted this bargaining process toward his objectives of frugality by bringing in two powerful players, George Humphrey and Joseph Dodge, who were committed to reducing expenditures so that there could be tax cuts. Eisenhower was thus insuring that pressures to lower defense outlays would not slacken and that any proposals for increases would have to run the gauntlet. Eisenhower also placed Treasury and budget representatives on the NSC's planning board, an advisory committee that channeled proposals to the NSC, and decreed that each policy paper presented to the NSC would include a financial appendix estimating the cost of implementing the proposal. These changes reflected Eisenhower's criticism of Truman's NSC, which had not "priced" its policies. Phillip Henderson correctly concludes, "The resulting integration of domestic and economic considerations is of fundamental importance in explaining

Eisenhower's success in keeping the defense budget from spiraling out of control in the Cold War environment of the 1950s."[53]

As a new member of the NSC, with no particular expertise in military weapons or strategy, George Humphrey might have been expected to be initially shy. But in spite of all the uncertainties of the Cold War and of rapidly changing military technology, he was one of the few officials who knew exactly what he wanted. With his concern for preserving business confidence, Humphrey was more frightened of an unbalanced budget than of the Communist menace.[54] He never claimed to know where the defense budget could be cut, but he knew that it had to be and that an effective secretary of defense could perform the necessary "surgery." At a May 22, 1953, cabinet meeting, Humphrey told Charles Wilson that at least $10 billion more would have to be cut from the defense department budget. Addressing Wilson, Humphrey thundered, "You've just got to get the best damn streamlined model you ever did in your life. And you have to do it in six months, not three years. This means a brand new model—we can't just patch up the old jalopy."[55]

Even in the usually sanitized minutes of NSC meetings, Humphrey's role is expressed in powerful language. At an October 13, 1953, NSC meeting, Humphrey objected to a defense department presentation by stating that "when all was said and done" the Pentagon proposal for FY 1955 "offered no cut at all." Later, at the same meeting, Humphrey argued that it was "absolutely essential" to clarify the issue of when atomic weapons would be used because "only their use on a broad scale could really change the program of the Defense Department and cut the costs of the military budget." "With some heat," according to the NSC minutes, "Secretary Humphrey pointed out to the Council that FY 1955 was *the* critical year. We are, of course, all dealing with the imponderable but we must preserve public confidence in the soundness of the economy and in the leadership of the president. If people begin to think that this administration is conducting its business in the same old way as the last, the American economy will go to hell and the Republican Party will lose the next election." At a subsequent NSC meeting on October 25, 1953, Adm. Robert Carney claimed that New Look manpower and budget reductions could not be made until United States military commitments were commensurately curtailed. "Secretary Humphrey inquired, with some heat, if the time had not come to make such changes, when did Admiral Carney imagine it would come? Admiral Carney replied, when you change our commitments."[56] The Joint Chiefs may have preferred to fight the Soviets than to confront George Humphrey in NSC meetings.

To meet his goal of balancing the budget, Eisenhower was also willing to fight the Congress with the veto. In August 1953, to maintain revenue, Eisenhower vetoed his first bill, a law that would have repealed the 20 percent excise tax on motion-picture tickets. In August 1956 the president vetoed a $1.6

Maurice Stans being sworn in by Justice William Brennan as director of the Bureau of the Budget (second from left), along with Robert Merriam as deputy director (left), March 18, 1958. Also attending were Eisenhower and Vice-President Nixon. (Courtesy Dwight D. Eisenhower Library/National Park Service.)

billion rivers and harbors pork barrel piece of legislation that would have authorized ninety-nine individual river, harbor, and flood control projects. He pocket vetoed the depressed areas bill in 1958 and formally vetoed it in 1959. After the Democrats decisively won the 1958 congressional elections, a more militant Eisenhower emerged, vowing to fight even more aggressively for his economic goals.

The centerpiece of that effort was the president's defense of the FY 1960 budget against the heavy Democratic majorities in both houses of Congress. The 1957–58 recession had caused the largest peacetime budget deficit in the history of the United States, a situation that embarrassed and aroused the combative instincts of the former general. He was determined to accomplish what most observers deemed impossible—change the $12.4 billion budget deficit of FY 1959 to a surplus. Eisenhower accomplished the impossible by focusing his powers on balancing the budget. Believing fervently that he was serving the nation's highest interest, Eisenhower vetoed bills that would finance classrooms and centers for the elderly. In addition, the new budget director, Maurice Stans, implemented Eisenhower's postelection pledge by publicizing the cost of Democratic legislative proposals. The president also threatened that if the Democrats succeeded in overriding his vetoes and increasing expenditures, he would call a special session of Congress to provide the necessary tax increase to balance the budget. However, no special session was required because the Democrats succeeded in overriding only the president's veto of an appropriation bill for the Bureau of Reclamation. Thus, Eisenhower and Stans succeeded in achieving a budget surplus of about one billion dollars in FY 1960.[57]

PRESSURES TO INCREASE EXPENDITURES

Maurice Stans once defined a budget as "a set of calculations that confirm your worst suspicions."[58] This definition was increasingly true for Eisenhower. Despite his strongest efforts, federal budget totals constantly expanded. As the president lamented to Humphrey, "Over the past five years it seems to me that I have put in two-thirds of my time fighting increased expenditures in government, yet only this morning we had mid-year review of the budget and we find that with the exception of one or two very unimportant agencies, the '57 expenditures for every single Department of government exceed comparable ones in the year '56."[59] These expanding budgets frustrated Eisenhower and his fellow Republicans because the increases suggested that such a trend was not a function of the fiscally irresponsible Democratic party. The Republicans had attributed the federal spending momentum to the reelection ambitions of the Democrats. Once in power, however, Republicans found they wanted to be reelected too. When Budget Director Brundage suggested cutting the Federal Old Age Assistance program, Republican Minority Leader Joseph Martin argued that such a proposal would damage the party in the upcoming 1958 congressional elections.[60] Even Eisenhower confessed to Humphrey, "I have already approved bills which I personally considered as imposing unwarranted drains on the Federal Treasury."[61]

In reality, the federal budget expanded because of both external and internal pressures. In chapter 3 some of the external pressures such as the Cold War and population growth were examined; here the focus will be on the internal pressures. Many of the internal pressures fed off the external pressures. That is, as the number of schoolchildren soared, bureaucrats in the Department of Health, Education, and Welfare were encouraged to promote federal aid to education. The awesome pressure to increase spending was nowhere better demonstrated than in the Department of Agriculture where, despite the efforts of Secretary Ezra Benson, a man who was more conservative than Humphrey, outlays rose from $2.5 billion in FY 1954 to $7 billion in FY 1959. The latter figure was a higher total than FDR's entire budget in 1935.

The two departments most able to generate pressure to increase their budgets were Defense and Health, Education, and Welfare. The secretaries of these two departments were in the best positions to take advantage of the opportunities provided by the Cold War, by recurring recessions, and by the political pressures of the Democrats.

The Department of Health, Education, and Welfare (HEW) was created in April 1953. As its name suggests, HEW was engaged in the widest array of programs of any department — everything from medical research on cancer, to testing food and drugs, to financial assistance for schools in federally-affected areas, to social security. Its bureaucrats had no problem justifying more money for, first, studies and then programs to benefit children, the sick, and the needy. The multitude of worthy causes served by HEW meant that it was politically painful to constrain its expenditures. No other department presented a greater challenge to policymakers to forge a politically acceptable balance between compassion and fiscal prudence.

As discussed in chapter 2, Eisenhower's modern Republican philosophy espoused liberalism in the field of human relations and conservatism in economic affairs. By its very nature, HEW highlighted the liberal componet of the president's outlook. Unfortunately for HEW secretaries, as Eisenhower became less liberal, there were increasing struggles within the administration over budget issues. Given Eisenhower's use of budget ceilings, any increase in the HEW budget would likely cut into the budgets of other departments.

During Eisenhower's presidency, HEW had three secretaries: Oveta Culp Hobby (April 1953 to August 1955), Marion B. Folsom (August 1955 to August 1958), and Arthur S. Flemming (August 1958 to January 1961). Eisenhower had the least conflict with Hobby. She was a southern Democrat from Texas who shared many of the conservative fiscal views of the president. Even so, Hobby submitted a memo to the president in November 1954 proposing an ambitious set of programs that would fulfill "your Administration's concern for the individual American."[62] Hobby's memo congratulated Eisenhower for establishing HEW and for proposing legislation that extended social security benefits to an additional ten million citizens. She suggested that in 1955 the administration concentrate on the health problems of the American people and in 1956 on educational issues. Proposed health programs included providing medical care for public assistance recipients, stimulating construction of more medical facilities, encouraging the training of more medical personnel, granting federal money to the states for mental health programs, and providing federal assistance for state and local programs in water and air pollution control. The education programs included federal scholarships to increase the number of scientists, engineers, and doctors; grants to the states to fight juvenile delinquency; and federal guarantees of local school bonds to overcome the shortage in classrooms. The memo indicated that more educational programs would emerge from the White House Conference on Education that was scheduled for 1955. Predictably,

Budget Director Hughes opposed Hobby's memo because of its budget-busting potential and its "undue paternalism."[63]

Eisenhower had more conflict with his second HEW secretary, Marion B. Folsom, a former Eastman Kodak executive from New York who served the first two and a half years in the Eisenhower presidency as an undersecretary in the Treasury Department. In 1955 when Folsom moved to HEW, he told BOB officials, "When I was in Treasury, I was on one side of these things; now I'm with HEW on the other side, the liberal side."[64] Folsom believed that the president wanted him to think liberally, and he did. "I felt the need for many of these (HEW) programs. Especially when they were trying to hold expenditures down, I was arguing with the Budget people all the time."[65] In discussing budget items with the president, Folsom always measured the program costs in relation to the GNP or to the size of the population, which generally displayed a downward trend of expenditures. For example, at the December 14, 1956, cabinet meeting, "Mr. Folsom emphasized that the non-security areas of government have been getting a constantly decreasing share of the GNP (1935 — seven percent; 1956 — three percent). He gave examples such as the Food and Drug Administration where enlarged action is necessary to a growing population."[66] From Folsom's bureaucratic perspective, "In a growing country and expanding economy, it was natural that programs would cost more, not to mention the new needs developing."[67] This was not the budget director's view.

Folsom felt that to be effective, he had to practice persuasion, perseverance, and patience and take advantage of personal meetings with the president. In these meetings Folsom tried to appeal to Eisenhower's liberal side: "Rather than trust somebody else to do it, invariably I would get an appointment and explain the program to him personally. If I put the National Defense [Education] proposal in the form of a memorandum to the White House, I probably wouldn't have gotten anything except very small parts of it, but by having a chance to present the whole program, well documented, I got his attention on each one of these. I could sell it by doing that."[68] Such advocacy antagonized budget officials and White House staff aides. One staff aide later commented, "I had the feeling, and I know General Persons a time or two commented on this, that Folsom — as did many others — would try to lead the President beyond where the President wanted to go, by pure persistence and just keeping after him and finally in desperation the President would throw up his hands and say 'okay.' But then he always would end up exploding in public indicating he really didn't believe that, which made it worse than ever."[69]

Folsom had his failures. He did not succeed in getting a bill passed by Congress for federal aid to construct classrooms. His crowning achievement, however, was to exploit the window of opportunity opened by Sputnik to attract the president's support for the National Defense Education Act, which

Congress passed in 1958. This law established a broad student loan program to enable talented students who needed financial help to obtain a higher education and a fellowship program to help overcome the national shortage of adequately trained college and university teachers. It also included grants to the states to strengthen instruction in science, mathematics, and modern foreign language in the public schools.

Eisenhower's third and final secretary of HEW, Arthur S. Flemming, proved the most difficult. Before becoming secretary on August 1, 1958, Flemming had served in Eisenhower's first administration as director of the Office of Defense Mobilization and then had been named president of Ohio Wesleyan University. A veiled hint of Flemming's bureaucratic conflicts within the administration was included in his letter of resignation submitted on January 12, 1961. "Under your far-sighted leadership, I have developed convictions as to how these [health, education, and welfare] issues should be resolved. I have believed, of course, that I had an obligation to conduct the affairs of this office in the light of these convictions."[70] Flemming's convictions were not necessarily those of the president.

Flemming had been in office less than two weeks when he sent the president a memo concerning the 1958 congressional elections. The new secretary suggested that the Republican National Committee prepare electoral material under the heading of "Liberal in the Field of Human Relations." "I believe that we can point to outstanding accomplishments in this area and that we can also project some forward-looking plans which will be consistent with our concept of being 'conservative in the field of economics.'"[71] A month before the 1958 elections Flemming sent Eisenhower another memo ostensibly about the budget for medical research. The secretary pointed out that appropriations for medical research throughout the National Institutes of Health had increased sharply during the past few years. Recent legislative history demonstrated that the administration had lost control in determining the costs of these programs to a network of officials in the medical field, federal bureaucracies, and congressional committees. To regain executive control, Flemming advocated that the administration develop a plan on how much the nation should be spending on medical research over the next twelve years and then hammer out an agreement on what share should be carried by the federal government, the states, the universities, and the private sector. Flemming concluded that this formula could serve as a model for other policy areas: "I think that this is the approach we should consider very carefully in other areas. If we as an administration can reach agreement on a national goal, and then if we talk to the nation about these goals and about the proportionate load that should be assumed by private groups, the state governments and the Federal government, we might be able to get on the offensive in dealing with these problems instead of always being put in a defensive position."[72] In essence, Flemming was offering Eisenhower a more effective political strategy for Modern Republicanism to meet the challenge of a resurgent Democratic party than just denying all reform proposals because of budget considerations.

After the poor Republican performance in the 1958 elections, Flemming pressed his case even more strongly. On November 7, 1958, Flemming submitted a memo to the president: "Your leadership over the past six years has provided the opportunity of creating an image of a Republican party that is liberal in the field of human relations. The 'right to work' battles have blurred that image in certain states. I feel that we must do everything possible to re-establish that image. I want to do everything possible to make a contribution to the achievement of that objective."[73] However, no such contribution could be made because of the rigid constraints imposed by the FY 1960 budget. On November 12, 1959, Flemming sent another memo to Eisenhower agreeing that the administration must present a budget which reflected fiscal responsibility but objecting to the stringent criteria being applied to the upcoming FY 1960 budget. These criteria included such guidelines as (1) no new construction starts; (2) no expansion of existing programs unless there was an immediate and urgent need; (3) no new programs unless there was an immediate and urgent need; (4) a program retrenchment in areas of low federal interest and priority, or where the federal government was supporting a disproportionately high share of the total cost. Flemming argued, "I do not see . . . how criteria of this kind can be applied in the preparation of the budget without putting the Administration in a position where it finds it impossible to present to the nation a positive on-going program in many areas that require such programs. The application of such criteria means that we will emerge with a budget which in many instances will freeze the status quo. In some instances this may be all right. In other instances the status quo may reflect, for example, a warped sense of values."[74]

The president, whose values were being questioned, responded to Flemming's memo with one of his own. Eisenhower agreed "that we must not be reactionary or static in our relations" and that these subjects raised by Flemming should be discussed in a future cabinet session. But the president was opposed to any tax increase to finance either the expansion of old programs or the development of new programs.[75]

A classic confrontation occurred in the cabinet meeting of January 16, 1959, in which the president and his advisers argued over whether to support Flemming's bill calling for federal aid for classroom construction. The transcript of the session presents clear evidence that Eisenhower had become more conservative and less inclined to support the Modern Republicans on domestic issues. The president's introduction of Flemming and his bill to help needy school districts service their debt on school construction was hardly an endorsement and set the stage for the most vigorous cabinet debate in the history of the Eisenhower administration. In his introductory remarks the president admitted that he had an "instinctive belief" that it was better for the federal government to stay out of schools "because I personally believe there has been a trend toward federal dependency. . . . But we must consider what the United States wants and what a few of us still believe. It is a hard decision." Eisenhower conceded that Flemming's bill would have no effect on the FY 1960 budget and would cost far less than the Democratic alternative. The president ended his introductory remarks by saying, "Now, having put you in that much of a halter, and having put that much of a noose around your neck, go ahead, Arthur."[76]

Flemming then read parts of his eleven-page statement in support of HEW's bill which had been largely prepared by Elliott Richardson, an assistant secretary. The secretary pointed out that there was a shortage of 430,000 classrooms for students attending elementary and secondary schools. The states were only building about 70,000 classrooms per year, which meant that in 1962 two million students would still not have adequate facilities. In addition, by 1970 the wave of baby boomers would double the number of college students. Flemming advocated that the federal government respond to these needs by aiding state governments in financing their school construction bonds. The estimated annual costs to overcome these two problems were quite low: $85 million for elementary and secondary schools; $25 million for college construction. Flemming concluded with a political argument: "Unless we make these plans a part of the Administration's program, we find ourselves in the completely indefensible position of opposing plans advanced by the opposition to meet a need that we will be forced to admit exists. . . . [These plans] are in harmony with the philosophy that we have stated on many occasions, namely, that the Government will step in on an emergency basis to help achieve national objectives that would not otherwise be achieved."[77]

After Flemming finished reading his statement, Treasury Secretary Robert Anderson spoke in opposition on several grounds. First, Flemming's bill would make it more difficult for the Treasury to refinance the national debt: "We are going into the poorest school districts in the country[;] these districts will be able to advertise . . . that these bonds are fully guaranteed by the Federal Government. The best bond I can sell to finance our debt will not exceed 4.25 percent — on which the full tax is paid. These school bonds will be tax exempt and will have an interest of 5.7 percent or so."[78] Second, Anderson was concerned that if this was perceived as a good way to finance schools, this approach would soon be applied to other problems: urban renewal, port construction, waste treatment plants, and so on. Finally, Anderson worried that the Democratic Congress might be so attracted to this approach that it would significantly increase the amount of funds available. Then the president would be confronted with the dilemma of vetoing a good principle because it was too expensive.

Anderson's position was supported by Budget Director Stans, who claimed the Flemming bill would soon be financing one out of five new classrooms. Secretary of Defense McElroy doubted whether Flemming's proposal would produce a net increase in the number of classrooms built because it would weaken incentives on the states to construct schools on their own. The most vehement opposition came from Secretary of Agriculture Ezra Benson, who condemned the proposal on ideological grounds. In Benson's view, education was solely a state responsibility, and to permit the federal government to become involved would only lead to an increase in income taxes and federal controls.

Flemming's bill was endorsed by Secretary of Labor James Mitchell, who argued that there was clearly a national need to construct more classrooms and that the federal government had to respond to that need. Perhaps thinking about his upcoming presidential campaign, Vice-President Richard Nixon supported Flemming's proposal on the basis of political reasoning. Nixon, the self-appointed political specialist in cabinet discussions, argued that because there was obviously a national need, the proposal could not be rejected for budgetary reasons. To turn it down on the principle that the federal government should not become involved in education was a difficult argument to sell because people did not distinguish between the responsibilities of the state and federal governments. Hence Nixon reluctantly supported the HEW program because, "Of all the plans I have seen, this hurts the least, and seems to offer some reasonable approach to a problem which somebody is going to do something about."[79]

But the one vote that counted at this cabinet meeting was the president's. Eisenhower conceded that educational needs were not being met by the states, but he was afraid that once the federal government jumped into this policy area, even if purportedly on a temporary basis to relieve an emergency situation, it would never be able to get out. He yearned for a way to force the states to meet their responsibilities. Flemming tried to convince the president that HEW was proposing a partnership between the national government and the states: "We do not have to 'take things over' in order to be intelligent partners." The president replied, "In some grant programs we carry on, we started out with 50 percent grants; now its 80 percent." The president was highly skeptical that the highest annual cost for this program would be $110 million, citing how expensive the farm program had become. Eisenhower lamented, "There may be a world trend toward socialism and we cannot get out of it. Perhaps we are like the armed guard with rusty armor and a broken sword, standing at the bridge and trying to stop progress." Eisenhower announced that he was "weary" from fighting for the principle of diminishing the number of federal programs and trying to get the states to assume more responsibility. "We are going to put up some kind of program. . . . I do not know of anything I hate as much, but I guess we must."[80] Flemming's bill was submitted to Congress but, unlike Eisenhower's three previous aid-to-education bills, this one was not accompanied by a presidential message of support. Not surprisingly, the bill was not treated seriously in Congress and quickly died.

Because of the Cold War, the defense department generated even greater pressures than HEW to increase its budget. Whereas HEW officals claimed that new programs were needed to respond compassionately to a national need, Pentagon officials often asserted that new weapons were needed to insure national survival. Eisenhower had to deal with an increasing number of such experts throughout the decade as the Soviet Union rapidly increased its military capabilities.

Part of Eisenhower's problem in controlling the defense budget was the acceleration of weapons development. In his memoirs Eisenhower compares the evolution of weapons from the time of his graduation from West Point in 1915 to his years as president. He was struck by how accelerated weapon development had become in the 1950s with the emergence of ICBMs and nuclear submarines. According to Eisenhower this called for a new decision-making guideline: "Our military structure and equipment were changing so rapidly that even the comforting old slogan 'tried and true' was gone. In its place had spring up a disquieting new one: 'If it works, it's obsolete.'"[81]

This meant that as the Eisenhower administration attempted to reduce the overall Pentagon budget expenditures for research and development steadily increased. Bureaucratic conflict over this issue emerged quickly. In 1953, when the chairman of the Atomic Energy Commission, Adm. Lewis Strauss, told an NSC meeting he was cutting funds available for research, he was chastised by Secretary of State Dulles. According to the NSC minutes, "Secretary Dulles reminded Admiral Strauss that, in the course of his presentation, he had referred to the fact that he was 'starving research'. . . . From the standpoint of the prestige of the United States perhaps our greatest single asset was the ability to keep ahead of the Soviet Union in the scientific and technological field. If we were to lose this advantage, it would be a grave blow to the security and to the leadership of the United States. He would much prefer . . . to see research and development pushed to the limit, as against adding to an already large stockpile of weapons." Secretary Humphrey then expressed his view that in both private industry and in government "there was no way you could spend money faster than on research, and unless this research was very carefully scrutinized, the results were often not worth the expenditures."[82]

But the greatest problem when it came to funding military research was deciding which project to fund. Each branch of the military had projects for which it could mobilize compelling evidence to justify financing. This tendency was tempered by the fact that under Eisenhower's rule of budget ceilings for each branch of the military, any money for new weapons would have to be paid for by cuts in other parts of its budget. For the president, however, it was very frustrating to be subjected to the conflicting pressures of reducing expenditures and yet spending millions on experiments with new weapons, some of which would never become operational. Which technological advance would work and which would not frequently could not be predicted. As an illustration, early in the Eisenhower presidency the air force wanted to develop an atomic plane and the navy a nuclear submarine that could launch missiles from under the water. Both proposals must have sounded equally fantastic. The Polaris submarine eventually became an essential component of the U.S. strategic triad; the atomic plane, although millions were spent on its development, did not.

To operate in this environment Eisenhower used the strategy of "parallel developments." Because the president could not be certain which new weapon would eventually prove effective, he allowed the air force and the army to each develop its own IRBM (the Thor and Jupiter, respectively). He also permitted the air force to develop two ICBMs—the liquid-fueled Atlas and the Titan. Defense Secretary McElroy explained, "We followed two parallel courses because we felt we didn't have time not to. If we failed on one, we just had to have another one, without losing time. This was expensive, but we had to do it."[83]

In no policy area was the president's judgment more criticized in the 1950s and in no policy area were his decisions later more vindicated than in the field of air defense. Because he saw that technological changes were accelerating, he avoided responding with crash programs to what turned out to be nonexistent bomber gaps (mid-1950s) and missile gaps (late 1950s). In 1956 it was estimated by the officer in charge of continental air defense that it would cost $65 billion by 1965 to provide the United States with an adequate air defense against Soviet attack.[84] Eisenhower had the foresight to see that offensive missile developments were moving so quickly it was unnecessary to produce an antimissile missile. His political courage to act on this belief saved the country billions.

THE BATTLE OF THE BUDGET FOR FY 1958

To understand the full range of budgetary politics during the Eisenhower presidency, it is informative to study what the media labeled "the battle of the budget." A short review of the episode is valuable because Richard Neustadt uses an analysis of Eisenhower's budgetary politics to substantiate his view that the presidency is no place for amateurs.[85] In Neustadt's widely read book, Franklin Roosevelt's presidency is portrayed as the model of a professional politician and Eisenhower's is used as a model of an amateur in the White House. Neustadt defines Eisenhower as an amateur because he tried to be a president who was "above politics"; consequently, he reigned but did not rule. To demonstrate the ineffectiveness of an amateur, Neustadt presents a case study on Treasury Secretary George Humphrey's criticism of the FY 1958 budget — criticism that was proclaimed at a press conference on the very day (January 15, 1957) that Eisenhower's budget message was delivered to Congress. By claiming that if such large and expanding budget expenditures were continued the United States would suffer a recession that would "curl your hair," Humphrey appeared to be breaking ties with the president. Instead, political observers were flabbergasted to learn that Eisenhower had approved — even edited — the Treasury secretary's press conference statement (though not Humphrey's off-the-cuff remark about a hair-curling depression.) In Neustadt's analysis, only an amateur in politics would have allowed such a blunder, which squandered the bargaining advantages earned from Eisenhower's 1956 electoral landslide victory and put the president on the defensive throughout 1957. Neustadt's book is one of the most perceptive studies of the modern presidency, but it is misleading in its analysis of Eisenhower and his style of leadership.

Some aspects of the battle of the FY 1958 budget can now be reexamined using evidence from the Eisenhower Library that was not available to Neustadt. The origin of this conflict was Humphrey's disgust with the FY 1958 budget and, ironically, his concern for public relations. In a series of letters and memos Humphrey laid out a political and economic strategy for his close friend, the president. Humphrey's letter of December 6, 1956, made the case that since monetary policy could no longer constrain inflation, the FY 1958 budget would have to be cut further to allow the administration to propose a substantial tax cut in January 1958 for FY 1959.[86] In essence, Humphrey urged Eisenhower to exploit his popularity in 1957 to curtail expenditures so that the president could provide a popular tax cut in 1958.

Twelve days later Humphrey wrote to the president complaining that too many people were willing to accept "creeping inflation." He suggested that "the idea that we 'Let the Federal government do it, then it won't cost anybody anything' is all too prevalent. We have just got to beat it down some way." Humphrey used an interesting metaphor: "We are sort of in the position of evangelists to get the more thoughtful sufficiently vocal to carry the crowd."[87] Knowing his friend well, Humphrey appealed to the president's sense of duty and morality, and advised him to avoid the easy road and to lead the country along the correct path of fiscal conservatism.

As the conservative conscience within the cabinet, Humphrey believed the administration was veering dangerously off this righteous path. In his January 8, 1957, letter to Eisenhower, Humphrey stressed that business confidence would be shaken by the size and trend of the budget: "Our reduction in Government expenditures three years ago made possible the largest tax reduction in our history and sparked the wave of national confidence which has carried us through the past two most prosperous years we have ever known." However, since FY 1956, expenditures had grown an estimated $7.2 billion and revenues had increased an estimated $13.2 billion — both discomforting trends. Military expenditures, while necessary to meet the Soviet threat, were, in Humphrey's eyes, an economic waste because they made "no additions to the permanent wealth of the country." On the other hand, rising income, inflation, and the progressive tax structure meant that the government was taking a larger share of the national income. Such expanding extractions from individuals and corporations could not be continued for long without causing a recession. Finally, since the usual procedures had failed over the past three years to reverse the trend of budget increases, Humphrey recommended a novel approach. He proposed that Congress be encouraged to cut the president's FY 1958 budget, scheduled to be released the next week, on January 15, 1957. Humphrey's plan was to defy conventional procedures by not giving the FY 1958 figures developed by the BOB full administration support in the initial bargaining with Congress in order to generate additional downward pressure on federal expenditures over the next eighteen months.[88]

When Humphrey read his four-page memo to the cabinet on January 9, 1957, he explained that he was troubled by the likelihood of a negative response from businesspeople and conservative Republicans to rising expenditures and no tax cut, and that timely action might become necessary to ward off serious decline in economic activity.[89] Without specifying where, Humphrey suggested that $4 billion worth of potential cuts still existed in the FY 1958 budget. Humphrey recommended that his memo be released as a public letter to the president calling for continued efforts by the administration, the Congress, and the public to reduce federal expenditures. Secretary of State Dulles responded by warning that Humphrey's proposal was an attack on a budget that had been shaped by the entire administration. Budget Director Brundage also objected to Humphrey's draft letter, claiming that, if publicized, it would be interpreted as a rift within the administration. Thus, in contrast to what Neustadt writes concerning the inadequacy of Eisenhower's advisory system, two red flags were raised about Humphrey's proposal.

As for Eisenhower, he was ambivalent and gloomy about the FY 1958 budget. Because of the 1956 presidential election and the crises of Hungary and Suez, he was out of touch with the budget figures and was therefore surprised and distressed when Brundage presented the final totals to him. There was not enough time for Eisenhower and Brundage to force further cuts before the executive budget had to be publicly released on January 15. Despite his efforts, Eisenhower was submitting the largest peacetime budget in the history of the United States. Eisenhower saw himself as a general who was losing the war to the enemy of ever-increasing expenditures. The president expressed his frustration by saying, "I've never felt so helpless."[90]

In response to the two warnings from Dulles and Brundage, Eisenhower agreed to personally edit Humphrey's memo and to change the means of transmittal from a letter to a press conference. Eisenhower accepted a revised version of Humphrey's proposal because he was dissatisfied with the outcome of the standard means of controlling the budget. Moreover, by permitting conservative criticism of his moderately liberal budget, the president could postpone the painful choice between competitive components of his belief system.

These events can now be viewed as an example of Eisenhower's hidden-hand leadership. The president had delegated considerable fiscal authority to Humphrey. On his own, Humphrey proposed a novel approach to mobilize public pressures to curtail the federal budget. Since Eisenhower knew this effort would generate political heat, he worked behind the scenes and used his language skills to edit Humphrey's press conference statement to insure that this effort would promote the president's objectives. Unlike Humphrey's original January 8 memo, the press release began with the words, "in support of the President's Budget Message. . . ."[91] Several other phrases were added indicating that Eisenhower, a careful editor, wanted to show that Humphrey was supporting him. The press release stressed more explicitly than Humphrey's original document that success in this difficult endeavor of trimming federal expenditures would be rewarded in 1958 with a tax cut. Unfortunately for the president, this sweetener was overshadowed by the media attention given Humphrey's extemporaneous remark about a hair-curling depression. Eisenhower's carefully crafted language was not the message that reached the public.

Thus, the Eisenhower we can now see does not consider himself above politics; he is a partisan Republican struggling against a Democratic-controlled Congress and his own bureaucrats to keep expenses down. He is plotting to exploit his popularity in 1957 to curtail expenditures so that he can provide a popular tax cut in 1958. He is concerned with how to convince Congress and the public of the need for a more disciplined budget.

This case illustrates the problem of presidential leadership when the chief executive is confronted by conflicting pressures. The FY 1958 budget symbolized how difficult, if not impossible, it was going to be to reconcile the contradictory expectations of Eisenhower's Modern Republicanism with his conservative concern for fiscal responsibility. Because of these conflicting pressures, Eisenhower acquiesced in submitting Brundage's budget and in supporting Humphrey's criticism that further cuts should be made. While Neustadt emphasizes the negative consequences of Humphrey's press conference, he also correctly suggests that it foreshadowed a chronic policy dilemma: "What caused the doubts in Eisenhower's mind were durable dilemmas we shall carry with us through the 1960s. By letting Humphrey speak for him in different words than his, Eisenhower . . . publicized the fact that he was forced to seek opposing objectives which had torn the patchwork holding them together throughout the earlier years: stability *and* growth, defense *and* welfare, funds for public services *and* funds in private hands."[92]

The faces of this issue that Eisenhower saw were the following: halting the upward trend of the budget, reducing the threat of inflation, conciliating conservative discomfiture, pleasing a trusted counselor, and generating countervailing power to reduce the budget. What he did not see, according to Neustadt, were the risks to his professional reputation. By ignoring the bargaining advantages that submitting a budget offers a president, Eisenhower failed to ask himself a clarifying question: "How may Humphrey's presentation make mine (and me) look when I have endorsed both?"[93] Neustadt's answer was that it made Eisenhower look foolish and weakened his bargaining position in the budgetary process.

The president did not ask Neustadt's clarifying question but he did go through a clarifying experience. In fighting the battle of the FY 1958 budget, Eisenhower discovered that his conservative values were stronger than his liberal ones. This allowed the New Eisenhower, the more conservatively committed president, to emerge from this episode.

During his first term, the president had boxed himself in because of his commitments to harmonize welfare liberalism with economic conservatism. But early in the second term, budgetary concerns and fears of inflation moved Eisenhower to the right. After Humphrey's press conference made the FY 1958 budget a front-page issue, Eisenhower had to defend his budget in numerous press conferences and speeches; this forced him to analyze budget trends in more detail than ever before. Such immersion in budgetary figures became a voyage of discovery and transformation for Eisenhower—a change in the president's outlook that did not go unnoticed. According to Arthur Larson, "If I were to select the point at which the graph of the Eisenhower administration began to turn from moderate progressivism to conservatism, it would be about Easter 1957. . . . To me, the most telling symptom of the change was the increasing obsession of President Eisenhower with the budget."[94] For Eisenhower, the scales were decisively tipped because the former general viewed balancing the budget as a national security issue and a necessity in what was likely to be a protracted Cold War struggle against the Soviet Union. A bankrupt or inflation-ridden United States could neither preserve its democratic political system nor defend itself and its allies.

Hence, as a result of this clarifying experience, Eisenhower became more aware of his own values and was able to make his choice. By 1959 the New Eisenhower had given up most of his domestic liberalism. The New Eisenhower was a conservative president.

CONCLUSION

This chapter has analyzed Eisenhower's efforts to achieve one of the strategic goals of his presidency—a balanced budget. Although he inherited a budgetary mess from President Truman, he was able to attain three balanced budgets—in FY 1956, FY 1957, and FY 1960. To balance the FY 1960 budget, after experiencing the recession-induced $12.4 billion deficit in FY 1959, was a truly remarkable feat. In addition, Eisenhower succeeded in lowering the ratio of federal expenditures to the GNP, although he was not able to reduce the size of the national debt. Nor was the president able to cut annual federal expenditures to $60 billion; instead, by the end of the 1950s the budget was breaking the $80 billion mark. As for the defense budget, he constrained and stabilized it for the "long haul" while developing a variety of new weapons under the New Look and maintaining the peace.

Nevertheless, the pressures to expand federal expenditures—especially from the Departments of HEW and Defense—steadily multiplied throughout the decade and eventually put the Eisenhower presidency on the political defensive. Regarding HEW policies, as the president became more rigidly conservative in his concerns for a balanced budget, he was no longer able to strike a politically acceptable balance between compassion and fiscal prudence. As for the defense department, the aftermath of Sputnik created pressures that even the former general could barely contain and only at great political cost. The president's response to the post-Sputnik hysteria was to initiate a few supplementary military appropriation bills and the National Defense Education Act of 1958. He avoided a number of crash programs, such as building air-raid shelters, thus saving the Treasury billions.

In reexamining the battle of the FY 1958 budget, this chapter tries to correct Richard Neustadt's misleading portrait of Eisenhower. Neustadt concludes that Eisenhower was a passive president who reigned above politics, an amateur who could not see his personal power stakes in the issues before him because he was surrounded by an overly protective staff and dominated by strong cabinet secretaries who had been delegated too much authority. But the new evidence shows that Eisenhower was more of a behind-the-scenes activist practicing the art of persuasion than Neustadt realized. Moreover, this case study reveals the effects of a clarifying experience on Eisenhower, who learned during a painful period of private and public discussion over the budget which of his conflicting values were the most important to him and should, therefore, determine subsequent policy choices. As a result of this clarifying experience, a New Eisenhower emerged who was a more conservative president.

The New Eisenhower was still popular, but he was less politically effective than he had been as the leader of the Modern Republicans in his first term. Eisenhower's budget priorities, bolstered by the use of the veto, created a logjam of legislative proposals in Congress. Eisenhower failed to preempt public policy space with Republican programs. He should have recognized that if there was great pressure to respond to certain national problems (such as health care for the elderly) within his administration as well as in Congress, sooner or later there were inevitably going to be federal programs in these policy areas. Modern Republicans like Folsom, Flemming, and Mitchell could have negotiated compromises with Democratic leaders like Rayburn and Johnson that would have created policy far closer to Eisenhower's preferences than the Great Society bills passed in the 1960s.

By the end of Eisenhower's second term, his budget priorities had placed him in the hopeless position of trying to stem the tide of progressive legislation designed to meet a number of national needs. One Modern Republican sadly describes the consequences: "Negativism was triumphant. Postpone, delay, or better still don't do anything. Stans was blocking everything, even progress that had previously been agreed upon. The president himself was obsessed with the sound fiscal idea, and that was that."[95] By 1958 even Nixon, according to Ambrose, "was coming to regard Eisenhower as an old fogy stuck in standpattism."[96] A White House staff aide paints this picture: "As Eisenhower fought this economic fight he became a symbol of conservatism embittered. And more and more he becme a contrast to the youthful senator from Massachusetts who . . . became a symbol of liberalism resurgent."[97] Ironically, although Eisenhower handed over the White House to Kennedy with the budget in better shape than the one he had inherited from Truman, the aging president received few accolades; indeed, he had to defend his budget policy against internal and external critics. After the frustration the Eisenhower administration encountered in pursuing its budgetary policy, it is not surprising that it increasingly looked toward monetary policy as the preferred instrument. That is the subject of chapter 5.

5
Monetary Policy—
The Battle against Inflation

The Eisenhower administration was as committed to preventing inflation as it was to balancing the budget. Indeed, it saw the latter as one of its principal means of preventing inflation. As the administration's economic policymakers learned how inflexible the budget was, they increasingly turned to and relied on monetary policy to combat inflation and stabilize the economy. Such a strategy required that the Eisenhower presidency forge closer ties with the Federal Reserve Board, the independent regulatory agency that largely administers monetary policy. For both the Eisenhower presidency and the FRB, fighting inflation during the general prosperity that prevailed throughout the 1950s turned out to be politically painful and technically difficult—an unpopular, never-ending struggle. Although price increases were small between 1953 and 1961 (in comparison with the rise in prices beginning after 1965 and continuing into the 1980s), prices did accelerate in the latter half of the 1950s. Inflation became a salient issue as press headlines frequently heralded that the consumer price index had reached an "all time high." Still, when the FRB, with the administration's silent blessing, employed "tight money" policies to curb inflation, many Democrats and consumers charged that the cure (high interest rates) was worse than the disease (inflation).

MONETARY POLICY

A former member of the FRB writes, "Monetary policy is among the most discussed but least understood of all major influences on the economy."[1] Even Eisenhower admitted that he did not comprehend the expansion and contraction of money and credit. In fact, Eisenhower first met Robert Anderson in January 1951 when Anderson was asked to explain the Treasury–Federal Reserve dispute to the general. And as late as September 1957, the president asked Treasury Secretary Anderson to submit a memo explaining the basic elements of the monetary and credit system.[2]

The Constitution gives Congress the power "to coin Money" and "regulate the Value thereof." In response to the bank panic of 1907, Congress in 1913 passed the Federal Reserve Act, which delegated monetary power to a new Federal Reserve System. Congress recognized that "money had to be managed" but that it lacked the time, the expertise, and the political will to regulate the banks. Consequently, Congress created an independent regulatory agency that was to be "self-financing and thus free from the appropriations process," operating under an exceptionally vague legislative mandate.[3] According to the Federal Reserve Act, the Fed (as it is called by the financial press) is supposed to conduct its operations "with a view of accommodating commerce and business." John Woolley stresses that "the Federal Reserve was not created for the purpose of macroeconomic stabilization. On the contrary, as in other Western settings, it emerged in response to the need for a central institution to serve other banks. Like other central banks, the Federal Reserve has a long and conservative heritage. It has been closely linked to the major financial institutions of the day, and its organizational ethos has been one of stressing stability."[4]

But the Federal Reserve, reflecting the American political culture, is a unique central bank. Structurally, it was given enough political independence so that it could act responsibly and in the financial interests of the nation and would be somewhat protected from the inevitable pressures to overexpand the money supply and from partisan manipulation of the monetary system. The Federal Reserve Act divided the United States into twelve districts, each with its own Federal Reserve Bank. These twelve regional banks were initially capitalized by the commercial bank members of the Federal Reserve System. Subsequently, Federal Reserve Banks have maintained their capitalization primarily by holding treasury securities rather than by lending out money as commercial banks do. The twelve banks are coordinated by the seven-member Board of Governors, known as the Federal Reserve Board, of the Federal Reserve System in Washington, D.C. The FRB's members are selected by the president, with the consent of the Senate, for fourteen-year, overlapping terms. In making the selections, the president is required to give due consideration to "fair representation of financial, agricultural, industrial, and commercial interests, and geographical divisions of the country," and not more than one member can be named from a single Federal Reserve District. The chair of the FRB is selected by the president for a four-year term that can be renewed. Members of the FRB can be removed for cause, but that power has never been publicly exercised. Thus insulated from direct political pressures, the FRB can regulate the money and credit system in a technocratic manner. This is considered necessary because easy money has a seductive appeal that labor, farmers, home buyers, and especially politicans before elections find impossible to resist.

The Banking Act of 1933 created another important component of the Federal Reserve System, the Federal Open Market Committee (FOMC). The FOMC is composed of twelve voting members: the seven members of the FRB; the president of the Federal Reserve Bank of New York, who has a permanent seat; and four other members selected by rotation from the other eleven district bank presidents. The other seven reserve bank presidents attend FOMC meetings as nonvoting members and participate in the discussions. At the monthly FOMC meetings—the chair of the FRB presides—the members analyze the financial markets and decide whether to pump more reserves into the banking system by buying treasury bills (i.e., short-term bonds maturing in less than a year) or longer-term bonds, or whether to tighten the money supply by selling government securities. Decisions of the FOMC to buy or sell government securities are carried out by the Federal Reserve Bank in New York, which is also in charge of buying and selling foreign currencies.

The FRB declined in influence during the early 1930s because it was not able to prevent the failure of many banks or avert the Depression. To combat the Depression, the Keynesians emphasized fiscal policy (tax and budget policies), sometimes denigrating monetary policy with the phrase "money doesn't matter." Many Keynesians felt that the only function of monetary policy was to keep interest rates low in order to facilitate investment. When World War II broke out, Treasury Secretary Henry Morganthau forced the FRB to accept for the duration of the war a fixed pattern of rates from ⅜ percent for ninety-day treasury bills, to 2½ percent for the longest-term treasury bonds, those maturing in twenty to twenty-five years. Donald Kettl explains: "The agreement, known as the 'peg,' guaranteed that no Treasury offering would fail during the war and that the Treasury would be assured of stable, low prices for its obligations during the campaign. If for any reason the public did not buy all the securities that Treasury needed to sell, the Fed was prepared to buy them itself."[5] The Fed's peg assured the success and low cost of the Treasury's financing but at the expense of the Fed's independence to control the money supply. The United States financed 60 percent of its wartime costs by borrowing, which tripled the money supply and created the potential for rampant inflation during the postwar period.[6] The national debt, which had stood at $48 billion in 1939, reached a peak of $280 billion by 1945. Managing that public debt has become an albatross for every subsequent Treasury secretary and a potential source of friction with the chair of the FRB.

After World War II, fears of inflation and the need to manage the public debt increased the influence of the FRB and of monetary policy. As G. L.

Bach explains, "The vast monetary expansion during the Second World War, combined with the bond pegging in the postwar years, highlighted the role of monetary expansion in producing inflation. Too much money and too few goods to buy with it turned out to be the major postwar economic problem — not the stagnant economy forecast by many Keynesians."[7] Truman's secretary of the Treasury, John Snyder, wanted to continue the peg because the United States had to borrow or reborrow $50 billion to $70 billion each year, and he naturally wished to guarantee the lowest interest rates. The Fed wanted to cooperate with the Treasury in managing the debt but not in a subordinate role as symbolized by the peg. The FRB was increasingly concerned that its lack of independence was preventing it from combating inflation. According to Kettl, "More than any structural tie between the Fed and the Treasury, the peg undermined the Fed's independence. Once it agreed to support the Treasury's pattern of rates, the Fed could take no action to tighten the money supply (and force rates up), since it would have to absorb the Treasury's offerings at the lower rate in any event."[8]

With the Korean War and the Cold War increasing both the need for deficit financing and the dangers of inflation, the Fed and the Treasury Department were on a collision course. Their conflict became a nasty, public squabble in January 1951, a counterproductive situation for both sets of officials, who agreed on the need to bolster business confidence. Treasury Secretary Snyder assigned William McChesney Martin, an assistant secretary of the Treasury, to negotiate an agreement with the FRB. Martin negotiated terms concerning the basic arrangements to guide future Fed-Treasury relations, which were publicized on March 3, 1951. This agreement, known as the "Accord," gradually liberated the FRB from the constraints of the peg. Shortly thereafter, President Truman appointed Martin to succeed Thomas McCabe as FRB member and chairman.[9] Martin was chair of the FRB throughout the Eisenhower years and beyond and was finally replaced in 1970 by Arthur Burns.

Martin largely institutionalized the modern role of the Fed during the Eisenhower presidency. The Federal Reserve System was created in 1913 to regulate the banks in order to prevent currency crises; in the 1950s the FRB joined the Treasury, the Bureau of the Budget, and the Council of Economic Advisers as a major — and the most independent — player in the formulation of macroeconomic policymaking. Martin helped to bring about this transformation because he and Eisenhower shared a similar economic philosophy and loathing of inflation. Although there were several disagreements between the FRB and the Eisenhower administration, the relationship was usually characterized by communication and cooperation.

Martin's personality was a unique blend of moralist and pragmatist. Sherman Maisel, who served with Martin as a board member during the 1960s, described him as a "money moralist." "Money as Martin sees it is a basic

William McChesney Martin, chairman of the Federal Reserve Board. (Courtesy Federal Board.)

moral force. Throughout history it has been misused by governments creating too much of it and depreciating its value. This is an immoral act. . . . [Hence] the Federal Reserve has the critical function of seeing that there is not too much money."[10] Other colleagues described Martin as a man of sincerity and personal charm. He chaired both the FRB and the FOMC in a collegial spirit. Interestingly, Martin was not an economist; he had a law degree from Columbia University and had made his money selling bonds on

Wall Street. Kettl stresses that Martin "did not have the training to lead the system's policies intellectually. His role, rather, was that of a consensus builder. He always spoke last and then tried to articulate a position on which nearly everyone could agree. His technique typically produced unanimous (or nearly so) votes, and he was willing to delay issues for one or two meetings until a clear consensus had emerged."[11] Martin's consensus-building style meant that policy changes emerged slowly and cautiously from the Fed.

Martin employed a pragmatic monetary philosophy as chairman of the Federal Reserve. In his view, no hard and fast rules could determine monetary policy; the FRB had to have discretionary authority to decide what was best for an economy that was always changing and always unpredictable. Experience had taught Martin that the law of supply and demand was particularly important. As Martin told the Joint Economic Committee in January 1957, "Interest rate charges, as well as other price movements, reflect supply-demand relationships. Rising rates, like rises in other prices, indicate that demand is exceeding supply. They discourage some borrowing on the one hand and encourage increased savings on the other. Thus they perform the vital function of balancing supply and demand. Current interest rates are a signal that the economy is straining its resources by trying to accomplish more at one time than resources permit."[12]

As the inflation rate inched up during the latter half of the 1950s, Martin became alarmed that too many economists and politicians believed that creeping inflation was a chronic and unavoidable condition in a modern economy. Martin considered that idea dangerous and believed that sound fiscal and monetary policies could prevent inflation while promoting economic growth. He also hoped that such policies would complement each other, but by 1958 he publicly recognized that "fiscal policy is less flexible than monetary policy."[13] This statement implied that the Federal Reserve would have to assume greater responsibilities in blocking inflation. As a "money moralist," representing an agency with close ties to banking interests, Martin was willing to assume this burden.

Under Martin's leadership, the FRB relied mainly upon three general quantitative instruments of credit control to influence monetary policy — reserve ratios, the discount rate, and open-market operations. The FRB has the authority to raise or lower the funds that member banks must keep in their district Federal Reserve Banks as reserves against various classes of deposits. If the Federal Reserve wants to tighten credit, it can raise the required reserve ratios for large and small banks up to the 22 and 14 percent statutory limits, respectively. If the Federal Reserve wants to ease credit conditions, it can reduce legal reserve ratios to as low as 10 and 7 percent, respectively, for large and small banks. Manipulating reserve ratios can be important because this influences how much money the banking system can lend, which, in turn, affects how much money is being created. Changing reserve requirements is a powerful device, but it is used infrequently because the FRB possesses other instruments that can achieve the same result more easily.

The second instrument at the FRB's disposal is the discount rate, the interest rate charged by the Federal Reserve for loans to member banks. By raising the discount rate, the Fed tends to constrain the expansion of bank deposits, and by lowering the discount, it tends to achieve the opposite effect. Maisel explains: "While a move in the discount rate is the most traditional, awesome, and newsworthy instrument in the Federal Reserve's portfolio, it in fact has a minimal real impact, since banks actually borrow very little from the Fed. A move in the discount rate can have a major impact, however, if it is intended to, and does, announce a shift in monetary policy and if it succeeds in changing expectations of future policy."[14]

The third and most-used instrument of monetary policy is the Fed's use of open-market operations. The FOMC determines open-market policy— that is, it decides whether to buy or sell government securities (bills, notes, and bonds). FOMC directives to ease or to tighten the money supply are implemented by the Open Market Desk of the Federal Reserve Bank in New York. To stimulate monetary growth, the Federal Reserve buys government securities, and, conversely, to tighten the money supply, it sells government securities. As Albert Rees explains, "When the Federal Reserve buys securities, it pays for them by creating deposits for the sellers in the Federal Reserve Banks; these deposits serve as additions to reserves for commercial banks. The added reserves permit commercial banks as a group to expand their loans and deposits by a multiple of the new reserves; this multiple is the inverse of the reserve ratio. For example, if reserves of 10 percent are required against all deposits, an additional dollar of reserves could ultimately support $10 of additional deposits."[15] And when the Federal Reserve sells government securities, it has the opposite effect.

Open-market operations are the most flexible of the three policy instruments because the FOMC can rapidly change the size and direction of its purchases or sales of government securities in order to nudge the financial markets in the desired direction. Under Martin's leadership, the FOMC increased the frequency of its meetings from about four times a year before 1955 to about once every three weeks after 1955."[16] This increase in the number of meetings reflected mainly the more dynamic use of open-market operations to influence the money supply.

In addition, in 1953, Martin succeeded in gaining the support of the FOMC (in spite of the opposition of the New York bank representative) for a policy known as "bills only." This policy called for the Federal Reserve, through its open-market operations, to influence banking reserves by buying or selling only short-term securities—that is, Treasury obligations maturing in a year or less. Kettl points out that "by limiting the FOMC's actions to bills . . . it would keep the Fed away from longer-term bonds and thus far away from the pegging issue that had dominated the previous decade. . . . Less clear was the fact that it would lessen the role of the Federal Reserve Bank of New York. . . . Prior to the 'bills only' policy it could, for example, deal in longer-term securities at its discretion to produce the same degree of 'tightness' or 'easiness' of the money supply."[17] The "bills only" policy was in effect from 1953 to 1961; it reflected both the Fed's independence from Treasury domination and Martin's political skills in centralizing authority.

One of the major monetary issues of the 1950s was how Martin and the Fed would use that increasingly independent and centralized authority. Freed from the requirement to support government bond prices, what criteria would the FRB use in making decisions? Although Martin refused to explain explicitly the Fed's decision-making criteria, Milton Friedman and Anna Jacobson Schwartz identify two: The first criterion was to provide "the appropriate secular growth of the stock of money . . . to amounts consistent with the requirements of a growing economy operating at a high level without inflation."[18] Martin declined to specify how much the supply of money would have to grow each year in order to satisfy that requirement.

According to Friedman and Schwartz, "The second criterion, which came to dominate short-term policy, was that the System should aim at producing countercyclical variations in credit conditions and, explicitly, in the money stock: that it should 'lean against the wind' by taking restrictive action during periods of economic expansion, and expansionary action during periods of economic contraction."[19] This second criterion reflected the new macroeconomic role of the Federal Reserve. Again, however, Martin refused to explain how to make this criterion operational. For example, how did the Fed determine which way the wind was blowing? At what point should the Fed begin leaning against the wind? How hard should the Fed lean against the wind? Martin believed that such decisions had to be made by the Federal Reserve policymakers who considered and balanced a variety of factors. Their decision-making rules could neither be explicitly nor publicly formalized.

Nor could the Fed's decisions always be popular. As Martin used to explain to noneconomists, the major task of the Federal Reserve had become taking away the punch bowl just when everyone was having a good time.

It must be stressed that monetary policy can exercise only a very indirect influence on the billions of economic decisions that millions of citizens make. As Kettl suggests, "The Fed . . . has great leverage over the economy, but its control is incomplete. In making monetary policy, the Fed faces enormous technical uncertainties that make it impossible for Fed officials to predict with precision what results their decisions will produce."[20] For example, although it is the Fed's responsibility to control the money supply, the increase in installment buying and use of credit cards has made it more difficult to define just what "money" is. In addition, the "velocity" of money spending must also be considered. Since most kinds of "money" are repeatedly spent each year, statisticians in the Fed must estimate how many times a typical dollar will be spent to ascertain how much economic growth any given level of money supply will support. Uncertainty is further increased when decisions have to be made on the basis of a bewildering array of economic statistics which may be, at best, several weeks old when processed and released. There is also the problem of interpreting the data. Does an increase in consumer demand portend healthy, sustainable economic growth or the first stage of inflation? The dilemma is that there are no reliable forecasting models which allow policymakers to analyze the statistics and trends of today and be fairly certain what they mean for the future. Thus, the Fed must play the role of a doctor who constantly prescribes medicines to cure his patients' ills, but who can never be sure how the remedies will work.

Despite these handicaps, the revival of monetary policy during the 1950s had a special appeal to conservatives because its influence was subtle and indirect. Monetary policy avoided direct controls administered by bureaucrats. The Fed only influenced the supply of money and credit; it did not control demand. As Galbraith wryly notes, "No businessman, or indeed no citizen, was told what to do. Instead they were guided by forces of which they were themselves not wholly aware. If the economy must be given guidance, how gratifying that it be done in this discreet and seemly way."[21] Conservatives also came to believe that monetary policy was the most effective means to curtail inflation. As Treasury Secretary Anderson spelled out for Eisenhower, "These three instruments give the Federal Reserve an effective means of restraint when excessive bank credit expansion threatens. They can also be used in reverse to provide greater credit ease in times of recession. They may be less effective then, however, as people may be unwilling either to make loans or borrow money if they are uncertain about the future, even if excess bank reserves are available. Monetary policy can be likened to a string. You can get better results when you are pulling on it in combatting inflation than pushing on it when the tables are turned."[22]

For conservatives, federal influence was sanitized and depoliticized by the technocratic decision-making style of Martin's Federal Reserve. Indeed, monetarists, under the leadership of Milton Friedman, the University of Chicago economist, believed that monetary policy could be more effective if it were less subject to human discretion. Friedman, who later won the 1976 Nobel Prize in economics, argued that the growth of the nation's supply of money determines the economy's future growth and inflation. Hence, the supply of money rather than interest rates should be the target and guide for monetary policy. Friedman's monetary theory holds that the Federal Reserve should increase the money supply according to a fixed rule at a constant rate. By maintaining steady, moderate growth of the money supply, the Fed could insure a healthy level of inflation-free economic growth.[23] Chairman Martin obviously opposed putting the Federal Reserve on the automatic pilot of Friedman's monetary theory.

Martin did believe in cooperation between the Fed and the administration to achieve the objectives of the Employment Act of 1946. Communication and cooperation through regular consultation increased during the 1950s. As mentioned in chapter 2, there was a Federal Reserve representative on Arthur Burns's Advisory Board on Economic Growth and Stability (ABEGS). George Humphrey and Robert Anderson frequently had lunch with Martin. Humphrey also appointed W. Randolph Burgess to a new position in the Treasury, the under-secretary for monetary affairs, which facilitated communication between the two agencies. Because of the growing importance of monetary policy to fight inflation and the need to respond to the balance of payments problem, the president, the chair of the FRB, the Treasury secretary, the chair of the CEA, and the budget director began to meet regularly in October 1957. In 1958, the president met with Martin twelve times.[24] This institutionalized communication and cooperation reflected a new framework of macroeconomic policymaking in which the Federal Reserve viewed its role as "independent within, but not independent from the administration." Robert Roosa, who coined these words, explains that this phrase meant that the Federal Reserve was a part of the government but "it had sufficient independence to serve as the conscience of, rather than just the servant of, any given administration."[25]

The independence of the Federal Reserve can be an invaluable political asset if the Fed cooperates with the president in pursuing the administration's objectives and takes the heat for tightening the money supply. And whenever the money supply is tightened and interest rates go up, there is considerable heat. For example, the Fed tightens the money supply to counter inflation, but the short-run effect of rising interest rates is an increase in prices. The housing and consumer credit component of the CPI will be especially hard hit. Albert Rees comments: "Most economists believe that this direct effect, except in the very short run, is smaller than the indirect effect through aggregate demand by which high interest rates reduce inflation. Much of the general public, however, holds the opposite view."[26]

Political controversy is also generated because the pain of monetary policy is not shared equally. Those hardest hit by high interest rates — small businesspeople, farmers, the construction industry, new homebuyers, and local governments — are not likely to endure their pain quietly. In June 1958, the AFL-CIO charged that the Federal Reserve's tight money policy did not stop inflation, but it did cause unemployment and bring about "windfalls" to bankers in the form of high interest rates while imposing higher prices on farmers, small businesspeople, and consumers. The AFL-CIO concluded that these results were too high a price to pay for the independence of the Federal Reserve Board.[27] However, the Eisenhower administration found that cooperation with the Fed was the most politically feasible means to achieve its anti-inflationary goals.

THE ANTI-INFLATIONARY GOALS
OF THE EISENHOWER ADMINISTRATION

In the 1952 election campaign, the Democrats were vulnerable on the issue of inflation despite the fact that price increases associated with the Korean War were tapering off. From July 1950 to April 1953, the CPI rose 12 percent, but there was only a moderate increase of 1.6 percent in 1952.[28] General Eisenhower attacked the Democrats on the decline in the purchasing power of the dollar while also promising to quickly terminate the unpopular price and wage controls that had helped to control inflation. He assumed office in 1953 with a commitment to stop inflation without employing centralized controls. With the Korean War winding down, Eisenhower could cut the military budget and follow Humphrey's advice to end most of the price and wage controls, which he did on February 6, 1953, with minimal fears of stirring up inflationary pressures. The president told Republican congressional leaders that he would like to have standby controls on consumer credit to combat inflation, but the legislators opposed this proposal. Other methods would have to be found and used.[29]

Although the Eisenhower administration was more concerned about the dangers of inflation than the Truman administration had been, the first economic challenge Eisenhower faced was the recession of 1953–54. By 1955, however, after the recession had been successfully stemmed, inflation began to emerge as the major threat to the economy. In Eisenhower's words, "Week by week we scrutinized stock prices, figures on credit expansion and debt, and other economic indicators for any sign of danger. In particular we continued to work to cut back on federal spending and produce a surplus for partial payment on the staggering national debt. 'If we cannot produce a surplus under conditions of such unprecedented prosperity,' Dr. Burns observed on August 12 [1955], 'a question can be raised as to whether the fiscal affairs of this country can ever be managed satisfactorily over the long run.'"[30] Eisenhower was beginning to realize the limitations of using budget reductions to control inflation.

In his 1957 State of the Union address, the president proclaimed that "even the optimistic analyst will realize that, in a prosperous period, the principal threat to efficient functioning of a free enterprise system is inflation."[31] By 1957, the goal of the administration was to defeat the spreading idea that a little inflation was necessary for prosperity and that attempts to curb inflation would inevitably cause recession and unemployment. Speaking for the administration, White House aide Gabriel Hauge defended both the Eisenhower presidency and the Federal Reserve for imposing some austerity on the economy to prevent inflation. To those who attacked high interest rates, he replied that interest is "the wage for saving" and is essential for investment. According to Hauge, this new emphasis on encouraging savings "requires a reorientation of some depression-born thinking, that the difficulty with our economy is oversaving and underconsumption." He condemned the idea that "creeping inflation is a tolerable price to pay for avoiding unemployment." Hauge responded to the higher level of economic expectations by claiming that the country ought to be able to tolerate "temporary periods of adjustment," and he concluded, "We must adjust our thinking to the realization that optimum prosperity and growth in the long run are not the same thing as maximum prosperity and growth in the short run. . . . A corollary to this viewpoint is that we regard the economy as a sturdy, though sensitive, mechanism capable of undergoing prudent restraint, when necessary, without being thrown into a tailspin. If we retain our depression psychosis about the tendency of the economy to run down, we become resigned to a more or less perpetual pumping up of our prosperity—hardly the way to keep it healthy."[32] Thus, Hauge argued that the anti-inflation policies of the administration and the Federal Reserve were inducing a prudent temporary adjustment that was necessary to promote a more durable and dependable period of economic growth in the future.

Eisenhower spent much of his second term rejecting Democratic legislative proposals because he considered them inflationary. His opponents claimed that he and his economic advisers were more concerned about sound dollars than sound people. No matter how often Eisenhower discussed how inflation hurt people such as the elderly living off the fixed income of a pension or social security, many felt that anti-inflationary policies aided the rich and the bankers and hurt the unions and consumers. It was tough, perhaps impossible, for Eisenhower to increase his popularity while fighting inflation.

Even George Humphrey recognized the public relations problem involved in mobilizing political support for the anti-inflation priorities of the administration. His response was to assert that the administration did not have a "hard money" policy but an "honest money" policy—that is, a commitment to maintaining the purchasing power of the dollar from month to month and year to year—and he pointed out that fulfilling that commitment would require the cooperation of several branches of government. He stressed that the Federal Reserve carried primary responsibility for managing money and credit, and he promised that the Treasury would offer "minimum interference" in the Fed's operations. In addition, the Treasury secretary strongly asserted that the termination of "pegging" was "the single most effective action in the battle against inflation."[33]

According to Humphrey, the Treasury's major role in promoting honest money was in managing the national debt. When Humphrey became secretary of the Treasury, the United States was saddled with over $267 billion in debt. The burden of this debt is revealed by the fact that, in 1953, $32 billion of it matured every ninety days. Humphrey's goal was to reduce the inflationary potential of this debt by gradually transforming the debt into longer-term issues and by transferring the debt from the banks, where it tended to be inflationary since it increased the quantity of available credit, to private investors.[34]

Humphrey's anti-inflation attitudes were based on his fear of the consequences of debasing the currency. Just as some Democrats feared that a rise in the unemployment rate might rapidly deteriorate into a depression, the secretary believed: "History demonstrates that, whenever deterioration has started, it tends to continue at an ever increasing rate. . . . Unless courageous, determined corrective action is taken in time, it finally speeds entirely out of control and finishes in utter collapse. The first half of the depreciation of our dollar has already occurred. The programs and conditions which this Administration inherited would have accelerated that pace. Stopping that spiral is imperative."[35]

Robert Anderson, Humphrey's second-term successor, was equally opposed to inflation, seeing it not as an ally of growth, but as the long-run "enemy of growth."[36] He stressed that "credit can be created by numerous devices: but capital has to be saved. Those who would provide capital through savings must be encouraged so that money saved will maintain its value."[37] With high inflation, a penny saved is not earned, it is lost, and real future growth cannot occur. Thus, as the rising inflation rate appeared to be a chronic attribute of the American economy in the latter part of the 1950s, Anderson dedicated himself to overcoming the "inflationary psychology" that was beginning to see such increases as inevitable. That is why he supported both the tight money policies of the Federal Reserve and the balanced budget in FY 1960 after the large deficit in FY 1959.[38]

Eisenhower's first chairman of the CEA, Arthur Burns, an expert in the business cycle, was also deeply concerned about inflation. By 1955, Burns recognized that inflation was likely to become a major problem and that credit restraint might provide the best available solution. By the time Raymond Saulnier replaced Burns as chairman in December 1956, the CPI was rising at an annual rate of 3½ percent; consequently, reducing the inflation rate became one of his top priorities. Although Saulnier did not always agree with the timing of Federal Reserve decisions, he was a strong believer in the efficacy of monetary policy: "Money policy is by far the most flexible, adaptable, useable instrument for achieving economic stability. I am satisfied to have that in the hands of a competent, experienced, so far as feasible depoliticized Federal Reserve Board."[39]

EISENHOWER'S ANTI-INFLATION ACHIEVEMENT

President Eisenhower's anti-inflationary record looks better in retrospect than it did in 1961. The United States uses two general price indices to measure inflation—the CPI and the overall deflator of the GNP. The CPI measures prices paid by a typical urban wage-earning family for a variety of goods and services. The GNP deflator monitors a much broader range of prices; it measures the prices of all newly produced goods and services. Both of these indices have generally shown price increases every year since 1933. Arthur Okun's 1970 study defined noninflationary years as those when both measuring tools have risen less than 1.75 percent. Using that standard, 1949, 1950, 1953–55, and 1959–64 were noninflationary years. Okun defined an inflationary year as one in which both indices rose by 2.75 percent or more. According to that standard, the Eisenhower presidency suffered one year of inflation—1957. In 1956 and 1958, the indices increased between 1.75 and 2.75 percent.[40] Eisenhower boasts in his memoirs that "whereas the 1939 dollar was worth 52 cents by January 1953, the 1953 dollar had lost only about 5-1/2 cents of its value by 1961."[41] During the Eisenhower presidency, the average annual rise of the CPI was only 1.5 percent; from 1967 to 1978, it averaged 6.3 percent. In 1979 and 1980, the United States experienced the double-digit inflation that contributed so heavily to President Jimmy Carter's electoral loss to Ronald Reagan.

However healthy the economy of the 1950s may look in retrospect, price increases were a cause of anxiety to Eisenhower and many others at the time. In spite of the president's willingness to impose budget austerity and the Federal Reserve's dedication to preventing inflation, prices continued to inch upward. Three recessions merely slowed the process; they did not reverse it. Between December 1956 and December 1960, the Federal Reserve increased the money supply (demand deposits and currency outside of the banks, which is called M-1) at an annual average rate of less than 1 percent. As Vatter explains, the money supply "rose much more slowly than GNP. The great bulk of the rise in GNP from 1955 to 1960 was accommodated by increases in the velocity of money, and a distinctly minor proportion by increases in its quantity."[42] No wonder there was so much discussion by the end of the decade about an "inflationary bias" built into the system.

The Treasury did not achieve much success in meeting its debt management goals. Despite repeated attempts to offer longer-term securities (about $51 billion worth that would mature in over five years was sold between 1953 and 1960), about 80 percent of the marketable public debt of $184 billion in 1960 was set to mature within five years, in contrast to 71 percent in December 1953. In 1960, $70 billion worth of debt would come to maturity within one year.[43] Borrowing requirements of this size and frequency, during a time of expanding private credit demands, made it very difficult for the Treasury to use debt management as an efficient anti-inflationary instrument. The Treasury blamed Congress for failing to pass in 1959 and 1960 administration proposals that would have eliminated the 4¼ percent ceiling on new long-term (more than five years) treasury bonds.[44]

THE EISENHOWER ADMINISTRATION'S
ANTI-INFLATIONARY POLICIES

The first step in the Eisenhower administration's attempt to prevent inflation was to increase communication with the FRB. Communication and cooperation with the always courteous William McChesney Martin was considered possible even though he was a Democrat. In a postelection memo Gabriel Hauge advised the president-elect: "At the Federal Reserve Board things are in pretty good shape under William McChesney Martin, an example of the right kind of Democrat. He has served as Assistant Secretary of the Treasury and understands the Treasury–Federal Reserve relationship."[45] Neither Eisenhower nor Martin wanted a repeat of the 1951 Truman–Federal Reserve squabble.

In 1953 regular consultation was instituted between Humphrey and Martin, and Federal Reserve officials were participants on Burns's ABEGS. Burns describes "frequent, honest consultation and communication" with the Federal Reserve during his chairmanship of the CEA.[46] When Raymond Saulnier replaced Burns, he had lunch every two weeks at the Fed with Martin and Vice-Chairman C. Canby Balderston. In September 1957, after a Treasury-Fed disagreement in April 1956 which will be discussed later, regular meetings in the White House of the president, Martin, Anderson, Saulnier, and Hauge were arranged. According to Saulnier, "Those meetings would almost invariably start with the President looking to me to describe the economic situation. Then if the Fed saw it differently, or the Treasury saw it differently, they had an opportunity to make their views known. I don't remember any cases in which there were really sharp differences."[47]

Martin recognized that if the Federal Reserve was going to play a more powerful role in macroeconomic policy, it would need to coordinate with—but not subordinate to—the administration. Similarly, the Eisenhower administration understood that it needed the Fed as an ally—one that would become essential as Democratic majorities in Congress impeded the administration's fiscal policies and inflation continued to creep upward. Still, it was probably easier for Martin to institutionalize closer relations with Anderson, a southern Democrat, than with the more blunt and partisan Humphrey.[48]

The second step in the Eisenhower administration's anti-inflation strategy was to achieve policy cooperation with the Federal Reserve. Early in Eisenhower's presidency, with the chief executive committed to a quick dismantling of price and wage controls and the Korean War still not settled, both the administration and the Federal Reserve were concerned about the threat of inflation. In January 1953, the Federal Reserve began tightening the money supply by raising the discount rate from 1¾ to 2 percent and by directing its open-market operations to sell government securities. In April 1953, Humphrey announced that the Treasury was offering a new 25–30 year 3¼ percent bond, the highest rate of interest offered by the United States since 1933, and the longest maturity issued since October 1941. According to Friedman and Schwartz, to the surprise and dismay of the Treasury and the Fed, "The market interpreted those developments as signs of greater restraint to come. A wave of selling of governments brought their prices down to new lows, the new 3¼ percent bond fell below par, and market interest rates rose. There was a quick change in monetary policy, when the System was confronted with more tightness than it had intended."[49] Hence, the Federal Reserve eased monetary policy by making open-market purchases in May and June, and reducing reserve requirements in July.

The April 1953 bond crisis had an unforeseen result. For the first time in its history the Federal Reserve had initiated a countercyclical easing of monetary policy before a peak of business activity had been reached. Such a peak occurred during the summer of 1953. These prerecession Federal Reserve actions probably triggered the monetary forces which eased the ensuing economic contraction. As the 1953–54 recession proceeded, Federal Reserve policy became one of "active ease," which brought about an increase in the quantity of credit available and a decline in interest rates. From June 1953 to June 1954 the money stock increased 2.8 percent and the interest rate on treasury bills was reduced from 2.11 percent to 0.64 percent. In the spring of 1954 the discount rate was reduced twice—from 2 percent to 1¾ percent, and then to 1½ percent. In April 1954, with the president's support, Treasury Secretary Humphrey pressured the Federal Reserve to further loosen the money supply. According to Kettl, "The Fed predictably resisted such pressure so soon after the accord—but only to the point of refusing to conduct open-market operations to ease the money supply; instead the board lowered reserve requirements. . . . To prove their argument on independence . . . Martin used a different tool to produce the result Eisenhower wanted."[50]

As can be seen from these monetary policy moves, the 1953–54 recession pushed the problem of inflation to the back burner of the administration's policy agenda. Of the twenty-three studies the CEA staff produced in 1954, none focused on inflation. Inflation would not again be a topic for discussion at weekly ABEGS meetings until June 27, 1956.[51] However, by 1955 Burns was again worrying about potential inflation and was critical of the Federal Reserve for not responding more vigorously to this potential threat. The Federal Reserve raised the discount rate from 1½ percent to 3 percent by six increments of 1/4 percentage point each in April, August, September, and November 1955, and in April and August 1956. Despite these efforts to tighten the money supply, "Total bank loans increased from $70.6 billion at the end of 1954 to $90.3 billion at the end of 1956; . . . not until the summer of 1957 did the rise in business loans come to a halt. The banks were able to finance this increase in their loans to business at a time when the monetary authorities were pursuing a disinflationary policy through reducing their holdings of United States Government securities."[52] The CPI rose by 6 percent between January 1955 and August 1957. Burns was so apprehensive that he advised Eisenhower in June 1956 to consider asking Congress for the authority to regulate the terms of installment credit on consumer purchases of durable goods. Humphrey successfully opposed Burns's proposal.[53]

William McChesney Martin also felt frustrated that four increases in the discount rate in 1955 had not prevented an increase in prices in 1956. As real economic growth slowed in 1956, Burns and Humphrey urged Martin not to increase the discount rate again. With a presidential election just seven months away, the administration was worried about rising unemployment and a possible recession. When the FRB did raise the discount rate in April 1956, there was a public outcry. The board's decision was attacked by Commerce Secretary Sinclair Weeks and Labor Secretary James Mitchell. Privately, but with the knowledge and support of the president, Humphrey sent Martin a letter that stressed the problems in the automobile, steel, and retail sectors of the economy which might soon produce an increase in the unemployment rate. Humphrey concluded, "Therefore, I recommend and urge, since you have increased your rate, that you now promptly begin, through open market operations, to make money and credit more plentiful. It will take some time for anything you do to become effective, even if you begin immediately, and I think before that time comes we will really need it. I fear that growing unemployment during the third quarter will be widely discussed if we don't begin promptly to do what we can now to prevent it."[54] Martin refused to comply.

The president was asked about the Fed's April decision at four press conferences, and in each case he endorsed the independence and integrity of the Federal Reserve but avoided giving support to this particular decision. Eisenhower's careful answers, unlike Truman's in 1951, quieted the dispute.

The April 1956 incident and its aftermath helped clarify the modern relationship between the Federal Reserve and the presidency. The episode established the ground rule that administration representatives could privately lobby FRB officials for policies they preferred. And administration officials would usually avoid criticizing the Fed publicly because that would have the effect of making presidential advisers look like apologists for inflation. According to Kettl's analysis, "The President believed his powers, especially in economic affairs, were limited, and he was only too happy to allow the Fed to take responsibility for economic stabilization—especially in an election year. Eisenhower's public comments solidified the Fed's position as the guardian against inflation, a role that had emerged as a result of the accord."[55]

The next test case in the relationship between the Fed and the presidency involved the shift from an anti-inflationary to an antirecession strategy. During the spring of 1957, CEA chairman Saulnier said that the Fed's monetary policy was "unnecessarily tight." At a lunch meeting on May 3, Saulnier told Martin that he would feel more comfortable "if credit policy were eased slightly." Saulnier conceded that the signals from the economy were mixed and that no forecast at this time could be made with certainty. However, if the economy was sliding into a recession, "now is the time to take the action to forestall this result." On the other hand, if the economy was about to move into a period of "renewed exuberance," then the current tight monetary policy was the correct one. In Saulnier's words, "I pointed out that in my position I would prefer to play the game modestly on the side of credit ease, believing that this would help to bring about the happier of these alternative courses and would not, considering the extent of unused capacity in our economy, induce any serious inflationary consequences."[56] Martin resisted this view because he felt that present price levels were too high and should not be validated. He claimed that some members of the FOMC were proposing a further tightening.

In August 1957 the Fed raised the discount rate despite the opposition of Saulnier. The FRB did not reverse this decision until November 1957, when it reduced the discount rate from 3½ to 3 percent. Still Saulnier argued that the Fed ought to be doing more since the economy was sinking into a recession. In December 1957 Saulnier wrote, "My fear is that we will find ourselves using Federal expenditures to revive an economic situation which is being dampened by an overly repressive credit policy."[57]

At the end of December 1957 the president called Saulnier to express his view that the Fed ought to be more vigorous in promoting a resumption of economic growth. According to Saulnier, the president "asked me to call Bill Martin and to say that he had been happy with the policy changes made in November and that he had expected that the follow up on those would be somewhat more vigorous than he had so far seen, and that in view of what we were doing through budget expenditures to help promote economic recovery, he thought the Fed ought to put its shoulder to the wheel and do something dramatic. . . . He asked me to tell Martin that if he had reservations about such a move that he ought to have a meeting very soon of the *ad hoc* financial group for a discussion of it."[58]

With unemployment mounting (to 7.4 percent, compared to the 1953–54 recession's high of 6 percent), the Fed did lower the discount rate in January, March, and April 1958 to a final 1¾ percent. Reserve requirements were reduced in February, March, and April. Beginning in March, open-market purchases also contributed to loosening the money supply. The combined effect of these three changes brought about a significant increase in the supply of money. According to Friedman and Schwartz, "Whereas the money stock had been virtually unchanged in the final five months of 1957, it rose 4.1 percent in the first six months of 1958 or at an annual rate of over 8 percent. One must go back to 1946 to find so high a rate of rise during a six month period. In the next six months it rose a further 2.4 percent, making the total rise for the year 6½ percent."[59] The vigor of the Fed's activities was partly a function of having responded to the recession so belatedly. The August 1957 decision to raise the discount rate was a blunder and the November 1957 decision to lower the discount rate was made four months after the cyclical peak of economic activity. Earlier responses to reverse policy and loosen the money supply might have done much to head off the short but severe recession of 1957–58.

In the final two years of the Eisenhower administration, anti-inflation policy was complicated by the balance of payments problem, the $12.4 billion budget deficit in FY 1959, and the long steel strike of 1959. In its retrospective examination of monetary policy following the 1953–54 recession, the Fed concluded that it had maintained an easy money policy for too long, which had led to the inflationary problems of 1956 and 1957. The Fed was determined not to repeat that mistake, so it raised the discount rate four times between September 1958 and September 1959 (from 1¾ percent to 4 percent). Between September 1959 and June 1960 there was a decline of 1.1 percent in the money stock. In 1960, with the economy recovering more slowly than expected following the steel strike, there was a decline in the money supply despite efforts by the Fed to increase it. From early March to November 1960, the Fed increased reserves of member banks through open-market purchases of government securities. In addition, the discount rate at the Reserve Bank of New York was cut in June and August.[60]

The tight money policies of the Federal Reserve during most of the final two years of the Eisenhower presidency split the members of the administration. Vice-President Nixon objected because a tight money policy would damage his electoral chances in 1960. Saulnier was opposed (but not as strongly as Arthur Burns might have been) because tight money inhibited economic growth. Anderson supported the Fed because he believed high interest rates would attract foreign capital and help correct the balance of payments. The Treasury secretary was also alarmed by the accelerating rise in prices. Anderson told the president that "we face a choice . . . [of] preventing a little more unemployment or preserving the value of the dollar. I favor the second course. Because if inflation ever starts snowballing, it will require so much unemployment to stop it that even a Dwight Eisenhower couldn't survive politically."[61] And the president, by this time a hardened conservative, felt it was his duty to side with Anderson.

Eisenhower's third anti-inflationary policy can be dealt with briefly because it was generally ineffective. It consisted of the formation of several committees to monitor rising prices and to educate the public on the evils of inflation.

To some observers, the inflation experienced after 1955 appeared to be different from that experienced after World War II and in the early months of the Korean War. Almost everyone agreed that in both of these earlier cases, inflation was caused by effective demand exceeding the capacity to supply in most sectors of the economy. By 1956, with the exception of the capital goods sector, the major cause of creeping inflation did not appear to be excess demand. This led to a vigorous debate concerning the causes of rising prices. Trade unions blamed business for raising administered prices while business representatives defined the problem as caused by trade union–induced cost inflation. Saulnier sided with the conservative business view that wage costs were rising faster than productivity and were, therefore, a major factor in causing inflation.[62] However, the prolabor Democratic majorities in Congress saw to it that legislative proposals to restrict wages had no chance of passing. Indeed, when the Eisenhower administration proposed to amend the Employment Act of 1946 by adding a provision committing the government to the goal of stable prices, labor, believing that its efforts to increase wages were being threatened, prevented its passage.

As inflation became a more salient issue, Eisenhower did respond administratively. In August 1958 the president created a special cabinet committee under Labor Secretary Mitchell "to consider the wage-cost-price spiral and possible measures for dealing with it."[63] In January 1959 the White House announced that the president had established two new committees to combat inflation: the Committee on Government Activities Affecting Prices and Costs (CGA) and the Cabinet Committee on Price Stability for Economic Growth (CCPSEG). Eisenhower appointed Saulnier as the chairman of the CGA. The CGA was charged with reviewing government operations of various agencies, especially those involved in procurement, construction, stockpiling, and price support, for the purpose of recommending changes that would promote price stability. Needless to say, the CGA's efforts were resisted by bureaucrats. H. Scott Gordon concludes, "There is no evidence that it actually played any role of significance in the Administration's anti-inflation policy."[64]

The CCPSEG was chaired by Vice-President Nixon and was directed to study the causes of rising prices and to educate the public about the evils of inflation. Eisenhower wanted to indoctrinate the American people with the idea that price stability was essential for sound economic growth. He also wanted to counter the seductive Democratic idea that a little inflation (say, less than 2 percent a year) was necessary to keep the economy expanding at a satisfactory rate (say, 4 or 5 percent a year). The administration argued that a 3 percent growth rate without any inflation was more in line with the nation's long-term interest. In any case, the CCPSEG was ineffective and was generally viewed as an electoral vehicle for Vice-President Nixon to develop an economic program for his presidential campaign.[65] No one in the administration enhanced their political reputation by fighting inflation.

President Eisenhower also tried to enlist the efforts of business and labor to fight inflation through the doctrine of "shared responsibility." This doctrine was spelled out in both the president's 1957 State of the Union address and his Economic Report of the same year. In the State of the Union speech,

Eisenhower stressed that the public interest must take precedence over temporary advantages which may be gained by particular groups at the expense of all citizens. He called upon business and labor leaders to be vigilant against inflationary tendencies and to cooperate in keeping prices down and wage increases constrained by improvements in productivity. "Freedom has been defined as the opportunity for self-discipline. This definition has a special application to the areas of wage and price policy in a free economy. Should we persistently fail to discipline ourselves, eventually there will be increasing pressure on Government to redress the failure. By that process freedom will step by step disappear. No subject on the domestic scene should more attract the concern of the friends of American working men and women and of free business enterprise than the forces that threaten a steady depreciation of the value of our money."[66]

By invoking the criterion of social responsibility in the private decisions of business and labor leaders, Eisenhower was probably unaware of how much he was departing from the general theory of a market economy. Instead of describing Adam Smith's invisible hand guiding private decisions in the public interest, Eisenhower was exhorting economic leaders to consider national concerns in the conduct of their affairs. When Eisenhower's doctrine of shared responsibility was used in the 1957 Economic Report, Milton Friedman, a market-oriented economist, complained to Saulnier: "You will not be surprised that my one really serious disagreement is with the assignment of responsibility to business and labor for restraining inflation. This seems to be not only analytically wrong, but politically dangerous. Heaven preserve us from a world of businessmen and labor leaders conducting their affairs in terms of 'social responsibility!'"[67] Eisenhower believed in the virtues of a market economy, but, like most politicians, he did not adhere religiously to any given economic theory.

THE BALANCE OF PAYMENTS PROBLEM

Eisenhower believed in international interdependence, and the nation he governed became increasingly interdependent with its worldwide trading partners and military allies during the 1950s. By 1958, monetary policy in particular, and economic policymaking overall, were made more complicated by the balance of payments problem. The U.S. balance of payments deficit was measured by the net sale of U.S. gold to foreigners in each year plus the accumulation by foreigners of liquid dollar assets (mostly bank deposits and treasury bills). The Federal Reserve Banks were required by law to maintain a gold reserve of 25 percent against their notes and deposit liabilities. The expanding balance of payments deficit reflected the net result of all U.S. economic transactions with the rest of the world for each calendar year.

Saulnier suggested that "with a large and continuing deficit in the balance of international payments and with a very large volume of foreign-held liquid claims outstanding against the U.S. dollar, there is little scope for the use of monetary ease as a means of promoting a higher rate of growth."[68] In other words, increasing the money supply when the United States was running a negative balance of payments might frighten foreign governments into cashing in their surplus dollars for gold.

The significance that Eisenhower attributed to foreign economic policy was indicated by his creation of the Commission on Foreign Economic Policy (popularly known as the Randall Commission) on August 7, 1953, and the U.S. Council on Foreign Economic Policy (CFEP) on December 11, 1954. The Randall Commission had seventeen members — seven appointed by the president, including its chairman, Clarence Randall; five appointed by the Speaker of the House from the House membership; and five appointed by the vice-president from the Senate. Sixty-three-year-old Clarence Randall had previously headed the Inland Steel Company and worked under Paul Hoffman in the administration of the Marshall Plan. George Humphrey and Sinclair Weeks had recommended that Eisenhower select Randall, a well-known supporter of free trade, as chairman. When the Randall Commission submitted its report to the president on January 12, 1954, three conservative Republican members objected to its free trade tendencies.

The Randall Commission report guided the administration's foreign economic policy. It recommended a three-year extension of the Reciprocal Trade Agreements Act (first passed in 1934) and authorized the president to cut current tariffs by 5 percent a year. Congress accepted these recommendations in 1955. In 1958 Congress renewed reciprocity for four additional years.[69] The report also urged that the federal government abandon the support of high farm prices and advocated that European countries move toward the free convertibility of their currencies. Eisenhower was pleased with Randall's efforts because he believed that the report reflected his own middle ground philosophy in the area of international trade policy.

In December 1954, Eisenhower appointed Joseph Dodge, the former budget director, as chairman of the CFEP. In July 1956 Dodge was replaced as chair by Clarence Randall. The CFEP consisted of the secretaries of state, Treasury, commerce, and agriculture and the director of the Foreign Operations Administration. The council also hired a small staff which was assisted by private consultants. The major function of the CFEP was to coordinate the executive agencies in the field of foreign economic policy; a secondary function was to initiate staff studies of specific problems. By the latter half of the decade, the most salient problem for the CFEP was the negative balance of payments.

The foreign economic policy of the United States was largely motivated by the memories of the short-sighted policies followed after World War I and by concern over potential Soviet influence in the industrialized nations of Western Europe and Japan, as well as in the Third World. Since the United States was considered the leader of the non-Communist bloc of nations and was also one of the few industrialized nations not devastated by World War II, the foreign policy elites in both the Truman and Eisenhower administrations were committed to supporting the internal economies and the international liquidity needs of Western Europe and Japan. Until 1950 or so, many of the industrialized nations suffered from a "dollar gap," a chronic shortage of dollars necessary to finance imports from the United States. For almost a decade after World War II, the United States, through foreign aid and loan programs, pumped billions of dollars into Western Europe and Japan, helping to fuel their economic recovery. At that time the American dollar was the key currency in the conduct of international trade and finance. Foreign private and governmental reserves were kept mainly in the form of dollar balances (i.e., in cash, bank deposits, and liquid short-term dollar securities). From 1945 to 1950 the U.S. dollar was undervalued at prevailing exchange rates. During this period the countries with overvalued currencies handled their dollar shortages by comprehensive exchange and import controls.

By the early 1950s the efforts of the United States and its allies were largely successful. The nations of Western Europe and Japan were no longer short of dollars; indeed, they began to build up their dollar reserves. Due to their own efforts and skills, plus some timely financial assistance from the United States, these nations could now compete more successfully against the United States in their own markets, in other markets, and sometimes even in U.S. markets. The balance of payments in the United States was also negatively affected by U.S. foreign military and aid programs, and the outflow of direct foreign investments by American corporations. What had been a dollar shortage for Western Europe and Japan at the beginning of the 1950s became a dollar glut by the end. What had begun as deliberate policy of the United States to aid its allies became a structural weakness it could not reverse. Although the United States still enjoyed a favorable balance of trade, the volume of its imports increased faster than the growth of its exports. The cost of U.S. imports soared as the country attempted to satisfy both its growing consumption needs and the demands of the defense programs. Sluggish export growth meant that it began to experience difficulty in financing international commitments.

The deterioration of the U.S. position is revealed when the decade is divided into two periods: 1951 to 1957 and 1958 to 1960. In the first period the balance of payments deficit averaged $957 million per year; in the second period it averaged over $3.7 billion per year.[70] The undervalued dollar of 1950 was an overvalued dollar by 1960. As foreign governments accumulated more dollars, there was a shift in their international liquidity preferences; that is, governments who were fearful of a devaluation of the dollar decided to exchange their dollars for gold. According to Vatter, "The United States gold stock, which had risen almost steadily from 1929 to an all-time high of $24.4 billion in 1949, dropped to a plateau at around $22–$23 billion between 1950 and 1957, then fell sharply to somewhat less than $18 billion in December, 1960."[71] Of that $18 billion in gold, $11.6 billion was required by law to be retained as backing for Federal Reserve notes and deposits. Furthermore, by 1960 the total volume of foreign-owned dollar claims against the U.S. gold supply reached $16.8 billion. As long as foreign governments had confidence in the United States, there was no danger that all of these dollar claims would be cashed in for gold, but one can understand that this situation caused feelings of anxiety at both the Treasury and the Federal Reserve.

In the 1940s the United States had overcome its isolationist heritage and assumed the burden of aiding other nations. Still, when the Employment Act was passed in 1946, the task of managing prosperity appeared to be a domestic problem. By the late 1950s, however, it was becoming clear that the United States would need the cooperation and help of other nations to remain a major player in the international economic arena. As Arthur Burns wrote, "Of late, many Americans have gained fresh awareness of a fact which fortune had permitted us to slight over a long generation, namely, that our nation is not self-sufficient. We are now relearning the lesson that, in order to manage our economic affairs successfully, we must be mindful of the needs and trading policies of other nations, of the size of our gold stocks and the short-term balances that foreign governments and citizens hold here, and of the levels of labor costs, interest rates, and prices in our country relative to those of other nations."[72] This truism of the need for international cooperation was driven home largely by the balance of payments difficulties the United States was experiencing.

As an emerging and murky issue, the balance of payments problem was not easy for the Eisenhower administration to handle. Neither its causes nor its possible policy solutions were clear. There was a tendency to believe that the problem might even simply disappear when foreign nations eliminated their discriminatory restrictions against U.S. exports and rising incomes in these countries increased demand for U.S. products.

The president did take the problem very seriously, however; he viewed the balance of payments as a national security issue. As he told the cabinet meeting of November 17, 1959, "We have got to meet this [threat of the Soviet Union] by keeping our economy absolutely healthy. . . . We are the world's banker. If our money goes pflooey, the whole thing collapses. Our vaunted high wages will turn into bread lines."[73] In his memoirs Eisenhower explained why balance of payments concerns caused him to strive so mightily to convert the budget deficit of FY 1959 into a balanced budget for FY 1960: "A number of respected business analysts, one of whom was Gabriel Hauge, cautioned me against the damaging effects that might result from trying to return too quickly to a balanced budget in FY 1960 after the $12 billion deficit of the previous year. I was impressed by Dr. Hauge's arguments but an overriding consideration, in my mind, was the worsening situation in our balance of payments. I felt that a rapid return to a balanced budget would help reassure other nations as to America's ability to pay her debts and lessen their desire to convert their dollars into gold."[74] Clearly, in this case Eisenhower was willing to make the effort — and bear the political heat — for his conservative beliefs and sense of duty.

The first of his advisers to warn Eisenhower about the balance of payments problem was George Humphrey. On April 15, 1955, the Treasury secretary sent a memo to the president that began, "We no longer need to worry ourselves about an excess of gold." Humphrey informed the president that U.S. gold stocks had shrunk by over $3 billion since 1949, and he concluded, "There is nothing to worry about yet, but this illustrates definitely how the monetary reserves of other countries have been strengthened and our own weakened to a point where we need to give careful thought to making sure of continued confidence in the U.S. dollar and safeguarding our remaining reserves."[75]

At a cabinet meeting in April 1956, Humphrey expressed increased concern about the problem. With the aid of several charts, Humphrey and his undersecretary, Randolph Burgess, demonstrated that there had been a definite trend since 1949 of depletion of U.S. gold reserves through foreign payments. If the trend were not stopped, they argued, the situation would become very serious. And Humphrey felt the trend might continue because the United States was about to enter a "severe period of competition" in both domestic and foreign markets with the rebuilt economies of Western Europe and Japan and even the Soviet Union. In this new era of competition, Humphrey believed that the United States was at a disadvantage because of high labor costs and the high taxes necessary to finance the military. Humphrey concluded that the United States had to recognize its "financial limitations" and work diligently to cut military expenditures so that taxes could be reduced.[76]

Arthur Burns, who was present at the meeting, disagreed with Humphrey's presentation, arguing that the balance of payments problem should indeed be closely monitored but that he did not believe it to be particularly worrisome.[77] Hauge supported Burns and expressed the hope that the problem would soon correct itself.

There was a temporary respite in the balance of payments issue in the aftermath of the Suez Crisis, but by 1958 the problem was obviously getting worse. By then, Treasury Secretary Robert Anderson had become very worried about the situation. His feeling was that since the United States had become the free world's banker, it was the country's primary responsibility to maintain the confidence of its trading partners. The world was watching; if the

United States did not set an example of "fiscal soundness," it would have a "serious impact on our dollar holdings."[78] Anderson recommended three courses of action. First, U.S. allies should be pressured to eliminate quotas and reduce tariffs on American goods, and these countries should bear a larger share of both defense costs and aid to the Third World. Second, corporations in the United States ought to be encouraged to be more export-oriented. Third, the administration should balance its budget to demonstrate its will and capacity to control inflation.[79] William Martin attended the August 7, 1959, cabinet meeting at which Anderson set forth his views, and he expressed his support for Anderson's analysis and recommendations. Clearly, this was now seen as a problem that would not correct itself; it would require a policy response.

However, the CEA continued to have a more sanguine outlook than the Treasury. The economists were committed to free trade, and they believed that market forces would soon correct the negative balance of payments. On December 6, 1958, Eisenhower recorded in his diary that "Saulnier takes a very much more optimistic view than Anderson does with regard to the gravity of this problem. Whereas Anderson believes that, unless we have a balanced budget, we are going to have very bad effects in foreign banking circles because of a diminishing faith in the dollar, Saulnier believes that there is very little danger of this at the moment. Moreover, he is not particularly concerned abouut the accelerated outward movement of gold. He believes that as corporate earnings go up—and he believes that the rate of increase is going to be higher than most people feel—corporations will have to find use for their money. Many of them will be purchasing notes and short-term securities, and this will greatly strengthen the bond market and tend to minimize our interest costs."[80]

By 1959, however, Saulnier agreed that the balance of payments deficit was "truly worrisome." International considerations were dictating that monetary policy be tightened more than what would be needed if only domestic factors were considered. As Saulnier later explained, "Remember that a major objective of policy was to eliminate cost and price inflation in the United States economy, and to eliminate the inflation psychology. In other words, we had to reestablish confidence in the stability of the United States dollar. By 1959, the job was done as regards domestic price indexes; but it was not done as regards the balance of payments."[81] Even so, Saulnier complained that the Federal Reserve tightened monetary policy too severely in 1959, causing sluggish economic growth and the mild recession of 1960–61. Politically, the major beneficiary of this policy was John F. Kennedy.

CONCLUSION

Keeping the inflation rate as low as possible was a strategic goal of the Eisenhower administration; accordingly, the president was willing to spend many of his political and administrative resources fighting inflation. After several years of trying to cut the federal budget, and after losing control of Congress to the Democrats, Eisenhower and his advisers recognized the limitations of fiscal policy. This created an atmosphere in which the Eisenhower administration increasingly turned to monetary policy as the best available means to control inflation. Because Eisenhower and William McChesney Martin both felt that inflation — not unemployment — was the chief threat to the economy, the Federal Reserve was able to create and institutionalize its modern macroeconomic policy role. Whereas the Federal Reserve was originally created in 1913 to be a regulatory agency, supervising the banks in order to prevent currency crises, after the March 1951 Accord, and under the leadership of Martin, the Fed became a major independent player in managing prosperity. Under Martin, the Fed came to see that the timely loosening of the money supply could help prevent a recession, but that its primary responsibility was to have the foresight and courage to restrict the money supply — which raised both interest rates and howls of protest — to prevent inflation. Only a politically independent agency could undertake such an unpopular but necessary role. Not surprisingly, the Eisenhower administration was willing to allow the Federal Reserve to take the lead — and a large portion of the political heat — in fighting inflation, and each subsequent administration has done the same.

The combined efforts of the Eisenhower administration and the Federal Reserve produced an impressive record in controlling inflation. Between 1953 and 1960 the average yearly rise of the CPI was 1.5 percent. However, the administration reaped few political rewards for this achievement. It appears that an administration is blamed when prices rise but is not rewarded when prices remain relatively steady. Indeed, the president and the Federal Reserve are sometimes condemned for the policies — budget austerity and a tightened money supply — that bring about a low inflation rate. There simply may not be a politically popular strategy for fighting inflation.

By 1958, combating inflation had become more complicated because the United States was suffering from a negative balance of payments with its trading partners. Since the United States had become the "free world's banker," Eisenhower saw the balance of payments issue as a national security issue. Both Treasury secretaries Humphrey and Anderson emphasized that maintaining our trading partners' confidence in the dollar should be a top priority in foreign economic policy. The president agreed. Eisenhower also believed in free trade and interdependence, and, under his administration, the country experienced a dramatic shift in trade relations with its allies. The reinvigorated economies of Western Europe and Japan transformed the dollar gap of the late 1940s into a dollar glut by the end of the 1950s. The United States had entered into what George Humphrey called a "severe period of competition." In this new era, our sluggish export growth rate and our expensive financial commitments overseas meant that we faced a chronic balance of payments problem. Managing prosperity was no longer primarily a domestic dilemma; it now demanded enhanced capabilities to compete successfully in international markets.

6

The Struggle against Recession:
1953–54 and 1957–58

President Eisenhower believed that inflation was the major economic threat
to the United States economy, but he quickly learned that the most politically
sensitive economic indicator was a rise in the unemployment rate. Any such
rise aroused fears of a possible recession or a dreaded depression. The prosperity of the 1920s had vanished in the Great Depression of the 1930s, and
there was a nagging fear following World War II that history might repeat
itself. The legacy of Herbert Hoover hung like a dark cloud over the first
Republican president in twenty years. Eisenhower's success would depend
largely on his ability to maintain economic prosperity.

This chapter will analyze and compare the Eisenhower administration's
responses to the recessions of 1953–54 and 1957–58. Such a comparison will
provide a "test" of some of the ideas developed in earlier chapters. Were expectations higher in the latter half of the 1950s than in the first half of what
could be done about recessions? Was Eisenhower politically more effective
in his first term? Was he more rigidly conservative and politically less effective in his second term? Some answers to these questions are suggested by
the following case studies of how Eisenhower dealt with these two recessions.

THE 1953–54 RECESSION

Although there was "statistical" prosperity in 1952, many voters were dissatisfied because of the Korean War, high taxes, fears of inflation, and concern about corruption in Washington, D.C. After the election of 1952, Hauge
sent the president-elect a memo indicating that the short-run business outlook was excellent. Unemployment was very low, and personal income was
rising. Hauge congratulated Eisenhower for winning by a landslide in the
face of such favorable economic indicators. He advised Eisenhower that the

economic outlook over the next six months was good, but then cautioned, "Past that, visibility isn't so good. This boom isn't going to last forever, of course. America hasn't found the secret of perpetual economic motion."[1]

Eisenhower recognized that the possibility of a recession was a strategic threat to his administration and to the Republican party. Before his inauguration, he told Humphrey that we "must not allow businessmen to be charged with indifference to the country."[2] Shortly after the inauguration, he ordered Hauge to work on the federal highway program and suggested that "the timing of construction should be such as to have some effect in leveling out peaks and valleys in our economic life."[3] As noted earlier, Eisenhower's sensitivity to the possibility of recession was also revealed in the selection of Arthur Burns, whose academic specialty was analysis of the business cycle, as chairman of the CEA. Before leaving New York to work for Eisenhower in March 1953, Burns told his colleagues at the National Bureau of Economic Research that the present boom would probably end soon. Shortly after assuming his post, Burns, with the president's support, requested the Bureau of the Budget to begin a study of budget flexibility as a possible counter to either inflation or recession.

The Korean armistice was signed on July 26, 1953. The end of the war and Eisenhower's budget cuts reduced federal expenditures by $10 billion from the second quarter of 1953 to the second quarter of 1954. After July 1953 the economy began to decline. By December the unemployment rate had risen to 3 percent; and by March 1954, the number of the jobless reached its recession peak of 3,725,000, or 5.8 percent of the civilian labor force.

When, in September 1953, Burns warned Eisenhower about the negative trends, the president told him, "Arthur, you are my chief of staff in handling the recession. You are to report every week at a cabinet meeting on where we are going and what we ought to be doing."[4] At the September 24, 1953, cabinet meeting, Burns reported that a series of economic indicators suggested that the economy was headed for a "readjustment," the administration's euphemistic term for recession. These indicators included a drop in the stock market, an increase in business failures, a reduction in the volume of orders for durable goods, a decline in residential construction, a drop in the average length of the work week, sagging farm prices, and excessive inventories. Burns attributed the decline to a combination of the reductions in government spending for the military and the adjustment of business inventories to current sales. Burns viewed the situation as not critical, but advocated "precautionary planning" in case conditions worsened. He formed the CEA staff into six task forces to study specific aspects of the recession and to make policy recommendations that might be used to reserve the economic downturn. Because the economy was still strong, the CEA was hopeful that relatively mild measures (a loosening of monetary policy and tax reductions instead of an increase in public spending) would be sufficient to meet the challenge. The president displayed his concern by reminding the cabinet that in 1952 the Republicans had promised to use the full constitutional authority of the government to forestall a recurrence of the 1929 events. Humphrey commented that he was in perfect accord with Burns, but with the economy at record-breaking levels, the only way for the economy to go was down. He believed that employment could decline for six or seven months without the situation becoming critical.[5]

Burns essentially designed the administration's strategy to combat the 1953–54 recession. Behind the automatic stabilizers (declining tax revenues, increasing expenditures for unemployment insurance), the first line of discretionary defense was to be a monetary policy designed to increase the availability and reduce the cost of credit to businesses, municipalities, and consumers. The second defense would be tax reductions for consumers and corporations to expand their purchasing power. Third, measures would be taken to encourage a high rate of public expenditure to offset the reduction in federal military outlays.[6] "Like a physician," according to the historian Saul Engelbourg, "Burns preferred to hold back the most drastic remedy as a last resort, lest the treatment do more harm than the disease."[7]

Critics charged, however, that the administration was failing to meet its responsibilities to maintain prosperity. In November 1953, Colin Clark, a British economist writing in the *Manchester Guardian*, predicted a painful American depression; his prediction was widely publicized in the United States. He recommended a $20 billion tax cut, with no reduction in federal expenditures. In January 1954, when unemployment reached three million, Walter Reuther urged Eisenhower to summon a national conference on unemployment, but the president declined. Senator Paul Douglas taunted administration witnesses appearing before the Joint Economic Committee in February over whether the present situation was a "readjustment" or a "recession." In April, David McDonald, head of the U.S. Steel Workers, called for a $5 billion public works program, a $5 billion home-building and slum-clearance program, $3 billion in increased unemployment benefits and pensions, and a $4 billion cut in income taxes. On May 11, Walter Reuther convened his own full employment conference and blasted the administration for "doing nothing" to relieve unemployment. Two days later, former president Truman told a union audience that the economy was suffering from "creeping McKinleyism" and urged a $3 billion increase for public works and welfare.[8] The Democrats charged that the Republicans were trying to ignore the recession. They ridiculed the administration's program as a "trickle down" policy that attempted to indirectly help the unemployed by granting tax relief to corporations and the rich. Eisenhower responded to these criticisms by repeatedly claiming that the administration's policies were sufficient to meet the present problem, but if further action was needed, he would not hesitate to act. The president asserted that he would not be stampeded into a "slam-bang emergency program." The administration accused opposition of reck-lessly propagating inaccurate "gloom and doom" forecasts solely for politi-cal advantage.

The Eisenhower administration favored monetary policy to combat the recession for a number of reasons. Assuming a cooperative Federal Reserve Board, monetary steps can be taken quickly and do not require any time-consuming action by the Congress. Monetary decisions are easily reversible if inflationary tendencies appear. Monetary decisions are indirect in their effects, providing a widespread stimulus without direct intervention in any sector of the economy except on the reserve balances of member banks. Finally, mone-tary action does not add to the budget. The latter was especially important to an administration dedicated to balancing the budget.[9] In brief, monetary policy was compatible with the economic philosophy of the administration.

Both Humphrey and Burns met often with the chairman of the Federal Reserve, William McChesney Martin, and were successful in gaining his sup-port to liberalize money and credit. However, there was conflict between the CEA and the Federal Reserve because Burns felt that Martin was not expand-ing credit as quickly as conditions required. On April 8, 1954, Eisenhower wrote in his diary, "I talked to the sec. of the t. in order to develop real pres-sure on the FRB for loosening credit still further. This is a project strongly supported by Dr. Burns, who believes that bankers have always acted 'too late and with too little' in the face of approaching recession."[10] Between the end of April 1953 and the end of July 1954, the Federal Reserve System added $900 million to its total holdings of U.S. government securities. In July 1953 required reserves on demand deposits were lowered for member banks of the Federal Reserve System, adding an estimated $1.2 billion to the commercial banking system. In February 1954, the discount rate of the Federal Reserve System banks was reduced from 2 to 1 3/4 percent, and in April 1954, it was further lowered to 1 1/2 percent. On June 21, 1954, the Federal Reserve an-nounced a $1.5 billion reduction in legal reserve requirements. The combined effects of these monetary actions expanded the potential lending powers of the commercial banking system by about $17 billion.[11] The loosening of credit also encouraged demand for housing during the recession. The combination of cheap credit and the reforms in the Housing Act of 1954, which autho-rized the FHA to insure mortgages with smaller deposits and longer repay-ment periods, helped create a housing boom in the second half of 1954.

In the realm of fiscal policy, a number of major tax revisions were already scheduled to take place when Eisenhower assumed the presidency. The excess profits tax was set to expire on June 30, 1953. Individual income tax rates were to decline by 10 percent on January 1, 1954. On April 1, 1954, corpora-tion income tax rates were to drop from 52 percent to 47 percent, and several temporary increases in excise taxes were to end. Social security taxes were scheduled to increase on January 1, 1954, from 1.5 percent to 2 percent on both employers and employees. Since Eisenhower still feared inflation and was committed to a balanced budget, he submitted a tax message to Congress on May 20, 1953, calling for the maintenance of all taxes during 1953, but suggesting that taxes be lowered in January 1954. Although some congressional Republicans considered it heresy to delay tax cuts, the president was able to get most of his proposals passed before Congress adjourned on August 3. By September it was evident that the danger was recession, not inflation, and that the reduction of federal expenditures would allow for tax cuts.[12]

In a speech before the American Bankers Association on September 22, 1953, Humphrey confirmed that the administration would not seek to prevent the expiration of the excess profits tax and the reduction of the individual income tax scheduled for January 1. Humphrey had resisted making such a definite statement, but was finally convinced by Burns, who argued that business confidence needed a boost during this early phase of the recession. This was a "cheap" promise since the administration probably would not have been able to forestall the scheduled tax reductions since Congress had already adjourned. Nevertheless, the Humphrey speech was considered significant enough to be given a two-column headline on page one of the *New York Times* for September 23. On January 1, 1954, the excess profits tax expired and individual income taxes were reduced by about 10 percent. These two reductions would cut federal revenue by $5 billion in calendar year 1954, but they would be partially offset by the $1.3 billion increase in social security contributions.[13]

The increases in the excise tax and the corporation profits tax, which had been enacted by the Revenue Act of 1951, were set to expire on March 31, 1954. Also scheduled for congressional deliberation was the proposed revision of the Internal Revenue Code, which had been the subject of review by Treasury and congressional tax experts since the spring of 1952. To fulfill its commitment to eventually balancing the budget, the administration proposed that existing excise and corporation taxes be maintained. The termination of the excise taxes on gasoline, tobacco, and automobiles and the reduction in the 52 percent corporate income tax scheduled for April 1 would decrease federal revenues by $3 billion in twelve months. In the revisions of the Internal Revenue Code, the administration proposed tax cuts of approximately $1.4 billion per year. These revisions were designed to promote a significant amount of business expenditure through more liberal depreciation allowances, longer carry-back of net business losses, more liberal treatment of research and development expenditures, and a limited credit for dividends. The administration stressed that its tax revision legislation was part of a long-range program of tax reform to aid the growth of the economy; it was not an emergency program of tax reduction to combat a depression because there was still no need for such a program.

However, in the context of a deepening recession and an upcoming congressional election, the administration found itself subject to enormous pressures to accept deeper tax cuts. The Democrats attacked the Republicans for trying to aid stockholders instead of wage earners. The Democratic alternative was to increase the personal income tax exemption from $600 to $800 in 1954 and from $800 to $1,000 in 1955. Humphrey vehemently opposed this proposal because it would expand the deficit by about $4.5 billion. On March 15, 1954, Eisenhower spoke to the nation on radio and televison in support of his tax reform bill and against the Democratic alternative. He asserted that the $1,000 exemption would remove one taxpayer in every three from all federal income taxes; all "real Americans," he felt sure, were willing to pay their fair share of taxes.[14] Privately, the administration was particularly concerned that if the personal exemption was raised to fight the recession, it could not be lowered again (because of political reasons) should recovery turn into inflation.

Political pressures also came from congressional Republicans, who were as anxious as the Democrats to cut taxes in an election year and who supported a bill to diminish excise taxes by about $1 billion annually. Humphrey did not like this bill, but Burns argued the economy needed this extra stimulus. Eisenhower did not mention this bill in his March 15 speech, thus signaling the administration's reluctance to accept it. The president signed the bill on March 31 and later claimed in the 1955 Economic Report that this was one of the policies the administration had pursued in defeating the recession. Edward Flash is correct when he writes, "In the final analysis, the Administration endured a $1 billion drop in luxury excise revenue in order to retain $3 billion of revenue from other sources, thereby achieving a net gain of $2 billion."[15] By accepting this compromise, the administration was able (barely) to defeat the Democratic personal exemption proposal and win its own tax reform legislation (the Tax Revision Act of 1954). Thus the total tax reductions accepted by the administration in 1954 approximated the reduction in defense expenditures of $6 billion for FY 1955.

The final line of defense against the recession was increased budget expenditures designed to stimulate aggregate demand. The paradox here is that while the administration was engaged in time-consuming efforts to plan expenditure increases, the actual budget was being cut in order to make progress toward balancing the budget. This ambivalence was reflected in the 1954 State of the Union address in which Eisenhower promised, on the one hand, that the transition from a wartime to a peacetime economy could be accomplished without serious interruption in economic growth because the administration was prepared to use the budget as a stabilizing factor; on the other hand, the president stressed his achievements in decreasing expenditures and vowed further reductions. The FY 1955 budget, submitted in January 1954, did not have any expenditures specifically designed to counter the recession. Eisenhower's budget message boasted that even with the scheduled tax cuts, the deficit for FY 1954 was probably going to be only $3.3 billion instead of the $9.9 billion estimated by Truman when he had submitted the budget in January 1953. Eisenhower's estimate for FY 1955 was for a decrease of about $5 billion in both revenue and expenditure, with a deficit of $2.9 billion. The expected reduction in defense expenditures was almost totally responsible for the projected decline in federal expenditures. Years later, Holmans showed that the actual decline in defense expenditures was underestimated by $2.2 billion in FY 1954 and $3.5 billion in FY 1955.[16] Because of the recession, the administration ran budget deficits of $3.1 billion in FY 1954 and $4.2 billion in FY 1955.

The continuing decline of defense expenditures during the recession was a measure of how dedicated Eisenhower was to gaining control of the largest component of the federal budget in order to balance it. Even Burns had cautiously advised the president on October 13, 1953, that the Department of Defense ought to develop a "shelf of desirable but postponable projects that could be activated quickly in the event of serious economic recession." Burns added, "At a time like the present, when a sizable federal deficit seems to be in the making for the fiscal year 1954–55, it is, of course, essential to scrutinize the demands of the Joint Chiefs with the greatest of care. We must not, however, lose sight of the very real possibility that some military demands, which might now appear to be of marginal significance, may deserve the very highest priority in any expansion of governmental spending in the future to relieve unemployment."[17]

The difference in perspectives concerning budget goals assured bureaucratic conflict between Burns and Budget Director Joseph Dodge. Dodge criticized sections in the 1954 Economic Report that advocated deficit financing to support public works projects if unemployment continued to rise while Burns stressed that successfully countering the recession necessarily "involved certain sacrifices of other values" (that is, balancing the budget).[18] Throughout this period Burns talked about "budget flexibility" — a euphemism for increased expenditures. The CEA decided in March 1954 to request public works funds when and if the number of unemployed reached six million; however, unemployment never reached even four million, and thus a major conflict with the budget bureau was avoided.

In the cabinet meeting of Feburary 5, 1954, Eisenhower announced that he had given Burns the responsibility of coordinating the plans of various departments for antirecession public works projects. Eisenhower declared that the administration should be prepared to launch a public works program by July 1 if economic conditions warranted such action. Robert Donovan points out that "an interesting aspect of this discussion, as well as of similar discussions in the next few months, was the muting of emphasis on balancing the budget. This goal had been emphasized before and was to be emphasized very strongly again. But with the fate of the economy in the balance, it was submerged under the determination of the President and of the Cabinet generally to undertake an expensive public works program if necessary and to prevent a serious depression at any cost."[19] At this same cabinet meeting, the politically sensitive Henry Cabot Lodge commented that such plans for projects to curb unemployment would counter Democratic party accusations that the administration was relying solely on the "trickle down theory of economics."[20]

On February 5, 1954, the cabinet discussed accelerating (but not increasing) expenditures. On May 14, accelerated expenditures for FY 1955 became the policy of the administration, although the decision was not announced publicly. Eisenhower is quoted in the handwritten minutes of that May 14 meeting: "Arthur's policy — if you have approp. — spend it."[21] Burns presented an optimistic report at the cabinet meeting on June 4, but Eisenhower was still apprehensive that the administration was not doing enough: "We've got to have good economics." Even though this "may jar our sense of logic," the president said, everything possible must be done to bring about a rapid recovery in order to avoid the fate of Hoover. He advised the members to "err on the side of doing too much."[22]

Wilfred Lewis estimates that the decision to accelerate expenditures raised the annual rate of federal spending by $.3 billion in the third quarter of calendar year 1954, $.8 billion in the fourth quarter, and $1.7 billion in the first quarter of 1955.[23] By the second quarter of 1955, the acceleration was reversed. These increases in expenditures occurred too late to affect the timing of the economic recovery but probably added to its strength. Actually, their greatest impact was felt when the chief enemy was no longer unemployment, but inflation. In brief, the administration had less to show for this effort than for any other recession-checking policy it engaged in during this period.

One of the reasons that Eisenhower was reluctant to request higher public expenditures for public works from Congress was the fear that this would damage business confidence, which the administration believed was essential for recovery. Sensitivity to maintaining such confidence caused the administration to speak one way internally and another externally. "The outside position," according to the economist Herbert Stein, "was one of calm and assurance. Much had been done, nothing more needed to be done now (whatever the date), and the government was alert and prepared to do anything more that might be needed later."[24] The administration wanted to portray itself as having a basic strategy to deal with the downward adjustment: It was monitoring the economic situation closely and, if conditions worsened, it would know exactly when and how to step up its efforts to reverse the downward spiral. Business need not worry because the administration had the policy expertise, the commitment, and the sensitivity toward business to prevent another 1929.

The administration's internal deliberations revealed much more apprehension. Agreement on the importance of maintaining business confidence in no way guaranteed consensus in selecting the best means to do so. Burns believed that the level of confidence was still high but "precariously held": "If it became known that the Administration lacked an antidepression policy, public confidence might be shaken. It is vitally important that the policy proposed by the Council, or some satisfactory alternative, be generally understood and accepted within the Administration, and that rough agreement be reached regarding the type of governmental action called for by the policy."[25] The 1954 Economic Report was essentially the chairman's effort to publicize the administration's economic strategy. The report stated that the federal government had a "continuous" responsibility to help maintain employment and prevent inflation. Government "must be prepared to take preventive as well as remedial action; and it must be ready to cope with new situations that may arise." Burns's report stressed that "the arsenal of weapons at the disposal of Government for maintaining economic stability is formidable. It includes credit controls administered by the Federal Reserve System; the debt management policies of the Treasury; authority of the President to vary the terms of mortgages carrying Federal insurance; flexibility in the administration of the budget; agricultural supports; modification of the tax structure; and public works. We shall not hesitate to use any or all of these weapons as the situation may require."[26] For Burns, in other words, business confidence was to be maintained by acknowledging that the government was ready and willing to employ its policy weapons to stabilize the economy.

Humphrey and his ideological allies had a different outlook on how to maintain business confidence. At the January 15, 1954, cabinet session, Humphrey objected to the tone of the Burns draft of the 1954 Economic Report because it suggested that government can "make or break prosperity." The Treasury secretary claimed that confident people, engaged in private enterprise, produce prosperity, not government. "What government can do is remove restrictions on enterprise, stimulate initiative." He was then interrupted by Eisenhower: "Now look. Let's not quote too much Mr. Hoover. I remember 1929 and prosperity around the corner, and basically sound economy." He went on to emphasize that they could not place themselves in the position of not being able "to act positively." Charles Wilson argued that the report should be more positive. Humphrey then expressed fear that Burns's report would trigger a negative headline: "Administration Girds for Depression." Wilson worried that "Socialists will rejoice that even Republicans see the need for a planned economy." Humphrey then raised the objection that the Burns report implied that much would be done *in the future* to fight a possible recession when, in reality, much was being done every day. Eisenhower responded, "You just don't hear this the same way I do." It is clear that at this meeting, Eisenhower supported Burns's approach in reassuring the public.[27]

At the March 12 cabinet session, Humphrey shared Eisenhower's concern that they should be prepared for all eventualities, but he did not feel the present situation was a crisis. "It will be April or May before I get excited." He recommended that the administration engage in "some little things that can be turned on and off. But don't start big things for radical moves can't be turned on and off easily—and can cause trouble." Eisenhower responded that "timely action would forestall more drastic action later."[28] Burns could not have said it any better. At the next cabinet meeting on March 19, Harold Stassen suggested that business confidence was still high because business believed that the administration would take timely action when necessary. Burns agreed; Humphrey disagreed, claiming that confidence remained high because business trusted the administration to follow sound fiscal policies instead of acting prematurely. Nixon supported Burns's more activist recommendations for political reasons: "If anything sound can be done today, do so now rather than three months later. Lines are drawn before an election. Challenge climate before Democratic argument is hammered in."[29]

On April 2, Burns presented a review of the economic situation to the cabinet meeting. In that ninth month of the decline, he recommended that if conditions continued to deteriorate, taxes be slashed further. For the present he urged cheaper credit. Eisenhower advised the cabinet to be extremely cautious in publicizing the administration's actions because "if you tell a soldier you're doing something to help his morale, he'll start running." The president told the members to emphasize the positive policies but directed them to avoid the term "pumppriming," which was associated with the New Deal.[30] Throughout these cabinet meetings, Eisenhower was very sensitive to the public relations aspects so as not to shatter public confidence and to avoid Democratic accusations that he was another Hoover.

This concern for business confidence posed a policy dilemma for the administration. Burns urged constant vigilance and stressed that the government could not "wait for indices to reach any magic point" before acting.[31] But Burns's inductive approach with its emphasis on how unique each recession was and how the administration was dealing with a new economy, made most previous experience inapplicable and prediction—except in the vaguest of terms—of when specific policies should be initiated impossible. Eisenhower, as an astute decision-maker, complained during the March 12, 1954, cabinet meeting about "the existence of counter-cyclical plans but the absence of recommendations as to when they should be put into effect."[32] Adding this sensitivity to business confidence to the uncertainty as to when counter-recession policies should be started, allows at least a partial understanding of why there was more talk than action during this period and why the administration avoided actions which required new congressional appropriations. Even the May 14 decision to accelerate FY 1955 expenditures was not publicly announced. Acknowledging the need for activist policies would threaten confidence. The "Catch 22" dilemma is nicely captured by Stein: "The desire not to acknowledge the existence of conditions calling for extraordinary action would have been an obstacle to taking extraordinary action of a kind that could not be concealed."[33] Fortunately, by April 1954 the economic indicators began to move in a positive direction, so there was no need to test whether the administration could have resolved this dilemma. The evidence suggests, however, that, if the economy had continued to decline, Eisenhower would have followed the next step of Burns's strategy and requested new congressional legislation calling for tax cuts and public works.

At the June 11, 1954, cabinet meeting Burns announced that there was finally evidence that recovery was underway. He urged the prudent course of strengthening the natural forces rallying the economy. An obviously pleased Eisenhower extended his highest accolade: "Arthur, you'd have made a fine Chief of Staff during the war."[34] On July 23, 1954, Burns told the cabinet that the economic decline — he still avoided the word recession — had definitely come to a close.

Burns deserved the president's praise. Although he underestimated the cuts in government expenditures for FY 1954 and overestimated administrative budget flexibility, Burns had correctly forecast a mild recession and mapped out an appropriate strategy to combat it. The recession lasted twelve months, during which total output diminished between 3 to 4 percent and employment declined 2½ percent. The key Keynesian concept of aggregate demand was maintained because of a combination of automatic stabilizers, loose monetary policy, and tax cuts. According to Holmans, "The fall in personal tax payments and the rise in transfer payments were more than enough to offset the fall in personal income before tax and transfer, disposable income rising by $1.0 billion. Although the level of personal income before tax and transfer in the second quarter of 1954 was the lowest reached in the recession, disposable income was higher than the prerecession peak, as was consumption."[35] Professor Burns had helped Eisenhower pass his first economics test.

THE 1957–58 RECESSION

Following the recession of 1953–54, the economy thrived in 1955 and 1956. But in the first half of 1957 inconsistent economic signals made it difficult to forecast future trends. On May 3, 1957, Raymond Saulnier announced to the cabinet that although business confidence was declining, "there is nothing in this picture to indicate clearly the outline of recession. At the moment it is more nearly the picture of an economy proceeding at a very high level . . . and making rather satisfactory adjustments. In my view, the economy is gathering strength during this period of sidewise [instead of up or down] movement."[36] Although Saulnier did not foresee a recession, he did argue that the Federal Reserve should ease credit restrictions; but he was stymied by William McChesney Martin, who still believed that the chief economic problem was rising prices. The Federal Reserve raised the discount rate on August 23, 1957 — perhaps its worst mistake of the 1950s.

By August 1957 Saulnier recognized that the United States was headed for a recession. Between August 1957 and April 1958, industrial production declined 14 percent, corporate profits fell by 25 percent, and the unemployment rate soared to 7.5 percent — the highest level since 1941. The number of the unemployed increased by over 2.4 million — nearly 700,000 workers lost their jobs in February 1958. By March almost 5.2 million people were unemployed. The 1957–58 recession was sharper but briefer than that of 1953–54. The decline in the quarterly GNP at constant prices from the pre-recession peak to the trough quarter was 3.7 percent in 1953–54 and 4.7 percent in 1957–58. But there were thirteen months of contraction in 1953–54 and only eight in 1957–58.[37] A perplexing aspect of this recession that deeply worried Eisenhower and Treasury Secretary Robert Anderson was that between September 1957 and May 1958 the consumer price index rose by 2.1 percent.[38] The recovery began in May 1958 and by December 1958 the number of unemployed was reduced by almost a million.

In Eisenhower's view, the 1957–58 recession was essentially following the pattern of the 1953–54 decline: "a dip in the economy, frenzied Democratic calls for action, the administration's determination not to panic, and the economy's gradual emergence from difficulty."[39] Eisenhower relied mainly on the automatic stabilizers to maintain a sufficiently high disposable income to overcome the recession. In fact, during the recession, personal disposable income fell less than one percent. In addition, on February 12, 1958, the president announced several antirecession proposals to increase federal hghway expenditures, accelerate defense contract awards, and modernize post offices. When the unemployment rate continued to climb, Eisenhower proposed, on March 25, a bill to extend unemployment benefits from the usual twenty-six to thirty-nine weeks, which Congress quickly passed and the president signed on June 4. Eisenhower rejected all Democratic proposals for tax cuts and emergency public works. He was determined, as he writes later, not to be "swayed from reason by the purveyors of doom" and to avoid any remedies that would "cause more acute trouble later on."[40] While the Democratic proposals for tax cuts were in the range of $5 to $10 billion, the Eisenhower policies to counter the recession resulted in an annual increase of expenditures of $1.1 billion in the fourth quarter of 1958. Stein concludes, "The largest and probably most important item of antirecession expenditure was the federal program to extend unemployment compensation payments which cost the federal government about $600 million. In general, activities on the expenditure side of the budget reduced pressure for an immediate decision on strong fiscal action but did not themselves constitute such action."[41]

Eisenhower wrote in his memoirs that as the economy began to recover in the early summer of 1958, "The storm was over."[42] But this was true only if one assumed, as the president did, that the target of this economic policy was to overcome the recession without encouraging inflation. For the increasing number of people who felt the real problem to be sluggish economic growth that was producing higher unemployment rates, the storm continued. Controversy persisted because the average unemployment rate for the last seven months of 1958 was 6.8 percent; for calendar year 1959 it was 5.5 percent. And the problem threatened to worsen as the annual accretions to the labor force grew from about 800,000 in 1955 to about 900,000 in 1960. Indeed, not until 1965 was unemployment as low again as it was in early 1957.

The context within which economic policy was made during the 1957–58 recession was far more complex and confusing than it had been in 1953–54. Eisenhower was now a lame-duck president, and because of Sputnik and the recession, his popularity had fallen below the 60 percent approval level for the first time during his presidency.[43] The Democrats, reflecting the higher expectations of the second half of the 1950s, and looking toward the 1958 congressional elections and the 1960 presidential race, argued that policies of their "New Economics" could either have prevented this "needless" recession or reversed it more quickly.[44] In addition, unlike the situation in 1954 when the end of the Korean War had meant that defense expenditures could be cut, the aftermath of Sputnik meant that defense costs would rise. And despite the 1957–58 recession, the cost of living continued to go up — an indicator seen as particularly ominous. Finally, the president who had to navigate a course through this complexity was less the Modern Republican of 1953–54 and more the rigidly conservative New Eisenhower. The New Eisenhower was disgusted by what he considered the hysterical reactions of demagogic politicians to both Sputnik and the recession and was less able to regain the political initiative. Under these circumstances, and believing that he had already compromised too much, Eisenhower was determined to do his duty. That meant fiscal and monetary measures that would not promote inflation.

The fact that Eisenhower believed that inflation was the fundamental economic problem and that the recession was a temporary storm that would largely cure itself strengthened the bargaining position of Treasury Secretary Anderson. From a bureaucratic point of view, usually the Treasury is more sensitive to inflation and the CEA more concerned with unemployment. The dilemma for policymakers in 1957–58 was that they were faced with both inflation and recession. It had been assumed that inflation and unemployment were mutually exclusive. Now they were occurring simultaneously — an early manifestation of what economists in the 1970s called "stagflation."

In this situation the chief issue within the administration was whether to propose a tax cut. Eisenhower and his top economic advisers always believed that taxes — especially on investment income — were too high. The president had planned to achieve a budget surplus and then propose a popular tax cut. These plans were dashed by the steady increases in federal expenditures and by the demands for an accelerated defense build up that followed Sputnik. Now the question was whether to take advantage of the recession to introduce a tax cut that could reverse the economic decline and promote more rapid economic growth. Both Democratic and Republican party leaders feared that the other side would be the first to propose a tax cut. Between February and March 1958 four members of the cabinet — Anderson, Mitchell, Brundage, and Nixon — made statements that there would be a tax reduction if it was needed.[45] At this delicate point the president was not ready to propose a tax cut, but he did not want the debate within his administration to incite a preemptive move by the Democrats to line up behind their tax bill. However, Eisenhower also wanted to retain the option of proposing an antirecession tax cut if that became necessary. The result of this period of uncertainty was an unappealing one for the administration: After tantalizing the public with the possibility of a tax cut, it never proposed one.

The intellectual leader of the tax cut advocates was Arthur Burns. Unlike in 1953–54, however, this time Burns was offering his advice from outside the administration — an enormous disadvantage. On March 10, 1958, Burns wrote a letter to Eisenhower that began, "As I see the political situation developing, I fear that there is a danger that we will gradually be drawn into a public works program of increasing scope." To avoid this trap, Burns recommended that the administration introduce a tax cut. "If it were not for politics, it might be well to wait for a while before enacting a tax reduction. But as things seem to be shaping up, I have come to the conclusion that a tax cut, to apply both to individuals and businesses, has now become desirable. A tax cut today can still be effective in checking the recession this year. Perhaps most important of all, it is a solution based on free enterprise, in contrast to the public works programs which can only serve to expand the role of government in our economy."[46] In his reply to Burns, the president wrote,

I trust that I am not getting stubborn in my attitude about logical Federal action in this business slump, but I am bound to say that I cannot help but feel that precipitate . . . action would be the worst thing that we could now do. I realize that to be conservative in this situation . . . can well get me tagged as an unsympathetic, reactionary fossil. But my honest conviction is that the greatest service we can do for our country is to oppose wild-eyed schemes of every kind. I am against vast and unwise public works programs . . . as well as the slash-bang kinds of tax cutting from which the proponents want nothing so much as immediate political advantage. Tax cuts may have to be made. . . . But how I pray that when and if such action is necessary, we may have some statesmen and economists in controlling positions, rather than demagogues.[47]

Several weeks later Burns sent Eisenhower another letter recommending that instead of individual antirecession measures, the president introduce a "concerted program." Burns suggested six measures, but the first and key proposal was a permanent $5 billion tax cut for both individuals and business firms designed to stimulate both consumption and investment.[48] Several days later in his reply to Burns Eisenhower agreed that an integrated package of measures to stimulate economic recovery would be better than piecemeal proposals. However, in response to Burns's recommendation for a tax cut, the president wrote, "When I contemplate the minimum size of the Federal Budget that we are now certain to have about 1961, I am alarmed by the amount of deficit spending we shall probably have to do. As I try to peer just a bit down the road into the future, I cannot fail but be impressed by the inflationary factors that we shall likely have to combat. A sizable tax reduction may become one of these; I have not yet been convinced of proof of its necessity. And if it is not needed at the moment then I am quite sure its future would be inflationary."[49]

On May 5, Burns wrote to urge a tax cut as part of a "rounded program for promoting the nation's long-range economic growth." Burns felt that it would be possible "to get a constructive tax bill from the present Congress in spite of the demagogues." Burns even proposed a political strategy: "The Congress has to write . . . some sort of tax bill this year. Or, more accurately, if they don't, the corporate income tax rate will come down automatically from 52 percent to 47 percent and some of the excises will also come down. This puts you in a strong position to get from the Congress something close to what you want. If they send you a socialistic bill, you can send it back with a healthy veto. They will then have to turn around and heed your wishes or take the risk of having the corporate tax rate come down by 5 points. Democrats cannot afford to do the latter."[50] The president replied to Burns with a short note that expressed skepticism over whether the administration could obtain the tax reform bill it needed from Congress. Burns's advice had been rejected.[51]

In spurning Burns's advice, Eisenhower was swayed by his growing doubts that anything rational could emerge from "the laborious and tortuous channels" of the legislative process. The president claimed that any administration tax bill would inevitably "be so loaded down with indefensible and illogical proposals that a veto would be practically compulsory." The president also expressed his own guilt over responding to, as well as his contempt for, political expediency: "As you know, I finally felt compelled to sign the latest

Housing Bill, even though certain of its provisions seemed to me to be unwise, if not completely stupid. The freezing of interest rates on veterans' mortgages with the requirements that the government purchase them at par, is demagoguery at its worst."[52] Thus, Burns's politically perceptive advice fell on deaf ears because the president felt he had already bowed too much to political expediency.

Burns's problem was that he was aiming his advice toward the president he had dealt with in the first term. If Burns had been in more intimate contact with Eisenhower in his second term, he might have recognized that to buttress his recommendations with political reasoning was now likely to be counterproductive. In 1958 Burns would have been wiser to express his advice in terms of Eisenhower's duty to propose a tax cut to help the United States match the Soviet Union's faster economic growth rate.

Burns was able to enlist the support of Labor Secretary Mitchell and Vice-President Nixon for a tax cut, but not that of Saulnier or Hauge. It is possible that Saulnier was estranged from Burns because of rumors circulating in Washington at the time that Eisenhower was dissatisfied with the CEA and was about to recall Burns.[53] To combat the recession, Saulnier argued that the Federal Reserve should expand the money supply. He was not an early advocate of a tax cut, preferring to keep this alternative in reserve if the recession did not bottom out by late spring. By late May, Saulnier had grown sufficiently apprehensive regarding the recovery to recommend a tax cut.[54] The president rejected Saulnier's advice and followed the recommendation of Treasury Secretary Anderson.

Anderson and Federal Reserve chairman Martin both believed that the fundamental threat to the economy was inflation and not recession. To confront the threat of inflation, Anderson believed that tax reform was needed. In September 1957 he had created an advisory committee of businesspeople under the chairmanship of Thomas B. McCabe, former chair of the Federal Reserve, to recommend a tax program to be proposed in 1958. This plan was shelved when Sputnik made it obvious that the administration was not going to be able to achieve the budget savings necessary to allow a tax cut. Still, Anderson remained committed to a tax reform that would reduce rates on the upper-income sector and corporations in order to stimulate the investment necessary for economic growth. What concerned Anderson was that the kind of tax bill most likely to be passed by Congress was one that targeted the lower- and middle-income sectors. In Anderson's view, this would promote consumption, not investment; it would engender inflation, not economic growth.[55]

Anderson recommended that the administration delay proposing a tax cut until other measures had time to take effect. He believed that an economic upturn would occur without a tax reduction, and he was afraid that if taxes were reduced too early, credit for the recovery would mistakenly be given to the tax reduction. Anderson would support a tax cut to head off the demand for public works projects if the unemployment rate continued to rise. Thus, once the economy began to show signs of recovery during the late spring of 1958, Anderson's position prevailed, and most of the pressure for a tax cut dissipated. After Eisenhower decided not to ask Congress for a tax reduction, Labor Secretary Mitchell lamented that he and Nixon had been defeated by Anderson and the Federal Reserve.[56]

Even when the Treasury Department was considering twenty alternative tax cuts during the spring of 1958, one suspects that Anderson wanted to kill the idea. In May, Anderson sent Eisenhower a document that analyzed only the revenue costs of various tax reduction proposals. The Treasury study claimed methodological difficulties and did not examine the possible effects of different kinds of tax reduction in expanding the national income. Such a glaring omission suggests that Anderson was not trying to interest the balanced-budget obsessed president with the tax cut option.[57]

The president was obviously pleased with the advice he received from Anderson. In his memoirs Eisenhower praised Anderson for the "solid support" he provided for the president's decision to rely on automatic stabilizers to overcome the recession.[58] Anderson's advice was compatible with the mindset of the New Eisenhower. That is, they both agreed that the principle problem was inflation, that fighting the recession should not burden the budget with permanent commitments that would impede balancing it once the recession was over, that political expediency was to be avoided, and that the long-range goal of tax reform designed to promote investment should not be jeopardized for the sake of a "quickie" tax cut. Stein explains why Eisenhower was so prone to follow Anderson's advice:

Anderson was a more consistent and effective barrier to action than Humphrey had been in 1954. While Humphrey had all the outward signs which made him the archetype of conservatism, . . . Anderson's conservatism was actually firmer. Humphrey's conservatism was instinctive and intuitive without much intellectual base; it could be moved or outflanked by argument. Morehover, Humphrey was a conservative second and a Republican first; he was willing to compromise his "principles" for the party. . . . Anderson was more ideological and less political. This was attractive to Eisenhower. He liked to think of himself, and have others think of him, as taking the long view rather than the short, the hard road rather than the easy, the nonpolitical course rather than the political.[59]

And so in 1958 the United States did not achieve a tax cut or a tax reform. The same was true in 1959 and 1960. As a result, the Republicans suffered in 1958 and 1960.

CONCLUSION

I have examined how the Eisenhower administration responded to two recessions. The first recession of 1953–54 was viewed as a crisis, and an enormous amount of time and effort was spent in debating strategy. Because that first recession was successfully handled, the second recession of 1957–58 was perceived as more of a recurrent problem—a temporary storm that would soon correct itself; there was much less fear of another 1929 and there were fewer mentions of Herbert Hoover in cabinet discussions. The memory of the 1953–54 recession made the 1957–58 recession less of a learning experience and did not encourage innovative thinking. But Eisenhower was not complacent; he was fearful of being stampeded into reckless acts that would further unbalance the budget and accelerate the inflationary trend, which he saw as the real threat to the economy.

But to experience one recession is not to have experienced them all. Eisenhower did not recognize that the public's higher expectations in the second half of the 1950s meant that the second recession required a different response. In addition to the conventional calling for emergency public works projects, the extension of unemployment benefits, the easing of credit, and tax cuts, the Democrats claimed in 1958 that policies derived from the New Economics could have prevented this "needless recession," or at least have shortened it. Even when the second recession turned out to be five months shorter than the first one, there was still growing criticism about the sluggish economic growth rate. By the end of the 1950s the attitude toward automatic stabilizers—which had been positive in 1954 when it was demonstrated how they "put a floor under recessions"—had become more ambivalent when it was shown how they also "put a ceiling on expansion."[60]

The New Eisenhower of 1958 was not as politically sensitive or as flexible as the Eisenhower of 1954. In the first recession, the president had recognized how politically sensitive a rise in the unemployment rate was; in the second, he did not. It was important that the Eisenhower administration be seen as doing more to overcome the second recession; instead, it was viewed as doing less. Holmans points out that "there is a striking contrast between the tone of the Economic Report of 1958 and that of the Economic Report of 1954. Whereas the latter had listed the 'formidable arsenal of weapons' available to deal with recession and emphasized that there would be no hesitation about using any or all of them if the situation should require, no such assurance was given in the 1958 Economic Report; its whole theme was that the economy would recover without any special action to this end by the Federal government."[61] A journalist who was politically friendly to Eisenhower wrote in May 1958, "Franklin Roosevelt, who loved to call himself 'Doctor New Deal,' became famous for his lavish use of the federal hypodermic. 'Doctor' Eisenhower was still stubbornly refusing the big needle that most of his critics, and many of his friends, wanted him to seize."[62] The president's commitment to a balanced budget, his fear of inflation, and his growing contempt for demagogues in Congress combined to inhibit his ability to act in the most politically rational manner.

In the first recession, Burns gave politically relevant advice and Eisenhower received that advice and recognized how politically relevant it was. In the second recession, Eisenhower rejected the best political advice he received because he felt that he had already compromised too much for political expediency. A president is in trouble when his mind is geared to reject politically perceptive arguments. While Burns, Mitchell, and Nixon believed that worthwhile tax legislation could be passed by Congress, Eisenhower and Anderson no longer believed that they could negotiate reasonable compromises with the Democrats in Congress. By losing faith in the legislative process, Eisenhower surrendered a large part of the presidency's power of initiative and placed himself and his party in a very vulnerable position. The political price for this was high in 1958 and 1960.

7

Conclusion

In the waning days of his presidency, a melancholy Eisenhower met with his top budget advisors to discuss his last budget message. Eisenhower wanted his final message (FY 1962) to be critical of Congress for having over-reacted (in terms of expenditures) to the "Sputnik hysteria." He also directed that the budget message and the economic report emphasize the eight-year effort of his administration "to preserve and stabilize the value of the dollar, bringing out the importance of this effort in light of the rapid decline in its value as a result of inflation just prior to 1953." The president told his budget advisers that his administration had achieved "a great measure of success" but he fantasized that "if he were a dictator he thought he could cut the budget before him 20% without damage to the country—by knocking out many sacred cows and completely useless but well-established activities."[1] It was time for this proud man to retire from the political struggles of the presidency, a role which was now more frustrating than fulfilling.

Certainly Eisenhower would have preferred more political rewards for his conservative economic policies, especially in his second term. Eisenhower did not succeed in creating the majority Modern Republican party he had talked about during his first term. Indeed, after 1957, the New Eisenhower frequently worked against the reform efforts of moderate Republicans. Both Treasury secretaries wanted to reduce federal expenditures to allow a tax decrease; they were also increasingly concerned about the rising national debt, creeping inflation, and the balance of payments problem. Humphrey and Anderson each overestimated what the political payoff would be for achieving balanced budgets. The two chairmen of the CEA were apprehensive about their inability to prevent recessions and the sluggish economic growth rate in the second half of the 1950s that was causing a rise in the unemployment rate. Both Burns and Saulnier had differences of opinion

Eisenhower and Bureau of the Budget director Percival Brundage conferring at Gettysburg, December 31, 1957. (Courtesy Dwight D. Eisenhower Library.)

with the Treasury secretary, the budget director, and the chair of the Federal Reserve Board. The directors of the Bureau of the Budget were frustrated that they could produce only three balanced budgets and were almost powerless to prevent the inexorable, incremental increases in the annual federal budget. Every one of these officials, but especially the chair of the Federal Reserve Board, believed that inflation was too great. Despite the frustrations of these policymakers, the economic record of the 1950s looks good to a contemporary audience because of the even more disappointing economic experiences of the following decades.

The most important member of the president's economic advisory system was Eisenhower himself. Eisenhower was a conviction politician who entered politics, at least partly, because of a sense of duty to serve the national interest that he felt was threatened by liberal big-spending Democrats on the left and reactionary Old Guard Republicans on the right. Eisenhower's philosophy generated an ambitious political agenda for the reluctant candidate: halting the leftward drift of public policies by defeating the Democratic party; constructing a moderately conservative Republican party that would hold majority control in Congress; balancing the budget; establishing that prosperity is not contingent on federal bureaucrats and inflation, but rather is dependent upon the self-discipline and cooperation of leaders of government, business, and labor; and preparing the nation for a long struggle with the Soviet Union, with the final chapter determined more by economics than military arms. After twenty years of Democratic party rule, Eisenhower wanted to close national political schisms by stressing consensus over conflict. By depoliticizing divisive issues and class conflict, he hoped to maximize his own freedom to maneuver while minimizing the opportunities for demagogic politicians. In his second term, however, Eisenhower became more conservative, which meant he had fewer opportunities to achieve consensual compromises. As his conservatism ossified, he became more self-righteous, more cynical about the motivation of others, and too prone to veto reform proposals, which he condemned as reflecting demagogic and bureaucratic interest. Thus Eisenhower's moral conservatism was a two-edged sword: It provided him with the energy and sense of direction that drove his presidency; but it also eventually inhibited his presidency from achieving more of its objectives.

The economic record of the Eisenhower administration during the 1950s is evaluated as a solid success by most observers today. It can even be speculated that many of Eisenhower's Democratic critics in 1952 would have been surprised to see how well the new Republican president would perform as manager of prosperity. Nevertheless, as he left office in January 1961 Eisenhower was seriously criticized because of the three recessions and the sluggish rate of economic growth during his second term. It was a shock to Eisenhower that although the standard of living steadily rose during the 1950s people were not satisfied, but wanted more. Economists of the period frequently talked about "rising expectations" in the Third World—that phenomenon was also occurring in the United States.

Eisenhower did not comprehend that the standards against which his performance as manager of prosperity was measured were rising during the 1950s. What was considered successful in the early 1950s was viewed as inadequate by 1960. The president's initial successes generated not satisfaction but demands that more and fairer prosperity by guaranteed. In the late 1950s, Eisenhower was criticized by Keynesian Democrats, proponents of the New Economics who believed that though the administration had achieved moderate success, the knowledge was available to achieve much more. Eisenhower may have avoided a 1929-type crash and a long recession in 1958, but his cautious economic interventions were considered by his critics to be too little and too late. His critics also believed that more timely interventions, less concern with a balanced budget, and a looser monetary policy would produce faster economic growth and a lower unemployment rate. Accelerating the growth rate was also necessary to deter aggression from the Soviet Union. The Soviet growth rate was twice that of the United States during this period, which frightened Americans almost as much as Sputnik. Prosperity was needed more than ever to finance the Cold War and to satisfy demands for higher standards of living for a wider variety of people. Recessions were now viewed as threats to national security and impediments to social progress. The crucial point that Eisenhower never recognized was that as economic growth was becoming viewed as the best response to the policy dilemmas of the 1950s, the growth rate was slowing down.

Eisenhower calmed the heated politics of the Truman era, but by the end of the 1950s the tranquilizing effects of his leadership were replaced by frustration at what was now considered an inadequate pace of progress. Senator Kennedy capitalized on this mood by proclaiming that he could get the country moving again through vigorous, heroic leadership. By the end of the 1950s the aging Eisenhower was still personally popular but less effective politically. His policy preferences were increasingly viewed as old-fashioned, the results of an overly structured advisory system that eliminated innovative proposals.

The conservative-defensive position of the second Eisenhower administration was influenced by several factors. Because of the Twenty-second Amendment and the depletion of intellectual capital in the first term, any administration is likely to find itself on the defensive during its second term. This natural tendency, however, was reinforced when Eisenhower and his economic advisers chose a balanced budget and anti-inflation as priorities. These issues compelled the administration to defend itself against a Congress which was increasingly controlled by liberal Democrats, and even against the bureaucracy, which was supposedly run by Republican political appointees. An administration that appeared old and tired in contrast with young and restless Democrats contributed to the image of a presidency that was no longer keeping up with the needs of the nation.

Eisenhower expended enormous effort to achieve one of the strategic goals of his administration—a balanced budget. The Eisenhower administration provided three balanced budgets, an accomplishment that no subsequent president has been able to attain; only Johnson managed to attain even one balanced budget—in FY 1969. This was a fundamental objective of Eisenhower's because he believed the budget measured the self-discipline necessary for a viable democracy. A budget deficit during a recesssion might be necessary to stimulate aggregate demand, but deficits during prosperous times indicated waste and a pandering to demagogic politicians that would inevitably lead to inflation. What limited Eisenhower's capacity to produce innovative policy responses in the second term was the view he shared with George Humphrey that U.S. economic and political systems were endangered by economic mismanagement. American democracy, however, was more institutionalized and adaptable than Eisenhower and Humphrey believed; it was less fragile than they feared.

Eisenhower took his campaign promises seriously, and in October 1952 he had pledged to balance the budget within four years. Unlike later presidents who made similar promises, Eisenhower succeeded in fulfilling his promise. In contrast to the Reagan administration, his aim was to reduce both the military and the domestic budgets; his three balanced budgets were achieved principally because he held down military spending. The former general's strategic economic objective was to maintain U.S. technological superiority over the Soviet Union without bankrupting the nation. A bankrupt or inflation-weakened nation could neither preserve its democratic form of government nor defend itself and its allies. Because Eisenhower believed military expenditures were a necessary evil that added nothing of value to the economy, he was the only post–World War II president who could – and did – emphasize that only a "minimum defensive structure" should be supported. The constraint he exercised over the military budget following Sputnik may have been the most remarkable budget achievement in recent U.S. history. No other politician could have done it.

In 1952 Eisenhower had also promised that whenever necessary, he would institute new progressive programs. The president was willing to make this promise because he perceived federal programs as temporary responses to national crises that he hoped would be solved within a few years, thus bringing such federal programs to an end. But most of the issues to which the federal government was responding were not temporary problems. One does not solve the problem of an aging population; one "copes" with it. Eisenhower's theory that his administration could generate a subtractive process that would match the additive process proved naive. Federal programs did not result in "final solutions"; they usually produced permanent bureaucracies and incrementally expanding expenditures. These outcomes increasingly exasperated the president.

Still, Eisenhower was relatively successful in holding down federal expenditures because he was uniformly tough in reviewing all proposals that would cost more money. He did not selectively exert downward pressure on one set of expenditures in order to allow another set to balloon. The president's patience – mistakenly interpreted by some as complacency – also saved money. All problems did not constitute crises that had to be solved immediately. Eisenhower was not willing to spend billions to see the other side of the moon; Kennedy and Johnson were willing and did.

Eisenhower's sensitivity to budget considerations plays well to Americans today. After watching the government allow budget deficits to soar for the past three decades, many citizens view Eisenhower's demand that all proposed policies be subject to strict budget scrutiny as necessary and proper. During the latter half of the 1950s, however, such scrutiny was criticized as reactionary and uncaring and as inhibiting economic growth and social progress. By his second term, Eisenhower's commitment to a balanced budget had put him and his administration on the defensive. The aging president was perceived as postponing progress, the nation's most important product. Eisenhower's budgetary concerns blinded him to opportunities suggested by Modern Republican advisers, including several HEW secretaries, to preempt policy space with Republican programs. The outcome of his stubborn refusal to adopt such proposals was that policy space in the fields of health, education, and welfare was eventually filled in the 1960s by Democratic programs.

In brief, Eisenhower's selection of balancing the budget as his top priority placed the administration in an uncomfortable box. The strategy was not compatible with public opinion nor with Congress, both of which increasingly wanted the government to do more. It also surrendered the power of proposing positive initiatives to the Democrats. By unilaterally giving up the executive's major political power to propose new legislative responses to national problems, Eisenhower severely damaged the possibilities for success of Modern Republicans.

While Eisenhower can properly be criticized for not responding adequately to social needs in the second administration, the Democrats deserve criticism for creating issues of nonexistent bomber and missile gaps that eventually proved costly. To a modern audience, some liberals of the 1950s look particularly naive, utopian, demagogic, and partisan in their complaints that Eisenhower made a fetish of balancing the budget. They demanded that the government simply provide as much national security, education, health, and urban renewal as they felt the country needed. While the conservative Eisenhower was guilty of being too concerned by limitations, some of his liberal opponents succumbed to the temptations of a party out of power by claiming their policies would resolve many of the problems of the 1950s without indicating the costs of their proposals. Eisenhower's postponement of necessary reforms and the rising expectations of the 1950s sowed the seeds that bloomed into the successes and excesses of the 1960s.

The Eisenhower presidency fell short in the eyes of most intellectuals because it stressed the necessity of moving toward a balanced budget in order to curtail inflation. Liberal Democrats saw Eisenhower as reactionary because he was more concerned about inflation than unemployment. For many Democrats, inflation was the greedy worry of bankers and businesspeople, and responding to it prevented the federal government from working to achieve more social equality. After experiencing continually rising prices in recent decades, most Americans no longer consider inflation a bogus issue.

William McChesney Martin, the chairman of the Federal Reserve Board, shared Eisenhower's view that inflation was the chief threat to the American economy. The rigidity of the budget helped turn the Eisenhower administration toward monetary policy as the preferred instrument to stem inflation. This provided a window of opportunity for Martin, who took advantage of it to forge the Federal Reserve's modern role. Today, it is understood that the relative independence of the Federal Reserve provides that agency with the freedom to make the always unpopular decision to tighten the money supply when it is deemed necessary. It is generally not remembered that the Federal Reserve became a major player in the making of macroeconomic policy during the Eisenhower administration. The combined efforts of the Eisenhower presidency and the Federal Reserve kept inflation at generally low levels during the 1950s, but at an increasingly high political cost.

One of the president's major objectives in the second administration was to dispute the spreading belief that a little inflation was a prerequisite for economic growth and that efforts to constrain inflation would inevitably bring about recession and unemployment. Eisenhower, Anderson, and Martin argued that inflation could be combated without causing the economy to go into a tailspin. A major political problem for Eisenhower was that his anti-inflation policies could not be easily explained to the American people. The Eisenhower administration's reliance on monetary policy to hold down inflation eroded popular support because of the pain inflicted on businesspeople, farmers, and consumers alike by high interest rates. While most people did not understand how the Federal Reserve contracts or expands the money supply, they did feel the impact of a decision to tighten credit in the form of either being turned down for a loan or paying higher monthly interest charges. The crucial political point is that for policymakers there is less external pressure to prevent inflation during a boom than to check unemployment in a recession.[2] Hence, Eisenhower feared that there was a structural tilt toward inflation in American democracy that could be checked only by a politically insulated FRB and a president determined to balance the budget.

The balance of payments problem, a murky issue for many, was a comparatively clear-cut matter for Eisenhower. For the president, a favorable balance of payments was a national security concern that deserved top priority. Slower economic growth than America's industrialized allies and sluggish increases in exports meant that the nation was having difficulty in financing its international obligations. The undervalued dollar of the early 1950s had become overvalued by the end of the decade. As the Free World's banker, the United States had to maintain international confidence in the dollar by balancing the budget and preventing inflation. By appealing to Eisenhower's sense of duty, Treasury Secretary Anderson used the balance of payments issue to move Eisenhower decisively to the right in his second term.

Politically, the responses of the Eisenhower administration to the recession of 1953–54 were more effective than those employed in 1957–58. In the first recession Eisenhower understood how politically sensitive a rise in the unemployment rate is and how fearful the people were of another depression. The president made sure his administration was seen as active, firm, and compassionate. In the second recession, he viewed the economic decline as a problem that would largely cure itself. Eisenhower's fear of inflation and his concern over the balance of payments issue meant that the administration responded less at a time when the population expected the government to do more. In the first recession, Eisenhower accepted politically perceptive advice; in the second recession, he rejected such advice because of his increasing disdain for political expediency. In 1958, he felt duty-bound to follow the advice of Treasury Secretary Anderson, who argued that the administration would not be able to obtain the kind of tax reform the economy needed from the Democratic-controlled Congresss. Arthur Burns's advice to propose a tax cut, which offered Eisenhower his best chance to regain the domestic political initiative, was rejected. Hence, no tax cut or tax reform was achieved; the recession ended, but the economic growth rate remained sluggish and continued to be a political liability. As a result, the Republicans suffered huge losses in the 1958 congressional elections and lost the presidency in 1960.

The frustration that Modern Republicans felt in 1958 is revealed in Emmet John Hughes's words:

> The whole performance reflected Eisenhower's constant, consoling faith in 'the long view.' Essentially, this was the same faith that had endowed him with such forbearance in confronting a McCarthy, such moderation in projecting future national defense plans and costs, such muting of tone in asserting leadership toward the Congress, such willful slowness in supporting the struggle for civil rights. In this instance, he defiantly insisted upon looking over, past, and beyond all the grim warnings of possible depression — to discover, farther ahead, the more distant and (to him) more ominous dangers of inflation. . . . Aside from all economic consequences and arguments, the political conduct of the President bespoke, again, one abiding quality of the man: the reserve of tenacity — so akin . . . to his physical resilience — that lay deep beneath all surface signs of irresolution . . . even while it defied, so often and so stubbornly, the most urgent efforts to reach it and to tap it in other causes.[3]

The picture of Eisenhower that emerges from this study is different from the one intellectuals painted in the 1950s and the one revisionists have drawn more recently. In these pages, Eisenhower appears as a conservative activist, more involved in domestic economic policy than his contemporaries or even many revisionists have claimed. Instead of being complacent, as accused by critics of his time, he is seen as haunted by the specter of the collapse of the nation if its people and politicians did not practice self-discipline. Eisenhower's problem with the intellectual community was that many intellectuals had developed a liberal bias when applying standards to presidential performance. In their view, Franklin Roosevelt had discovered the "one best way" to operate as a modern president; any other model or style of leadership was considered inferior. Intellectuals and Democrats were disappointed, first, that Eisenhower was so popular, and second, that he did not use his popularity to achieve liberal reforms. On the other hand, many arch-conservatives, such as William Buckley and Barry Goldwater, evaluated Eisenhower negatively because they applied reactionary and/or impossible standards. That is, they faulted Eisenhower for not reversing the New Deal, selling the Tennessee Valley Authority, liberating Eastern Europe, significantly reducing the federal bureaucracy, and producing budget surpluses each year to reduce the national debt. Thus, because Eisenhower did not use his popularity to promote liberal reforms *or* reactionary policies, both sides assumed he was not using his popularity at all. But Eisenhower did not merely hoard his popularity; he "spent" it to hold down federal expenditures and to prevent what he considered nonessential reforms. These activities also require energy; passive presidents cannot bring about balanced budgets.

In contrast to the revisionists' image of Eisenhower, this book argues that Eisenhower's style of political leadership was more effective in his first term than in his second. The Eisenhower of the early 1950s was more in harmony with the mood of the population than the embittered president of the second half of the decade, who did not adapt to rising public expectations. When Eisenhower was trying to reconcile welfare liberalism with economic conservatism, he was a very difficult target for the Democrats. Admittedly, such a reconciliation may not be possible, but the variety of policies used in the attempt and the finesse of effective public relations may be the best political strategies. In any case, after the clarifying experience of fighting for the FY 1958 budget, the "new" and more conservative Eisenhower became a more stationary target for the Democrats' barbs.

The key point missed by many of the revisionists is that as Eisenhower became more conservative, he was less likely to employ hidden-hand tactics. Whereas few people perceived how Eisenhower plotted to weaken Senator Joe McCarthy, many saw Eisenhower leading the struggle to balance the budget and combat inflation. There was nothing hidden about Eisenhower's efforts to keep federal expenditures down. These efforts included making blunt statements regarding federal spending in the State of the Union address and in press conferences, presenting austere budgets to Congress, and vetoing any congressional legislation that he felt was too expensive. For a conviction politician, the major dilemma is how to balance moral zeal with political finesse. Eisenhower handled this problem more skillfully during his first term than his second.

The New Eisenhower was so contemptuous of demagogic politicians that he was less capable of exerting positive executive leadership. He became less Machiavellian, more moral, and less effective. The strength of his conservative convictions reduced his tactical flexibility. The records of Eisenhower's meetings make clear that the number and intensity of his complaints about government, the budget, the Congress, and demagogic politicians steadily increased in his second four years. If Eisenhower's political sensitivities had not deteriorated in the second administration, he might have been able to score some major victories for the Modern Republicans, including a tax cut and the passage of a federal aid to education bill. Whereas many presidents can be accused of allowing short-term political considerations to impinge upon their view of the long-range national interest, the opposite was true of Eisenhower during his second term.

In rethinking the Eisenhower presidency, one encounters a paradox — Eisenhower's conservatism seems more "modern" than his opponents' liberalism. His philosophy allowed him to hold the contemporary, post-Vietnam view regarding national limitations. His liberal adversaries were less bound by restraints. They believed that government could promote rapid economic growth, prevent recessions, thrive under moderate inflation, eliminate poverty, promote social justice, increase the defense budget, defeat Third World guerrilla movements, and negotiate arms control agreements with the Soviet Union — all at the same time, without confronting conflicting choices or long-term consequences to the federal budget. Eisenhower's more limited agenda can now be evaluated more favorably. As Robert Wright wryly observes, "In the sixties Eisenhower seemed culpable for problems that were just then surfacing. In the seventies the attempted solutions created more problems, and his restraint suddenly seemed judicious."[4]

In this nation's history, there have been times that called for liberal leadership and others that needed conservative guidance. After twenty years of the New Deal and Fair Deal, the 1950s required conservative leadership, and Eisenhower provided it. For the most part, Eisenhower, a man of contradictions, handled the paradoxes of the presidency and the conflicting pressures of the 1950s with a great deal of skill. War was avoided; the economy grew stronger. Still, in his second term especially, he allowed himself to be placed in the position of seeming to postpone Progress, which made him a vulnerable target in a country where progressive change is such an integral part of the political culture. What embittered Eisenhower in the late fifties was his belief that his conservative policies were not being politically rewarded. The nation was moving in a direction that Eisenhower found increasingly distasteful. He attributed his growing problems to the Republican party's lack of public relations skills, which freed him of the responsibility to reexamine his own decisions and to possibly alter his policies.[5] In assuming the role of a lonely moralist, he became a less effective politician and ended up achieving fewer of his objectives.

Eisenhower was a good president who might have been a great president if his selection of goals had not put him on the defensive for so much of his second term. In this optimistic country, with its faith in progress, it goes against the cultural grain to stress limits as much as Eisenhower did. Modern presidents have to demonstrate they have "vision"; they are under pressure to "do something" about an ever-expanding list of problems. In his first term, as he attempted to reconcile social compassion and fiscal conservatism, Eisenhower demonstrated a vision that was compatible with the needs of the period. But by the end of the 1950s, Eisenhower's presidency seemed to lack the required vision, and he left office with feelings of rejection. This study has suggested that Eisenhower could have felt better about his own contributions. As an effective conservative manager of prosperity, Eisenhower left the country in better economic shape than it had been when he assumed office in 1953. The bitter irony for Eisenhower, however, was that he bequeathed to his Democratic opponents a healthy economy that would finance a number of the policies he opposed.

Notes

ABBREVIATIONS

AWAS   Ann Whitman Administration Series
AWCS   Ann Whitman Cabinet Series
AWNS   Ann Whitman Name Series
DDE Diary Series   Dwight D. Eisenhower Diary Series
EL   Eisenhower Library
NSCS   National Security Council Series
OHT   Oral History Transcripts

CHAPTER 1. INTRODUCTION

1. Emmet John Hughes, *The Ordeal of Power* (New York: Dell Publishing Co., 1964), 299. See also Rexford Tugwell, *The Enlargement of the Presidency* (Garden City, N.Y.: Doubleday, 1960), 465.
2. William V. Shannon, "Eisenhower as President," *Commentary* 26 (Nov. 1958): 390.
3. A sampling of the revisionist literature would include Stephen E. Ambrose, *Eisenhower: The President,* vol. 2 (New York: Simon and Schuster, 1984); Vincent P. De Santis, "Eisenhower Revisionism," *Review of Politics* 38 (April 1976): 190–208; Robert A. Divine, *Eisenhower and the Cold War* (New York: Oxford University Press, 1981); Fred I. Greenstein, *The Hidden-Hand Presidency: Eisenhower as Leader* (New York: Basic Books, 1982); Anthony James Joes, "Eisenhower Revisionism: The Tide Comes In," *Presidential Studies Quarterly* 15 (Summer 1985): 561–571; Murray Kempton, "The Underestimation of Dwight D. Eisenhower," *Esquire* 68 (Sept. 1967): 108–109, 156; Mary S. MacAuliffe, "Eisenhower, the President," *Journal of American History* 68 (Dec. 1981): 625–632; and Elmo Richardson, *The Presidency of Dwight D. Eisenhower* (Lawrence: University Press of Kansas, 1979).
4. Greenstein, *The Hidden-Hand Presidency,* 58–59.
5. MacAuliffe, "Eisenhower, the President," 627.
6. Clinton Rossiter, *The American Presidency* rev. ed. (New York: Harcourt, Brace and World, 1959), 36–37.

7. Walter W. Heller, *New Dimensions of Political Economy* (New York: Norton, 1966), 59.

8. Stephen K. Bailey, *Congress Makes a Law: The Story behind the Employment Act of 1946* (New York: Columbia University Press, 1950).

9. Erwin C. Hargrove and Samuel A. Morley, eds., *The President and the Council of Economic Advisers* (Boulder, Colo.: Westview Press, 1984), 185.

10. Ibid., 13.

11. Heller, *New Dimensions*, 69, 80.

12. Neil H. Jacoby, "The President, the Constitution and the Economist in Economic Stabilization," *History of Political Economy* 3 (Fall 1971): 400.

13. Graham T. Allison, *Essence of Decision: Explaining the Cuban Missile Crisis* (Boston: Little, Brown and Co., 1971), 164.

14. Ibid., 144.

15. Dan Caldwell, "Bureaucratic Foreign Policy-Making," *American Behavioral Scientist* 21 (Sept. 1–1 Oct. 1977): 97.

16. Stephen Krasner, "Are Bureaucracies Important?" *Foreign Policy* 3 (Summer 1972): 166. See also Jerel A. Rosati, "Developing a Systematic Decision-Making Framework: Bureaucratic Politics in Perspective," *World Politics* 33 (Jan. 1981): 234–252.

17. I. M. Destler, *Presidents, Bureaucrats and Foreign Policy: The Politics of Organizational Reform* (Princeton, N.J.: Princeton University Press, 1975), 60.

18. Eisenhower letter to Arthur Burns, April 2, 1958, DDE Diary Series, EL. See also Eisenhower letter to Nelson Rockefeller, April 24, 1958, DDE Diary Series, EL.

CHAPTER 2. ECONOMIC PHILOSOPHY AND ADMINISTRATION IN THE EISENHOWER PRESIDENCY

1. Robert Griffith, "Dwight D. Eisenhower and the Corporate Commonwealth," *American Historical Review* 77 (Feb. 1982): 88.

2. Gabriel Hauge, Oral History Interview, July 10, 1976, p. 97, OHT, EL. See also Charles Murphy, "The Eisenhower Shift," pt. 1, *Fortune* (Jan. 1956): 85.

3. Charles Murphy, "The Eisenhower Shift," pt. 4, *Fortune* (April 1956): 114.

4. Gary W. Reichard, *The Reaffirmation of Republicanism: Eisenhower and the Eighty-third Congress* (Knoxville: University of Tennessee Press, 1975), 10.

5. *New York Times*, Oct. 26, 1952.

6. Eisenhower letter to William E. Robinson, Aug. 4, 1954, AWNS, EL.

7. Sherman Adams, *First Hand Report: The Inside Story of the Eisenhower Administration* (London: Hutchinson and Co., 1962), 135.

8. Eisenhower letter to Milton Eisenhower, Jan. 6, 1954, AWNS, EL.

9. Eisenhower letter to Milton Eisenhower, May 25, 1959, AWNS, EL.

10. Eric F. Goldman, *The Crucial Decade—And After: 1945–60* (New York: Vintage Books, 1960), 268.

11. Richard H. Rovere, Oral History Interview, Feb. 22, 1968, p. 38, OHT, EL.

12. Stephen E. Ambrose, *Eisenhower: The President*, vol. 2 (New York: Simon and Schuster, 1984), 115–116.

13. Fred I. Greenstein, *The Hidden-Hand Presidency: Eisenhower as Leader* (New York: Basic Books, 1982), 46–47.

14. Elmo Richardson, *The Presidency of Dwight D. Eisenhower* (Lawrence: University Press of Kansas, 1979), 195.

15. Quoted in Ambrose, *Eisenhower*, 48.

16. Griffith, "Dwight D. Eisenhower and the Corporate Commonwealth," 91.

17. Ibid., 93.

18. Eisenhower letter to George Humphrey, July 22, 1958, AWAS, EL.

19. Eisenhower letter to John Eisenhower, Oct. 23, 1953, DDE Diary Series, EL.

20. Robert J. Donovan, *Eisenhower: The Inside Story* (New York: Harper and Row, 1956), 38.

21. *New York Times*, June 12, 1953.

22. Arthur Larson, *A Republican Looks at His Party* (New York: Harper and Row, 1956), 39.

23. Ibid., 201.

24. Emmet John Hughes, *The Ordeal of Power* (New York: Dell Publishing Co., 1964), 288.

25. Arthur Larson, *Eisenhower: The President Nobody Knew* (New York: Charles Scribner's Sons, 1968), 141. See also William Bragg Ewald, Jr., *Eisenhower the President: Crucial Days, 1951-1960* (Englewood Cliffs, N.J.: Prentice Hall, 1981), 289.

26. Eisenhower letter to Mrs. Edgar Eisenhower, May 6, 1960, DDE Diary Series, EL.

27. Greenstein, *The Hidden-Hand Presidency*, 53. See also Piers Brendon, *Ike: His Life and Times* (New York: Harper and Row, 1986), 406.

28. Richardson, *The Presidency of Dwight D. Eisenhower*, 22.

29. *Time*, Jan. 26, 1953, 22.

30. Ambrose, *Eisenhower*, 23.

31. Robert H. Ferrell, ed., *The Eisenhower Diaries* (New York: Norton, 1981), entry for May 14, 1953, p. 237.

32. Robert H. Ferrell, ed., *The Diary of James C. Hagerty* (Bloomington: Indiana University Press, 1983), entry for Dec. 14, 1955, p. 243.

33. Eisenhower letter to George Humphrey, March 7, 1956, AWAS, EL.

34. Eisenhower letter to George Humphrey, July 29, 1957, AWAS, EL.

35. Hughes, *Ordeal of Power*, 64.

36. Larson, *Eisenhower*, 26.

37. Steve Neal, *The Eisenhowers* (Lawrence: University Press of Kansas, 1984), 320.

38. Neil Jacoby, Oral History Interview, Dec. 5, 1970, pp. 79-81, OHT, EL.

39. Office of Staff Secretary, L. Arthur Minnich, Cabinet Series (handwritten notes), cabinet meetings on June 4, 1954, and Nov. 5, 1954.

40. U.S. Congress, Joint Committee on the Economic Report, Hearings on the January 1954 Economic Report of the President, 83d Congress, 2d session, p. 82.

41. Joe Alsop, *Washington Post*, March 13, 1959.

42. Nathaniel R. Howard, ed., *The Basic Papers of George M. Humphrey* (Cleveland: The Western Reserve Historical Society, 1965), 49-51.

43. Ibid., 275.

44. Ibid., 282.

45. Ewald, *Eisenhower the President*, 192.

46. Dwight D. Eisenhower, *Mandate for Change* (Garden City, N.Y.: Doubleday and Co., 1963), 235.

47. Robert Griffith, ed., *Ike's Letters to a Friend: 1941-1958* (Lawrence: University Press of Kansas, 1984), 138.

48. Ferrell, *The Eisenhower Diaries*, 308.

49. Eisenhower letter to Robert Anderson, Jan. 13, 1961, AWAS, EL.

50. Robert Anderson memo to President Eisenhower, "The Money and Credit System of the U.S. and How It Works," Sept. 1957, AWAS, EL.

51. Eisenhower letter to Robert Anderson, Nov. 3, 1958, AWAS, EL.

52. Robert Anderson speech to American Finance Association and American Economic Association, Washington, D.C., Dec. 29, 1959, p. 7, AWAS, EL.

53. Office of Staff Secretary, L. Arthur Minnich, Cabinet Series (handwritten notes), cabinet meeting on May 2, 1958, EL.

54. See for example Robert Anderson's presentations to the cabinet on Dec. 12, 1958, and March 13, 1959. Office of Staff Secretary, L. Arthur Minnich, Cabinet Series, EL.

55. Robert Merriam, Oral History Interview, Jan. 13, 1969, p. 69, OHT, EL.

56. Larry Berman, The Office of Management and Budget and the Presidency, 1921-1979 (Princeton, N.J.: Princeton University Press, 1979), 49.

57. Ibid., 56.

58. Rowland Hughes to President Eisenhower, May 10, 1954, AWAS, EL.

59. For example, see the cabinet minutes of the Oct. 11, 1957, meeting, AWAS, EL.

60. Percival Brundage memo to President Eisenhower, May 23, 1956, AWAS, EL.

61. Maurice Stans, "The Eisenhower Presidency and Beyond," in The Eisenhower Presidency: Eleven Intimate Perspectives of Dwight D. Eisenhower, ed. by Kenneth W. Thompson (Lanham, Md: University Press of America, 1984), 215-216.

62. Berman, The Office of Management and Budget, 56.

63. "Republicans Need Economists Too," Fortune (April 1953): 250.

64. Arthur Burns letter to President Eisenhower, Nov. 12, 1956, Arthur Burns Papers, EL.

65. Office of Staff Secretary, L. Arthur Minnich, Cabinet Series (handwritten notes), cabinet meeting on Nov. 21, 1956, EL.

66. "Republicans Need Economists Too," Fortune (April 1953): 116.

67. Erwin C. Hargrove and Samuel A. Morley, eds., The President and the Council of Economic Advisers (Boulder, Colo.: Westview Press, 1984), 112.

68. Eisenhower, Mandate for Change, 118.

69. Sherman Adams, Oral History Interview, April 12, 1967, p. 192, and June 19, 1970, p. 246, OHT, EL. See also Gabriel Hauge, Oral History Interview, May 31, 1976, p. 86, OHT, EL.

70. Eisenhower memo to Arthur Burns, Jan. 14, 1955, Arthur Burns papers, EL.

71. Arthur Burns letter to President Eisenhower, Dec. 28, 1954, Arthur Burns Papers, EL.

72. Hargrove and Morley, The President and the Council of Economic Advisers, 107-108.

73. Arthur F. Burns, Prosperity without Inflation (New York: Fordham University Press, 1957), 26.

74. For an excellent study of the Hoover presidency see Martin L. Fausold, The Presidency of Herbert C. Hoover (Lawrence: University Press of Kansas, 1985).

75. Arthur F. Burns, "Recent Trends in the Business Cycle Policy of the Government," speech presented to the Conference of Pennsylvania Economists, Pennsylvania State University, June 16, 1955, AWAS, EL. See also Arthur F. Burns, "Progress towards Economic Stability," American Economic Review 50 (March 1960): 13.

76. Economic Report of the President, January 1954 (Washington, D.C.: Government Printing Office, 1954): 52.

77. Herbert Stein, The Fiscal Revolution in America (Chicago: University of Chicago Press, 1969), 294.

78. Arthur F. Burns, "Recent Trends in the Business Cycle Policy of the Government," p. 3, AWAS, EL.

79. Economic Report of the President, January 1956 (Washington, D.C.: Government Printing Office, 1956): 43.

80. Economic Report of the President, January 1955 (Washington, D.C.: Government Printing Office, 1955): 2.

81. Neil H. Jacoby, "Recent Trends in the American Economy," speech presented to the Conference of the National Association of Purchasing Agents, Oct. 5, 1954, Washington, D.C., p. 5, Arthur Burns Papers, EL.

82. Hargrove and Morley, *The President and the Council of Economic Advisers*, 123.

83. This quote and the remaining quotes in this paragraph are taken from Raymond J. Saulnier, *The Strategy of Economic Policy* (New York: Fordham University Press, 1962), 3, 21, 27.

84. Hargrove and Morley, *The President and the Council of Economic Advisers*, 156.

85. Ibid., 160.

86. Raymond J. Saulnier, Oral History Interview, Aug. 31, 1967, pp. 25–26, OHT, EL.

87. Charles Walcott and Karen M. Hult, "Organizing The White House: Structure, Environment, and Organizational Governance," *American Journal of Political Science* 31 (Feb. 1987): 109–110.

88. Gabriel Hauge memo to President-elect Eisenhower, Nov. 13, 1952, AWAS, EL.

89. Hargrove and Morley, *The President and the Council of Economic Advisers*, 95.

90. Ibid., 96.

91. Office of the Staff Secretary, L. Arthur Minnich, Cabinet Series (handwritten notes), cabinet meeting on March 12, 1954, EL.

92. Hargrove and Morley, *The President and the Council of Economic Advisers*, 104.

93. Bryce Harlow, Oral History Interview, May 30, 1974, OHT, EL.

94. Hargrove and Morley, *The President and the Council of Economic Advisers*, 129.

95. Robert Anderson memo to President Eisenhower, Sept. 19, 1957, AWAS, EL.

96. Hargrove and Morley, *The President and the Council of Economic Advisers*, 128–131.

97. Ibid., 140.

98. Arthur F. Burns, "Heller's New Dimensions of Political Economy," *National Banking Review* 4 (June 1967): 374. For Saulnier's similar role see Raymond J. Saulnier, "On Advising the President," *Presidential Studies Quarterly* 15 (Summer 1985): 583–588.

99. Arthur Burns letter to Rowland Hughes, June 28, 1954, Arthur Burns Papers, EL.

100. Arthur Burns letter to George Humphrey and Randolph Burgess, June 23, 1956, Arthur Burns Papers, EL. See also Saulnier, "On Advising the President," 586.

101. Memorandum of conference with the president, Oct. 14, 1957, DDE Diary Series, EL.

102. Saulnier, "On Advising the President," 586–587.

CHAPTER 3. THE POLITICAL ECONOMY OF THE 1950s

1. Paul Light, "The Presidential Policy Stream," in *The Presidency and the Political System*, ed. by Michael Nelson (Washington, D.C.: Congressional Quarterly Press, 1984), 429.

2. *New York Times*, June 6, 1957.

3. Harold G. Vatter, *The U.S. Economy in the 1950s* (Chicago: The University of Chicago Press, 1963), 10.

4. Ronald Lora, "Education: Schools as Crucible in Cold War America," in *Reshaping America: Society and Institutions, 1945–1960*, ed. by Robert H. Bremner and Gary W. Reichard (Columbus: Ohio State University Press, 1982), 232.

5. William L. O'Neill, *American High: The Years of Confidence, 1945–1960* (New York: The Free Press, 1986), 288. See also Vatter, *The U.S. Economy*, 22–23.

6. O'Neill, *American High*, 288. See also Robert Wright, "Eisenhower's Fifties," *Antioch Review* 38 (Summer 1980): 277–290.

7. Dwight D. Eisenhower, *Waging Peace: 1956-1961* (Garden City, N.Y.: Doubleday and Co., 1965), 464-465.

8. Vatter, The U.S. Economy, 7. See also Bernard Sternsher, "Reflections on Politics, Policy and Ideology," in *Reshaping America: Society and Institutions, 1945-1960*, ed. by Bremner and Reichard (Columbus: Ohio State University Press, 1982), 383.

9. Vatter, *The U.S. Economy*, 120. See also Herbert Stein, *Presidential Economics: The Making of Economic Policy from Roosevelt to Reagan and Beyond* (New York: Simon and Schuster, 1984), 90.

10. Eisenhower letter to Everett E. ("Swede") Hazlett, July 20, 1954, in *Ike's Letters to a Friend*, ed. by Robert W. Griffith (Lawrence: University Press of Kansas, 1984), 129.

11. *New York Times*, April 29, 1959.

12. George H. Gallup, *The Gallup Poll: Public Opinion, 1935-1971* (New York: Random House, 1972), 989-991.

13. Fred I. Greenstein, *The Hidden-Hand Presidency: Eisenhower as Leader* (New York: Basic Books, 1982), 4.

14. Gary W. Reichard, "Eisenhower as President: The Changing View," *South Atlantic Quarterly* 77 (Summer 1978): 279-280.

15. Stephen E. Ambrose, *Nixon: The Education of a Politician* (New York: Simon and Schuster, 1987), 385.

16. Richard H. Rovere, *Affairs of State: The Eisenhower Years* (New York: Farrar, Straus and Cudahy, 1956), 309.

17. Herbert S. Parmet, *Eisenhower and the American Crusades* (New York: Macmillan, 1972), 175.

18. Greenstein, *The Hidden-Hand Presidency*, 57.

19. Quoted in Elmo Richardson, *The Presidency of Dwight D. Eisenhower* (Lawrence: University Press of Kansas, 1979), 25.

20. Angus Campbell, Phillip E. Converse, Warren E. Miller, Donald E. Stokes, *Elections and the Political Order* (New York: John Wiley, 1966), 326.

21. Kathleen H. Jamieson, *Packaging the Presidency* (New York: Oxford University Press, 1984), 80.

22. *Time*, Nov. 10, 1952, p. 21.

23. Richardson, *The Presidency of Dwight D. Eisenhower*, 58.

24. Stephen E. Ambrose, *Eisenhower: The President*, vol. 2 (New York: Simon and Schuster, 1984), 218.

25. Ambrose, *Nixon*, 353.

26. John Bartlow Martin, *Adlai Stevenson and the World*, vol. 2 (Garden City, N.Y.: Doubleday and Co., 1979), 360.

27. Jamieson, *Packaging the Presidency*, 50-121.

28. Kenneth S. Davis, *The Politics of Honor: A Biography of Adlai E. Stevenson* (New York: G. P. Putnam's Sons, 1967), 329.

29. Martin, *Adlai Stevenson*, 358.

30. Campbell et al., *Elections*, 71.

31. Eisenhower, *Waging Peace,* 376.

32. Cornelius P. Cotter, "Eisenhower as Party Leader," *Political Science Quarterly* 98 (Summer 1983): 260.

33. Ibid., 280.

34. Quoted in Robert Griffith, "Dwight D. Eisenhower and the Corporate Commonwealth," *American Historical Review* 77 (Feb. 1982): 102.

35. Greenstein, *The Hidden-Hand Presidency*, 51.

36. Eisenhower letter to William Phillips, June 5, 1953, DDE Diary Series, EL.

37. Ambrose, *Eisenhower*, 221.

38. Eisenhower letter to Robert Anderson, Dec. 9, 1960, AWAS, EL.

39. Robert J. Donovan, *Eisenhower: The Inside Story* (New York: Harper and Row, 1956), 152; Sherman Adams, *First Hand Report: The Inside Story of the Eisenhower Administration* (London: Hutchinson and Co., 1962), 39.

40. Jacob Javits, Oral History Interview, Jan. 30, 1968, pp. 3-4 Oral History Collection of Columbia University. See also Emmet John Hughes, *The Ordeal of Power* (New York: Dell Publishing Co., 1964).

41. James L. Sundquist, *Politics and Policy: The Eisenhower, Kennedy, and Johnson Years* (Washington, D.C.: Brookings Institution, 1968), 416.

42. William F. Buckley, "The Tranquil World of Dwight D. Eisenhower," *National Review* 5 (Jan. 18, 1958): 59.

43. Rovere, *Affairs of State*, 356; Marion D. Irish, "The Organization Man in the Presidency," *Journal of Politics* 20 (May 1958): 269; Richard Neustadt, *Presidential Power: The Politics of Leadership* (New York: John Wiley, 1960), 117.

44. Richardson, *The Presidency of Dwight D. Eisenhower*, 127. See also John W. Sloan, "The Management and Decision Making Style of President Eisenhower," *Presidential Studies Quarterly* 20 (Spring 1990): 295-313.

45. Adlai Stevenson letter to Agnes Meyer, July 9, 1955, quoted in Martin, *Adlai Stevenson*, 193.

46. Davis, *Politics of Honor*, 307.

47. Parmet, *Eisenhower*, 576.

48. George Reedy, *The U.S. Senate: Paralysis or a Search for Consensus* (New York: Crown Publishers, 1986), 150.

49. Sundquist, *Politics and Policy*, 405.

50. John Kenneth Galbraith, *The Affluent Society* (Boston: Houghton Mifflin Co., 1958), 257.

51. Sundquist, *Politics and Policy*, 385.

52. Walter W. Heller, *New Dimensions of Political Economy* (New York: Norton, 1966), 28.

53. Davis, *Politics of Honor*, 384.

54. Ibid., 384.

CHAPTER 4. THE BATTLE OVER THE BUDGET

1. Samuel P. Huntington, *The Common Defense: Strategic Programs in National Politics* (New York: Columbia University Press, 1961), 70.

2. Charles J. V. Murphy, "The Eisenhower Shift," pt. 1, *Fortune* (Jan. 1956): 87.

3. Sherman Adams, *First Hand Report: The Inside Story of the Eisenhower Administration* (London: Hutchinson and Co., 1962), 134.

4. *New York Times*, Oct. 3, 1952.

5. Eisenhower letter to Everett E. ("Swede") Hazlett, July 2, 1953, DDE Diary Series, EL.

6. Letter of Transmittal, *Economic Report of the President, January 1956*, (Washington, D.C.: Government Printing Office, 1956), v; Gabriel Hauge, "The Economics of Eisenhower Conservatism," speech presented to the Commonwealth Club of California, San Francisco, Oct. 14, 1955, AWAS, EL.

7. Dwight D. Eisenhower, *Mandate for Change, 1953-1956* (Garden City, N.Y.: Doubleday and Co., 1963), 127.

8. Eisenhower memo to Joseph Dodge, Nov. 5, 1953, DDE Diary Series, EL.

9. Joseph Dodge memo to President Eisenhower, Feb. 25, 1953, AWAS, EL.

10. Murphy, "The Eisenhower Shift," 208.

11. Cabinet meeting, May 22, 1953, AWCS, EL.

12. Nathaniel R. Howard, ed., *The Basic Papers of George M. Humphrey* (Cleveland: The Western Reserve Historical Society, 1965), 63-64.

13. Cabinet meeting, Nov. 4, 1955, AWCS, EL.

14. George Humphrey letter to President Eisenhower, Sept. 7, 1956, AWAS, EL.

15. *U.S. News and World Report*, June 28, 1957, 138.

16. Adams, *First Hand Report*, 141; Cabinet meeting, Nov. 4, 1955, AWCS, EL.

17. Eisenhower letter to Brig. Gen. Benjamin Caffey, July 27, 1953, DDE Diary Series, EL.

18. Adams, *First Hand Report*, 20. See also Richard H. Rovere, *Affairs of State: The Eisenhower Years* (New York: Farrar, Straus and Cudahy, 1956), 69.

19. Stephen E. Ambrose, *Eisenhower: The President*, vol. 2 (New York: Simon and Schuster, 1984), 87; see also Herbert S. Parmet, *Eisenhower and the American Crusades* (New York: Macmillan, 1972), 220.

20. E. Bruce Gellhoed, *Charles E. Wilson and Controversy at the Pentagon, 1953-1957* (Detroit: Wayne State University Press, 1979), 16. See also Donald R. McCoy, *The Presidency of Harry S. Truman* (Lawrence: University Press of Kansas, 1984), 214-216.

21. Quoted in Ambrose, *Eisenhower*, 88. See also Douglas Kinnard, *President Eisenhower and Strategy Management: A Study in Defense Politics* (Lexington: The University Press of Kentucky, 1977), 8.

22. *New York Times*, Jan. 8, 1954.

23. Elmo Richardson, *The Presidency of Dwight D. Eisenhower* (Lawrence: University Press of Kansas, 1979), 63.

24. Notes on Legislative Leadership Meeting, March 10, 1959, DDE Diary Series, EL.

25. Eisenhower letter to Charles Wilson, Jan. 5, 1955, AWAS, EL.

26. Ibid. See also Lawrence J. Korb, "The Budget Process in the Department of Defense: The Strengths and Weaknesses of Three Systems," *Public Administration Review* 37 (July–Aug. 1977): 337.

27. National Security Council Meeting, Oct. 13, 1953, NSCS, EL.

28. Quoted in Fred. I. Greenstein, *The Hidden-Hand Presidency: Eisenhower as Leader* (New York: Basic Books, 1982), 83.

29. Gellhoed, *Charles E. Wilson*, 19.

30. Douglas Kinnard, "Eisenhower and the Defense Budget," *Journal of Politics* 39 (August 1977): 598. See also Eisenhower, *Mandate for Change*, 445-447.

31. Huntington, *The Common Defense*, 67, 87.

32. Ambrose, *Eisenhower*, 225.

33. Matthew B. Ridgeway, *Soldier: The Memoirs of Matthew B. Ridgeway* (New York: Harper and Brothers, 1956); Maxwell D. Taylor, *The Uncertain Trumpet* (New York: Harper and Row, 1959).

34. Kinnard, *President Eisenhower*, 57.

35. Huntington, *The Common Defense*, 102.

36. Maurice Stans to President Eisenhower, Jan. 9, 1961, "Report of the Bureau of the Budget in the Fields of Fiscal and General Management of the Federal Government, 1953-1961," AWAS, EL.

37. Ibid.

38. Harold G. Vatter, *The U.S. Economy in the 1950s* (Chicago: University of Chicago Press, 1963), 6.

39. Huntington, *The Common Defense*, 278-283.

40. Thomas Gates to President Eisenhower, Jan. 4, 1961, "Department of Defense

1953–1960," AWAS, EL. See also Duane Windsor, "Eisenhower's New Look Reexamined: The View from Three Decades," in *Dwight D. Eisenhower: Soldier, President, Statesman*, ed. by Joann P. Krieg (New York: Greenwood Press, 1987), 151.

41. Windsor, "Eisenhower's New Look Reexamined," 147.

42. Wilfred Lewis, Jr., *Federal Fiscal Policy in the Postwar Recession* (Washington, D.C.: Brookings Institution, 1962), 134.

43. Office of Staff Secretary, L. Arthur Minnich, Cabinet Series (handwritten notes), cabinet meeting on May 3, 1957, EL.

44. Memorandum for the record, meeting of President Eisenhower and Maurice Stans, Sept. 14, 1959, DDE Diary Series, EL.

45. Office of Staff Secretary, L. Arthur Minnich, Cabinet Series (handwritten notes), cabinet meeting on Jan. 9, 1957, EL.

46. Office of Staff Secretary, L. Arthur Minnich, Cabinet Series (handwritten notes), cabinet meeting on Nov. 1, 1957, EL.

47. Memorandum for the record, meeting of President Eisenhower, Adm. Arthur Radford, and Roland Hughes, March 20, 1956, AWAS, EL.

48. "Paraphrase of Remarks of the President on Future Budgets and Programs at the Cabinet Meeting of November 27, 1959," AWCS, EL.

49. *New York Times*, Jan. 18, 1961. See also George H. Quester, "Was Eisenhower a Genius?" *International Security* 4 (Fall 1979): 168.

50. Eisenhower, *Mandate for Change*, 376.

51. Memorandum of conference with the president, March 29, 1947, DDE Diary Series, EL.

52. Kinnard, *President Eisenhower*, 125–26. See also Windsor, "Eisenhower's New Look Reexamined," 159; Korb, "The Budget Process," 335; Quester, "Was Eisenhower a Genius?," 165.

53. Phillip G. Henderson, "Advice and Decision: The Eisenhower National Security Council Reappraised," in *The Presidency and National Security Policy*, ed. by R. Gordon Hoxie (New York: Center for the Study of the Presidency, 1984), 170. See also Joseph Dodge and Robert Cutler memo to President Eisenhower, July 10, 1953, "Preparation and Use of Financial Data in Connection with NSC Procedures," AWAS, EL.

54. Office of Staff Secretary, L. Arthur Minnich, Cabinet Series (handwritten notes), cabinet meeting on April 20, 1956, EL.

55. Quotes from Emmet John Hughes, *The Ordeal of Power* (New York: Dell Publishing Co., 1964), 121.

56. National Security Council meetings, Oct. 13, 1953, and Oct. 29, 1953, NSCS, EL.

57. Dwight D. Eisenhower, *Waging Peace, 1956–1961* (Garden City, N.Y.: Doubleday and Co., 1965), 386.; James L. Sundquist, *Politics and Policy: The Eisenhower, Kennedy, and Johnson Years* (Washington, D.C.: Brookings Institution, 1968), 428; Richardson, *The Presidency of Dwight D. Eisenhower*, 144–145.

58. Address of Maurice Stans before the Houston chapter of the American Society of Chartered Life Underwriters, Houston Club, Houston, Tex., April 9, 1958, AWAS, EL.

59. Eisenhower letter to George Humphrey, Nov. 22, 1957, AWAS, EL.

60. Office of Staff Secretary, Legislative Leaders Meeting Series, Dec. 4, 1957, EL.

61. Eisenhower letter to George Humphrey, July 22, 1958, AWAS, EL.

62. Oveta Culp Hobby memo to President Eisenhower, Nov. 18, 1954, AWAS, EL.

63. Rowland Hughes memo to President Eisenhower, Nov. 18, 1954, AWAS, EL.

64. Marion B. Folsom, Oral History Interview, Jan. 10, 1968, p. 47, OHT, EL.

65. Ibid., p. 96.

66. Cabinet meeting, Dec. 14, 1956, AWCS, EL.

67. Folsom, Oral History Interview, p. 157.

68. Ibid., pp. 156-157.

69. Robert Merriam, Oral History Interview, Jan. 13, 1969, p. 152, OHT, EL.

70. Arthur S. Flemming letter of resignation to President Eisenhower, Jan. 12, 1961, AWAS, EL.

71. Arthur Flemming memo to President Eisenhower, Aug. 11, 1958, AWAS, EL.

72. Arthur Flemming memo to President Eisenhower, Oct. 2, 1958, AWAS, EL.

73. Arthur Flemming memo to President Eisenhower, Nov. 7, 1958, AWAS, EL.

74. Arthur Flemming memo to President Eisenhower, Nov. 12, 1958, AWAS, EL.

75. President Eisenhower memo to Arthur Flemming, Nov. 15, 1958, AWAS, EL.

76. James C. Duram, "'A Good Growl': The Eisenhower Cabinet's Jan. 16, 1959, Discussions of Federal Aid to Education," *Presidential Studies Quarterly* 8 (Fall 1978): 435. This article contains a full transcript of the Jan. 16, 1959, cabinet meeting.

77. Statement of Arthur Flemming before the cabinet meeting of Jan. 16, 1959, AWCS, EL.

78. Duram, "'A Good Growl,'" 436.

79. Ibid., 438.

80. Ibid., 435, 437, 440, 441, and 442.

81. Eisenhower, *Mandate for Change*, 458.

82. National Security Council meeting, Oct. 13, 1953, NSCS, EL.

83. Neil McElroy, Oral History Interview, May 8, 1967, p. 26, OHT, EL.

84. James Tobin, "The Eisenhower Economy and National Security," *Yale Review* 47 (March 1958): 325.

85. Richard E. Neustadt, *Presidential Power: The Politics of Leadership* (New York: John Wiley, 1960).

86. George Humphrey letter to President Eisenhower, Dec. 6, 1956, AWAS, EL.

87. George Humphrey letter to President Eisenhower, Dec. 18, 1956, AWAS, EL

88. George Humphrey letter to President Eisenhower, Jan. 8, 1947, AWAS, EL.

89. Cabinet meeting, Jan. 9, 1957, AWCS, EL.

90. Office of Staff Secretary, L. Arthur Minnich, Cabinet Series (handwritten notes), cabinet meeting on Jan. 9, 1957, EL.

91. George Humphrey's press conference transcript, Jan. 15, 1957, AWAS, EL.

92. Neustadt, *Presidential Power*, 108.

93. Ibid., 88.

94. Arthur Larson, *Eisenhower: The President Nobody Knew* (New York: Charles Scribner's Sons, 1968), 141. See also William Bragg Ewald, Jr., *Eisenhower the President: Crucial Days, 1951-1960* (Englewood Cliffs, N.J.: Prentice-Hall, 1981), 289; Sundquist, *Politics and Policy*, 424.

95. Larson, *Eisenhower*, 143.

96. Stephen Ambrose, *Nixon: The Education of a Politician* (New York: Simon and Schuster, 1987), 484.

97. Ewald, *Eisenhower the President*, 294.

CHAPTER 5. MONETARY POLICY—THE BATTLE AGAINST INFLATION

1. Sherman J. Maisel, *Managing the Dollar* (New York: Norton, 1973), ix.

2. Robert Anderson memo to President Eisenhower, Sept. 19, 1957, "The Money and Credit System of the U.S. and How It Works," AWAS, EL.

3. Donald F. Kettl, *Leadership at the Fed* (New Haven, Conn.: Yale University Press, 1986), 3.

4. John T. Woolley, "The Federal Reserve and the Politics of Monetary Policy," in *The President and Economic Policy*, ed. by James P. Pfiffner (Philadelphia: Institute for the Study of Human Issues, 1986), 244.

5. Kettl, *Leadership*, 59.

6. Ibid., 60.

7. G. L. Bach, *Making Monetary and Fiscal Policy* (Washington: Brookings Institution, 1971), 87.

8. Kettl, *Leadership*, 59.

9. Ibid., 66-75. See also Milton Friedman and Anna Jacobson Schwartz, *A Monetary History of the United States, 1867-1960* (Princeton, N.J.: Princeton University Press, 1963), 593.

10. Maisel, *Managing*, 115.

11. Kettl, *Leadership*, 84.

12. January 1957 Economic Report of the President, Hearings before the Joint Economic Committee, Congress of the United States, 85th Congress, 1st Session, Jan. 18, Feb. 6, 1957, p. 588.

13. January 1958 Economic Report of the President, Hearings before the Joint Economic Committee, Congress of the United States, 85th Congress, 2d Session, Feb. 6, 1958, p. 387.

14. Maisel, *Managing*, 36.

15. Albert Rees, *Striking a Balance: Making National Economic Policy* (Chicago: University of Chicago Press, 1984), 71.

16. Kettl, *Leadership*, 85.

17. Ibid., 86-87; Robert Roosa, Oral History Interview, Nov. 13, 1972, p. 47, OHT, EL.

18. Friedman and Schwartz, *A Monetary History*, 628.

19. Ibid., 631.

20. Kettl, *Leadership*, 6.

21. John Kenneth Galbraith, *The Affluent Society* (Boston: Houghton Mifflin Co., 1958), 227.

22. Robert Anderson memo to President Eisenhower, Sept. 19, 1957, AWAS, EL.

23. Maisel, *Managing*, 256.

24. Kettl, *Leadership*, 84.

25. Robert Roosa, Oral History Interview, Nov. 13, 1972, p. 44, EL.

26. Rees, *Striking a Balance*, 73.

27. *Wall Street Journal*, June 11, 1958.

28. Donald R. McCoy, *The Presidency of Harry S. Truman* (Lawrence: University Press of Kansas, 1984), 264; John W. Snyder, "The Treasury and Economic Policy," in *Economics and the Truman Administration*, ed. by Francis H. Heller (Lawrence: Regents Press of Kansas, 1981), 31.

29. Robert J. Donovan, *Eisenhower: The Inside Story* (New York: Harper and Row, 1956), 32-34; H. Scott Gordon, "The Eisenhower Administration: The Doctrine of Shared Responsibility," in *Exhortation and Controls: The Search for a Wage-Price Policy, 1945-1971*, ed. by Craufurd D. Goodwin (Washington, D.C.: The Brookings Institution, 1975), 97.

30. Dwight D. Eisenhower, *Mandate for Change: 1953-1956* (Garden City, N.Y.: Doubleday and Co., 1963), 489.

31. *New York Times*, Jan. 11, 1957.

32. Address by Gabriel Hauge before the Economic Club of Detroit, March 11, 1957, "Problems of Prosperity," AWAS, EL.

33. A. E. Holmans, *U.S. Fiscal Policy, 1949 to 1959: Its Contribution to Economic Stability* (London: Oxford University Press, 1961), 270; Nathaniel R. Howard, ed., *The Basic Papers of George M. Humphrey* (Cleveland: Western Reserve Historical Society, 1965), 111.

34. Howard, *The Basic Papers of Humphrey*, 49, 111.

35. Ibid., 51.

36. Robert Anderson speech to American Finance Association and American Economic Association, Washington, D.C., Dec. 29, 1959, AWAS, EL.

37. Robert Anderson speech to Republican Finance Committee, Detroit, Mich., Oct. 3, 1957, AWAS, EL.

38. Robert Anderson remarks at cabinet meeting, Aug. 26, 1960, AWCS, EL.

39. Raymond J. Saulnier interview, in *The President and the Council of Economic Advisers: Interviews with CEA Chairmen*, ed. by Erwin C. Hargrove and Samuel A. Morley (Boulder: Westview Press, 1984), 161; Raymond J. Saulnier Oral History Interview, Aug. 31, 1967, p. 26, OHT, EL.

40. Arthur Okun, "Inflation: The Problems and Prospects before Us," in *Inflation: The Problems It Creates: The Policies It Requires*, ed. by Arthur Okun (New York: New York University Press, 1970), 3-4.

41. Dwight D. Eisenhower, *Waging Peace 1956-1961* (Garden City, N.Y.: Doubleday and Co., 1965), 464.

42. Harold G. Vatter, *The U.S. Economy in the 1950s* (Chicago: University of Chicago Press, 1963), 121.

43. Robert Anderson, "Debt Management and Advance Refunding," Sept. 1960, AWAS, EL.

44. Friedman and Schwartz, *A Monetary History*, 635.

45. Gabriel Hauge memo to President-elect Eisenhower, Nov. 13, 1952, AWAS, EL.

46. Arthur F. Burns interview in Hargrove and Morley, *The President and the Council of Economic Advisers*, 120.

47. Raymond J. Saulnier interview in Hargrove and Morley, *The President and Council of Economic Advisers*, 135. See also Kettl, *Leadership*, 92.

48. Maisel, *Managing*, 116.

49. Friedman and Schwartz, *A Monetary History*, 613.

50. Kettl, *Leadership*, 88.

51. Gordon, "The Eisenhower Administration," 99.

52. Holmans, *U.S. Fiscal Policy*, 268.

53. Arthur Burns letter to President Eisenhower, June 25, 1956, Arthur Burns Papers, EL.

54. George Humphrey letter to William McChesney Martin, April 24, 1956, AWAS, EL.

55. Kettl, *Leadership*, 89.

56. Memorandum for the record, Raymond Saulnier meeting with William McChesney Martin, May 3, 1957, Raymond Saulnier Papers, EL.

57. Memorandum for the record, Raymond Saulnier meeting with William McChesney Martin, Dec. 5, 1957, Raymond Saulnier Papers, EL.

58. Memorandum for the record, president's telephone call, Dec. 31, 1957, Raymond Saulnier Papers, EL.

59. Friedman and Schwartz, *A Monetary History*, 617.

60. Ibid., 619.

61. Quoted in William Bragg Ewald, Jr., *Eisenhower the President: Crucial Days, 1951-1960* (Englewood Cliffs, N.J.: Prentice-Hall, 1981), 291.

62. Office of Staff Secretary, L. Arthur Minnich, Cabinet Series (handwritten

notes), cabinet meeting on Aug. 1, 1958, EL. See also R. T. Selden, "Demand-Pull versus Cost-Push Inflation," *Journal of Political Economy* 67 (Spring 1959): 1-20.

63. Gordon, "The Eisenhower Administration," 122.

64. Ibid., 123.

65. Ibid., 123; *Wall Street Journal*, Aug. 17, 1959.

66. *New York Times*, Jan. 11, 1957.

67. Milton Friedman letter to Raymond Saulnier, Feb. 8, 1957, Raymond Saulnier Papers, EL.

68. Raymond J. Saulnier, *The Strategy of Economic Policy* (New York: Fordham University Press, 1962), 38.

69. Herbert S. Parmet, *Eisenhower and the American Crusades* (New York: Macmillan, 1972), 290-291.

70. Vatter, *The U.S. Economy*, 260.

71. Ibid., 21.

72. Arthur F. Burns, "Some Reflections on the Employment Act," *Political Science Quarterly* 77 (Dec. 1962): 485. See also Andrew Shonfield, *Modern Capitalism: The Changing Balance of Public and Private Power* (New York: Oxford University Press, 1965), 14; and John J. McCloy, "Foreign Economic Policy and Objectives," in *Goals for Americans*, President's Commission on National Goals (Englewood Cliffs, N.J.: Prentice-Hall, 1960), 331, 355.

73. "Paraphrase of Remarks of the President on Future Budget and Programs at the Cabinet Meeting of November 27, 1959," AWCS, EL.

74. Eisenhower, *Waging Peace*, 460.

75. George Humphrey memo to President Eisenhower, April 15, 1955, AWAS, EL. See also Burton I. Kaufman, *Trade and Aid: Eisenhower's Foreign Economic Policy, 1953-61* (Baltimore: Johns Hopkins University Press, 1982), 178.

76. Office of Staff Secretary, L. Arthur Minnich, Cabinet Series (handwritten notes), cabinet meeting on April 20, 1956, EL. See also George Humphrey letter to President Eisenhower, May 14, 1957, AWAS, EL.

77. Office of Staff Secretary, L. Arthur Minnich, Cabinet Series (handwritten notes), cabinet meeting on April 20, 1956, EL.

78. Office of Staff Secretary, L. Arthur Minnich, Cabinet Series (handwritten notes), cabinet meeting on Dec. 12, 1958, EL.

79. Robert Anderson remarks, cabinet meeting, Aug. 7, 1959, AWCS, EL.

80. Robert H. Ferrell, ed., *The Eisenhower Diaries* (New York: Norton, 1981), entry for Dec. 6, 1958, p. 359.

81. Raymond Saulnier, Oral History Interview, Dec. 21, 1967, p. 61, OHT, EL.

CHAPTER 6. THE STRUGGLE AGAINST RECESSION:
1953-54 and 1957-58

1. Gabriel Hauge memo to President Eisenhower, Nov. 13, 1952, AWAS, EL.

2. Office of the Staff Secretary, L. Arthur Minnich, Cabinet Series, reorganization meeting, Jan. 14, 1953, EL.

3. Eisenhower memo to Gabriel Hauge, Feb. 4, 1953, AWNS, EL.

4. Arthur F. Burns, Oral History Interview, in *The President and the Council of Economic Advisers Interviews with CEA Chairmen*, ed. by Erwin C. Hargrove and Samuel A. Morley (Boulder, Colo.: Westview Press, 1984), 116.

5. Office of the Staff Secretary, L. Arthur Minnich, Cabinet Series (handwritten notes), cabinet meeting on Sept. 25, 1953, EL. See also Robert J. Donovan, *Eisenhower: The Inside Story* (New York: Harper and Row, 1956), 210.

6. Minutes of Advisory Board on Economic Growth and Stability meeting, April 1, 1954, Arthur F. Burns Papers, EL.

7. Saul Engelbourg, "The Council of Economic Advisers and the Recession of 1953-54," *Business History Review* 54 (1980): 206.

8. Donovan, *Eisenhower*, 218-219; Dwight D. Eisenhower, *Mandate for Change, 1953-56* (Garden City, N.Y.: Doubleday and Co., 1963), 306.

9. R. J. Saulnier memo to Neil H. Jacoby, April 8, 1954, Arthur F. Burns Papers, EL.

10. Robert H. Ferrell, ed., *The Eisenhower Diaries* (New York: Norton, 1981), entry for April 8, 1954, p. 278.

11. Neil Jacoby memo to Gabriel Hauge, Aug. 9, 1954, Arthur F. Burns Papers, EL. See also Edward S. Flash, Jr., *Economic Advice and Presidential Leadership: The Council of Economic Advisers* (New York: Columbia University Press, 1965), 150.

12. A. E. Holmans, *U.S. Fiscal Policy, 1949 to 1959: Its Contribution to Economic Stability* (London: Oxford University Press, 1961), 225-226.

13. Flash, *Economic Advice*, 148.

14. *New York Times*, March 16, 1954.

15. Flash, *Economic Advice*, 150.

16. Holmans, *U.S. Fiscal Policy*, 218.

17. Arthur Burns memo to President Eisenhower, Oct. 13, 1953, Arthur F. Burns Papers, EL.

18. Engelbourg, "The Council of Economic Advisers," 204.

19. Donovan, *Eisenhower*, 214.

20. Office of the Staff Secretary, L. Arthur Minnich, Cabinet Series (handwritten notes), cabinet meeting on Feb. 5, 1954, EL.

21. Office of the Staff Secretary, L. Arthur Minnich, Cabinet Series (handwritten notes), cabinet meeting on May 14, 1954, EL.

22. Office of the Staff Secretary, L. Arthur Minnich, Cabinet Series (handwritten notes), cabinet meeting on June 4, 1954, EL.

23. Wilfred Lewis, Jr., *Federal Fiscal Policy in the Postwar Recessions* (Washington, D.C.: The Brookings Institution, 1962), 184.

24. Herbert Stein, *The Fiscal Revolution in America* (Chicago: The University of Chicago Press, 1969), 302.

25. Minutes of Advisory Board on Economic Growth and Stability meeting, April 1, 1954, Arthur F. Burns Papers, EL.

26. *Economic Report of the President*, Jan. 1954 (Washington, D.C.: Government Printing Office, 1954): IV.

27. Office of the Staff Secretary, L. Arthur Minnich, Cabinet Series (handwritten notes), cabinet meeting on Jan. 15, 1954, EL.

28. Office of the Staff Secretary, L. Arthur Minnich, Cabinet Series (handwritten notes), cabinet meeting on March 12, 1954, EL.

29. Office of the Staff Secretary, L. Arthur Minnich, Cabinet Series (handwritten notes), cabinet meeting on March 19, 1954, EL.

30. Office of the Staff Secretary, L. Arthur Minnich, Cabinet Series (handwritten notes), cabinet meeting on April 2, 1954, EL.

31. Office of the Staff Secretary, L. Arthur Minnich, Cabinet Series (handwritten notes), cabinet meeting on Jan. 15, 1954, EL.

32. Office of the Staff Secretary, L. Arthur Minnich, Cabinet Series (handwritten notes), cabinet meeting on March 12, 1954, EL.

33. Stein, *The Fiscal Revolution*, 306-307.

34. Office of the Staff Secretary, L. Arthur Minnich, Cabinet Series (handwritten notes), cabinet meeting on June 11, 1954, EL.

35. Holmans, *U.S. Fiscal Policy*, 228.

36. Notes for cabinet presentation, cabinet meeting, May 3, 1957, Raymond Saulnier Papers, EL.

37. Holmans, *U.S. Fiscal Policy*, 273; Dwight D. Eisenhower, *Waging Peace 1956-1961* (Garden City, N.Y.: Doubleday and Co., 1965), 304; Charles J. V. Murphy, "The White House and the Recession," *Fortune* 57 (May 1958): 106-109; Arthur F. Burns, "Progress towards Economic Stability," *American Economic Review* 50 (March 1960): 8; R. Alton Lee, "Federal Assistance to Depressed Areas in the Postwar Recessions," *Western Economic Journal* 2 (Fall 1963): 19; and Harold G. Vatter, *The U.S. Economy in the 1950s* (Chicago: University of Chicago Press, 1963), 120.

38. Holmans, *U.S. Fiscal Policy*, 293.

39. Eisenhower, *Waging Peace*, 305.

40. Eisenhower, *Waging Peace*, 307. See also Lee, "Federal Assistance," 20.

41. Stein, *The Fiscal Revolution*, 329.

42. Eisenhower, *Waging Peace*, 310.

43. Elmo Richardson, *The Presidency of Dwight D. Eisenhower* (Lawrence: University Press of Kansas, 1979), 134.

44. Kenneth S. Davis, *The Politics of Honor: A Biography of Adlai E. Stevenson* (New York: G. P. Putnam's Sons, 1967), 376-377.

45. Stein, *The Fiscal Revolution*, 330.

46. Arthur Burns letter to President Eisenhower, March 10, 1958, AWAS, EL.

47. President Eisenhower letter to Arthur Burns, March 12, 1958, AWAS, EL.

48. Arthur Burns letter to President Eisenhower, March 31, 1958, AWAS, EL.

49. President Eisenhower letter to Arthur Burns, April 2, 1958, AWAS, EL.

50. Arthur Burns letter to President Eisenhower, May 5, 1958, AWAS, EL.

51. President Eisenhower letter to Arthur Burns, May 7, 1958, AWAS, EL.

52. President Eisenhower letters to Arthur Burns, April 2, 1958, and May 7, 1958, AWAS, EL.

53. See the *Wall Street Journal*, Oct. 9, 1957, and Drew Pearson's column in the *Washington Post*, Feb. 28, 1958.

54. Raymond Saulnier memo to President Eisenhower, May 23, 1958, AWAS, EL.

55. Murphy, "The White House," 250; Stein, *The Fiscal Revolution*, 331; Office of the Staff Secretary, L. Arthur Minnich, Cabinet Series (handwritten notes), cabinet meeting on May 2, 1958, EL.

56. *New York Times*, June 14, 1958; Stein, *The Fiscal Revolution*, 344.

57. "Revenue Costs of Various Tax Reductions in Individual Income Tax," May 2, 1958, Robert Anderson Files, AWAS, EL.

58. Eisenhower, *Waging Peace*, 310.

59. Stein, *The Fiscal Revolution*, 332.

60. Vatter, *The U.S. Economy*, 118.

61. Holmans, *U.S. Fiscal Policy*, 278.

62. Murphy, "The White House," 246.

CHAPTER 7. CONCLUSION

1. A. J. Goodpaster memorandum of conference with President Eisenhower, Dec. 30, 1960, DDE Diary Series, EL.

2. Arthur F. Burns, "Some Reflections on the Employment Act," *Political Science Quarterly* 77 (Dec. 1962): 488.

3. Emmet John Hughes, *The Ordeal of Power* (New York: Dell Publishing Co., 1964), 230.

4. Robert Wright, "Eisenhower's Fifties," *Antioch Review* 38 (Summer 1980): 278.

5. "Notes in Legislative Leaders Meeting," Dec. 15, 1958, DDE Diary Series, EL.

Bibliography

BOOKS AND ARTICLES

Adams, Sherman. *First Hand Report: The Inside Story of the Eisenhower Administration.* London: Hutchinson and Co., 1962.

Allison, Graham T. *Essence of Decision: Explaining the Cuban Missile Crisis.* Boston: Little, Brown and Co., 1971.

Ambrose, Stephen E. *Eisenhower: The President.* Vol. 2. New York: Simon and Schuster, 1984.

Bach, G. L. *Making Monetary and Fiscal Policy.* Washington, D.C.: Brookings Institution, 1971.

Bailey, Stephen K. *Congress Makes a Law: The Story behind the Employment Act of 1946.* New York: Columbia University Press, 1950.

Berman, Larry. *The Office of Management and Budget and the Presidency, 1921–1979.* Princeton, N.J.: Princeton University Press, 1979.

Bremner, Robert H., and Gary W. Reichard, eds. *Reshaping America: Society and Institutions, 1945–1960.* Columbus: Ohio State University Press, 1982.

Brendon, Piers. *Ike: His Life and Times.* New York: Harper and Row, 1986.

Buckley, William F. "The Tranquil World of Dwight D. Eisenhower." *National Review* 5 (Jan. 18, 1958): 57–59.

Burns, Arthur F. "Heller's New Dimensions of Political Economy," *National Banking Review* 4 (June 1967): 373–375.

————. "Progress towards Economic Stability." *American Economic Review* 50 (March 1960): 1–19.

————. *Prosperity without Inflation.* New York: Fordham University Press, 1957.

————. "Some Reflections on the Employment Act." *Political Science Quarterly* 77 (Dec. 1962): 481–504.

Caldwell, Dan. "Bureaucratic Foreign Policy-Making." *American Behavioral Scientist* 21 (Sept.–Oct. 1977): 87–109.

Campbell, Angus, Phillip E. Converse, Warren E. Miller, and Donald E. Stokes. *Elections and Political Order.* New York: John Wiley, 1966.

Cotter, Cornelius P. "Eisenhower as Party Leader." *Political Science Quarterly* 98 (Summer 1983): 255–283.

Davis, Kenneth S. *The Politics of Honor: A Biography of Adlai E. Stevenson.* New York: G. P. Putnam's Sons, 1967.

De Santis, Vincent P. "Eisenhower Revisionism." *Review of Politics* 38 (April 1976): 190–208.

Destler, I. M. *Presidents, Bureaucrats and Foreign Policy: The Politics of Organizational Reform.* Princeton, N.J.: Princeton University Press, 1975.

Divine, Robert A. *Eisenhower and the Cold War.* New York: Oxford University Press, 1981.

Donovan, Robert J. *Eisenhower: The Inside Story.* New York: Harper and Row, 1956.

Duram, James C. "'A Good Growl': The Eisenhower Cabinet's January 16, 1959, Discussions of Federal Aid to Education." *Presidential Studies Quarterly* 8 (Fall 1978): 434–444.

Economic Report of the President. Annual publication of the Council of Economic Advisers, 1952–1961. Washington, D.C.: Government Printing Office.

Eisenhower, Dwight D. *Mandate for Change 1953–1956.* Garden City, N.Y.: Doubleday and Co., 1963.

————. *Waging Peace 1956–1961.* Garden City, N.Y.: Doubleday and Co., 1965.

Engelbourg, Saul. "The Council of Economic Advisers and the Recession of 1953–54." *Business History Review* 54 (1980): 192–214.

Ewald, William Bragg, Jr. *Eisenhower the President: Crucial Days, 1951–1960.* Englewood Cliffs, N.J.: Prentice-Hall, 1981.

Fausold, Martin L. *The Presidency of Herbert C. Hoover.* Lawrence: University Press of Kansas, 1985.

Ferrell, Robert H., ed. *The Diary of James C. Hagerty.* Bloomington: Indiana University Press, 1983.

————. *The Eisenhower Diaries.* New York: Norton, 1981.

Flash, Edward S., Jr. *Economic Advice and Presidential Leadership: The Council of Economic Advisers.* New York: Columbia University Press, 1965.

Friedman, Milton, and Anna Jacobson Schwartz. *A Monetary History of the United States, 1867–1960.* Princeton, N.J.: Princeton University Press, 1963.

Galbraith, John Kenneth. *The Affluent Society.* Boston: Houghton Mifflin Co., 1958.

Gallup, George H. *The Gallup Poll: Public Opinion, 1935–1971.* New York: Random House, 1972.

Gellhoed, E. Bruce. *Charles E. Wilson and Controversy at the Pentagon, 1953–1957.* Detroit: Wayne State University Press, 1979.

Goldman, Eric F. *The Crucial Decade—and After: 1945–1960.* New York: Vintage Books, 1960.

Gordon, H. Scott. "The Eisenhower Administration: The Doctrine of Shared Responsibility." In *Exhortation and Controls: The Search for a Wage-Price Policy, 1945–1971,* edited by Craufurd D. Goodwin, 95–135. Washington, D.C.: Brookings Institution, 1975.

Greenstein, Fred I. *The Hidden-Hand Presidency: Eisenhower as Leader.* New York: Basic Books, 1982.

Griffith, Robert. "Dwight D. Eisenhower and the Corporate Commonwealth." *American Historical Review* 77 (Feb. 1982): 87–122.

Griffith, Robert, ed. *Ike's Letters to a Friend: 1941–1958.* Lawrence: University Press of Kansas, 1984.

Hargrove, Erwin C., and Samuel A. Morley, eds. *The President and the Council of Economic Advisers: Interviews with CEA Chairmen.* Boulder, Colo.: Westview Press, 1984.

Heller, Walter W. *New Dimensions of Political Economy.* New York: Norton, 1966.

Henderson, Phillip G. "Advice and Decision: The Eisenhower National Security Council Reappraised." In *The Presidency and National Security Policy*, edited by R. Gordon Hoxie, 153–187. New York: Center for the Study of the Presidency, 1984.

Holmans, A. E. *U.S. Fiscal Policy, 1949 to 1959: Its Contribution to Economic Stability*. London: Oxford University Press, 1961.

Howard, Nathaniel R., ed. *The Basic Papers of George M. Humphrey*. Cleveland: The Western Reserve Historical Society, 1965.

Hughes, Emmet John. *The Ordeal of Power*. New York: Dell Publishing Co., 1964.

Huntington, Samuel P. *The Common Defense: Strategic Programs in National Politics*. New York: Columbia University Press, 1961.

Irish, Marion D. "The Organization Man in the Presidency." *Journal of Politics* 20 (May 1958): 259–277.

Jacoby, Neil H. "The President, the Constitution and the Economist in Economic Stabilization." *History of Political Economy* 3 (Fall 1971): 398–414.

Jamieson, Kathleen H. *Packaging the Presidency*. New York: Oxford University Press, 1984.

Joes, Anthony James. "Eisenhower Revisionism: The Tide Comes In." *Presidential Studies Quarterly* 15 (Summer 1985): 561–571.

Kaufman, Burton I. *Trade and Aid: Eisenhower's Foreign Economic Policy, 1953–61*. Baltimore: Johns Hopkins University Press, 1982.

Kempton, Murray. "The Underestimation of Dwight D. Eisenhower." *Esquire* 68 (Sept. 1967): 108–109, 156.

Kettl, Donald F. *Leadership at the Fed*. New Haven, Conn.: Yale University Press, 1986.

Kinnard, Douglas. "Eisenhower and the Defense Budget." *Journal of Politics* 39 (August 1977): 596–623.

———. *President Eisenhower and Strategy Management: A Study in Defense Politics*. Lexington: University Press of Kentucky, 1977.

Korb, Lawrence J. "The Budget Process in the Department of Defense: The Strengths and Weaknesses of Three Systems," *Public Administration Review* 37 (July–Aug. 1977): 334–346.

Krasner, Stephen. "Are Bureaucracies Important?" *Foreign Policy* 3 (Summer 1972): 160–170.

Larson, Arthur. *Eisenhower: The President Nobody Knew* (New York: Charles Scribner's Sons, 1968.

———. *A Republican Looks at His Party*. New York: Harper and Row, 1956.

Lee, R. Alton. "Federal Assistance to Depressed Areas in the Postwar Recessions." *Western Economic Journal* 2 (Fall 1963): 3–20.

Lewis, Wilfred, Jr. *Federal Fiscal Policy in the Postwar Recessions*. Washington, D.C.: Brookings Institution, 1962.

Light, Paul. "The Presidential Policy Stream." In *The Presidency and the Political System*, edited by Michael Nelson, 423–448. Washington, D.C.: Congressional Quarterly Press, 1984.

Lora, Ronald. "Education: Schools as Crucible in Cold War America." In *Reshaping America: Society and Institutions, 1945–1960*, edited by Robert H. Bremner and Gary W. Reichard, 223–260. Columbus: Ohio State University Press, 1982.

MacAuliffe, Mary S. "Eisenhower, the President." *Journal of American History* 68 (Dec. 1981): 625–632.

McCloy, John J. "Foreign Economic Policy and Objectives." In *Goals for Americans*. The President's Commission on National Goals, 330–357. Englewood Cliffs, N.J.: Prentice Hall, 1960.

McCoy, Donald R. *The Presidency of Harry S. Truman.* Lawrence: University Press of Kansas, 1984.

Maisel, Sherman J. *Managing the Dollar.* New York: Norton, 1973.

Martin, John Bartlow. *Adlai Stevenson and the World.* Vol. 2. Garden City, N.Y.: Doubleday and Co., 1979.

Murphy, Charles J. V. "The Budget—and Eisenhower." *Fortune* (July 1957): 96–99, 228–231.

———. "The Eisenhower Shift." Parts 1–4. *Fortune* (Jan., Feb., March, April 1956).

———. "Republicans Need Economists Too." *Fortune* (April 1953): 83–87, 206–208.

———. "The White House and the Recession." *Fortune* 57 (May 1958): 106–109, 242–252.

Neal, Steve. *The Eisenhowers.* Lawrence: University Press of Kansas, 1984.

Neustadt, Richard E. *Presidential Power: The Politics of Leadership.* New York: John Wiley, 1960.

Okun, Arthur. "Inflation: The Problems and Prospects before Us." In *Inflation: The Problems It Creates: The Policies It Requires,* edited by Arthur Okun, 3–43. New York: New York University Press, 1970.

O'Neill, William L. *American High: The Years of Confidence, 1945–1960.* New York: Free Press, 1986.

Parmet, Herbert S. *Eisenhower and the American Crusades.* New York: Macmillan, 1972.

Quester, George H. "Was Eisenhower a Genius?" *International Security* 4 (Fall 1979): 159–179.

Reedy, George. *The U.S. Senate: Paralysis or a Search for Consensus.* New York: Crown Publishers, 1986.

Rees, Albert. *Striking a Balance: Making National Economic Policy.* Chicago: University of Chicago Press, 1984.

Reichard, Gary W. "Eisenhower as President: The Changing View." *South Atlantic Quarterly* 77 (Summer 1978): 265–282.

———. *The Reaffirmation of Republicanism: Eisenhower and the Eighty-third Congress.* Knoxville: University of Tennessee Press, 1975.

Richardson, Elmo. *The Presidency of Dwight D. Eisenhower.* Lawrence: University Press of Kansas, 1979.

Ridgeway, Matthew B. *Soldier: The Memoirs of Matthew B. Ridgeway.* New York: Harper and Brothers, 1956.

Roosa, Robert. Interview by John Richard, Nov. 13, 1972. Oral History Collection of Columbia University.

Rosati, Jerel A. "Developing a Systematic Decision-Making Framework: Bureaucratic Politics in Perspective." *World Politics* 33 (Jan. 1981): 234–252.

Rossiter, Clinton. *The American Presidency.* Revised edition. New York: Harcourt, Brace and World, 1959.

Rovere, Richard H. *Affairs of State: The Eisenhower Years.* New York: Farrar, Straus and Cudahy, 1956.

———. Interview by John T. Mason, Jr., Feb. 22, 1968. Oral History Collection of Columbia University.

Saulnier, Raymond J. "On Advising the President." *Presidential Studies Quarterly* 15 (Summer 1985): 583–588.

———. *The Strategy of Economic Policy.* New York: Fordham University Press, 1962.

Saulnier, Raymond J. Interview by John Luter, Aug. 7 and Aug. 31, 1967. Oral History Collection of Columbia University.

Selden, R. T. "Demand-Pull versus Cost-Push Inflation." *Journal of Political Economy* 67 (Spring 1959): 1–20.

Shannon, William V. "Eisenhower as President." *Commentary* 26 (Nov. 1958): 390–398.

Shonfield, Andrew. *Modern Capitalism: The Changing Balance of Public and Private Power*. New York: Oxford University Press, 1965.

Sloan, John W. "The Management and Decision Making Style of President Eisenhower." *Presidential Studies Quarterly* 20 (Spring 1990): 295–313.

Snyder, John W. "The Treasury and Economic Policy." In *Economics and the Truman Administration*, edited by Francis H. Heller, 23–37. Lawrence: Regents Press of Kansas, 1981.

Stans, Maurice. "The Eisenhower Presidency and Beyond." In *The Eisenhower Presidency: Eleven Intimate Perspectives of Dwight D. Eisenhower*, edited by Kenneth W. Thompson, 211–229. Lanham, Md.: University Press of America, 1984.

Stein, Herbert. *The Fiscal Revolution in America*. Chicago: University of Chicago Press, 1969.

———. *Presidential Economics: The Making of Economic Policy from Roosevelt to Reagan and Beyond*. New York: Simon and Schuster, 1984.

Sternsher, Bernard. "Reflections on Politics, Policy and Ideology." In *Reshaping America: Society and Institutions, 1945–1960*, edited by Robert H. Bremner and Gary W. Reichard, 375–390. Columbus: Ohio State University Press, 1982.

Sundquist, James L. *Politics and Policy: The Eisenhower, Kennedy, and Johnson Years*. Washington, D.C.: Brookings Institution, 1968.

Taylor, Maxwell D. *The Uncertain Trumpet*. New York: Harper and Row, 1959.

Tobin, James. "The Eisenhower Economy and National Security." *Yale Review* 47 (March 1958): 321–334.

Tugwell, Rexford. *The Enlargement of the Presidency*. Garden City, N.Y.: Doubleday and Co., 1960.

United States, Congress, Joint Committee on the Economic Report, *Hearings on the January 1954 Economic Report of the President*, 83d Congress, 2d session.

———, Joint Economic Committee, *Hearings before the Joint Economic Committee*, 85th Congress, 1st session, Jan. 18 and Feb. 6, 1957.

———. *Hearings before the Joint Economic Committee*, 85th Congress, 2d session, Feb. 6, 1958.

Vatter, Harold G. *The U.S. Economy in the 1950s*. Chicago: University of Chicago Press, 1963.

Walcott, Charles, and Karen M. Hult. "Organizing the White House: Structure, Environment, and Organizational Governance." *American Journal of Political Science* 31 (Feb. 1987): 109–125.

Windsor, Duane. "Eisenhower's New Look Reexamined: The View from Three Decades." In *Dwight D. Eisenhower: Soldier, President, Statesman*, edited by Joann P. Krieg, 143–173. New York: Greenwood Press, 1987.

Woolley, John T. "The Federal Reserve and the Politics of Monetary Policy." In *The President and Economic Policy*, edited by James P. Pfiffner, 240–264. Philadelphia: Institute for the Study of Human Issues, 1986.

Wright, Robert. "Eisenhower's Fifties." *Antioch Review* 38 (Summer 1980): 277–290.

ORAL HISTORY TRANSCRIPTS

Adams, Sherman. Interview with Ed Edwin, April 10, April 11, and April 12, 1967, and June 19, 1970. Oral History Transcripts of Eisenhower Library.

Folsom, Marion B. Interview with John T. Mason, Jr., Jan. 10, 1968. Oral History Collection of Columbia University.

Harlow, Bruce. Interview with Stephen J. Wayne and James F. C. Hyde, Jr., May 30, 1974. Oral History Transcripts of Eisenhower Library.

Hauge, Gabriel. Interview with Ed Edwin, March 10, April 24, May 31, and July 10, 1976. Oral History Transcripts of Eisenhower Library.

Jacoby, Neil. Interview with James V. Mink, Dec. 5, 1970. Oral History Collection of Columbia University.

Javits, Jacob. Interview with Peter Corning, Jan. 30, 1968. Oral History Collection of Columbia University.

McElroy, Neil. Interview with Ed Edwin, May 8, 1967. Oral History Collection of Columbia University.

Merriam, Robert. Interview with John T. Mason, Jan. 13, 1969. Oral History Collection of Columbia University.

Roosa, Robert. Interview with John Richard, Nov. 13, 1972. Oral History Collection of Columbia University.

Rovere, Richard H. Interview with John T. Mason, Jr., Feb. 22, 1968. Oral History Collection of Columbia University.

Saulnier, Raymond J. Interview with John Luter, Aug. 7, and Aug. 31, 1967. Oral History Collection of Columbia University.

PRESIDENTIAL PAPERS

Papers of Dwight D. Eisenhower as president of the United States, Eisenhower Library, Abilene, Kansas:
Ann Whitman Administration Series
Ann Whitman Cabinet Series
Ann Whitman Name Series
Dwight D. Eisenhower Diary Series
National Security Council Series

Index

ABEGS, 46, 114, 119, 120
Adams, Sherman, 43, 45; on Burns, 34; photo of, 39, 84; quote of, 15; role of, 64; scandal involving, 60; on Taft, 73
Additive process, use of, 72
Advisory Board on Economic Growth and Stability (ABEGS), 46, 114, 119, 120
AFL-CIO, 114
Aggregate demand, 143; inflation and, 36; manipulation of, 5
Allison, Graham, 9, 10; work of, 7-8
Alsop, Joseph, 24
Ambrose, Stephen: on Nixon, 104; quote of, 16, 21
American Bankers Association, Humphrey speech to, 137
Anderson, Robert B., 40, 42, 45, 47, 105, 114, 119, 131, 144, 145, 151; on balanced budgets, 152; on balance of payments, 129-30; conservatism of, 27-28; on education spending, 95-96; on FRB, 113; on inflation, 117, 158; monetary policy of, 106, 123; photo of, 25; style of, 26-28; on tax cuts, 146, 148-49; work of, 25-28, 159
Anti-inflationary policies, 116, 117-25, 158
Army Industrial College, 14
Austerity, 115, 118, 131
Authority, delegating of, 55-56, 64-65

Baby boom, impact of, 49
Bach, G. L.: quote of, 108
Balanced budgets, 9, 11, 14, 15, 19, 24, 28, 32, 36, 44, 47, 51, 52, 67-69, 72-73, 78, 80, 98-102, 103, 105, 117, 129, 136, 137, 153, 154, 158, 160; commitment to, 70-71,
139-40, 149, 151, 155-57; national security and, 102; techniques for, 83-90
Balance of payments, 12, 114, 132, 152; Eisenhower and, 129, 130, 158; national security and, 128-29, 131, 158; problem with, 123, 125-30
Balderston, C. Canby, 119
Bank deposit insurance, 18
Banking Act of 1933, 107
Benson, Ezra Taft, 43, 90, 96
Berman, Larry: on budget directors, 29
Big business: criticism by, 124; dependence on, 58-59; Eisenhower and, 65
Big government, Eisenhower on, 14-15
BOB. See Bureau of the Budget
Bomber gap, 98; Democrats and, 157
Bond crisis, FRB and, 120
Bonds, 130, 136; long-term, 111-12, 117, 118, 119; selling, 120
Brennan, William: photo of, 89
Brownell, Herbert, 44
Brownlow Committee, 28
Brundage, Mrs.: photo of, 30
Brundage, Percival, 90, 100, 101; BOB and, 29; photo of, 30, 153; on tax cuts, 146
Buckley, William, 160; quote of, 63
Budget and Accounting Act (1921), 28
Budget battles, 9, 11, 19, 98-102. See also Balanced budgets
Budget directors: Eisenhower and, 32; role of, 29, 30
Bureaucracy: freeze on, 83; growth of, 84; reduction of, 71-72, 80, 84
Bureaucratic politics approach: description of, 7-8; Eisenhower and, 8-10
Bureau of the Budget (BOB), 6, 9, 12, 100,

185

Bureau of the Budget (*continued*)
108; ABEGS and, 46; description of, 28–32; flexibility and, 134; influence of, 47. *See also* Office of Management and Budget
Burgess, W. Randolph, 114, 129
Burns, Arthur F., 10, 23, 28, 41, 42, 47, 108, 114, 115, 121, 134, 136, 137, 138, 152; ABEGS and, 46; appointment of, 43; on balance of payments, 129; on CEA, 45; on confidence, 141; on deficits, 139; on economic management, 128; Eisenhower and, 34, 35, 44, 148; on flexibility, 143; FRB and, 119; Humphrey and, 34–35, 37; on inflation, 117; influence of, 34; money policy and, 123; Nixon and, 142; philosophy of, 35–36; photo of, 33, 39; quote of, 35, 37; on recession, 135; rejection of, 147–48; skills of, 44; on taxation, 36; on tax cuts, 146, 159; work of, 32–38, 151
Burton, Harold V.: photo of, 30, 84
Byrd, Harry, 73

Cabinet Committee on Price Stability for Economic Growth (CCPSEG), 124
Caldwell, Dan: quote of, 8
Carney, Robert: on New Look, 88
Carter, Jimmy, 118
CCPSEG, 124
CEA. *See* Council of Economic Advisers
Centralization, 41
CFEP, 126
CGA, 124
Churchill, Winston, 61
Civil rights, 2, 159
Clark, Colin, 135
Clay, G. Lucius D., 20
Cold War, 70; budgets and, 90–91, 102; domestic politics and, 53; Eisenhower and, 16, 53; financing of, 68, 97, 108, 155; influence of, 52–53; prosperity and, 15
Commission on Foreign Economic Policy, 126
Committee on Government Activities Affecting Prices and Costs (CGA), 124
Confidence, 128, 142; maintaining, 130, 141
Consensus building, 110, 154
Conservatism, 11, 16, 19, 35, 103, 104; Eisenhower and, 11, 19, 62, 103, 154, 161; liberal humanitarianism and, 62; welfare liberalism and, 102, 160
Consumer goods, 49–50
Consumer price index (CPI), 114; growth of, 105, 115, 118, 120–21, 144
Containment, 63
Conviction politician, 16–17

Coolidge, Calvin, 2
Corporate tax rate: drop in, 147; increase in, 137
Council of Economic Advisers (CEA), 9, 12, 23, 43, 108, 119, 120, 130, 139, 145, 148; Burns on, 32–33; 35; description of, 5–6; FRB and, 136; influence of, 7, 44, 47; recession and, 134; Saulnier on, 39, 41, 45
Countercyclical policies, 35–38, 67, 120, 142
CPI. *See* Consumer price index
Credit: liberalizing, 135, 136, 150; restrictions on, 141, 144

DAC, 66–67
Davis, Kenneth: quote of, 59, 67
Debt: management of, 27, 107–8, 141; transferring, 117. *See also* National debt
Defense spending, 24, 53, 73, 75, 100, 103; controlling, 76–77, 85–88, 156; cutting, 81, 82, 84, 139; Eisenhower and, 74–78, 97–98; increasing, 69–70, 161; for research, 86, 97–98; Sputnik and, 145, 156. *See also* Expenditures
Deficits, 27, 69–70, 79, 80, 89, 103, 125, 128, 129, 139, 155, 156; elimination of, 73; growth of, 138; inflation and, 30–31. *See also* Surpluses
Democratic Advisory Council (DAC), 66–67
Democratic National Committee, 66
Democratic party: description of, 63–68; majority for, 58, 60–61, 66; partisan loyalty to, 56
Democrats: criticism by, 64–65; Eisenhower and, 56, 60, 65–68; presidential campaigns of, 58
Demographics: changes in, 48–49
Depression, 15, 35, 50, 68; avoiding, 3, 17, 61, 107, 137, 140; of 1930s, 4, 38, 133
Destler, I. M.: quote of, 8
Dewey, Thomas, 42, 56
Dillon, Douglas: photo of, 25
Discount rate, 110; description of, 111; FRB and, 121; lowering, 123, 136; raising, 120–23, 144. *See also* Interest rates
Dodge, Joseph, 44, 70, 71, 74, 86, 87, 139; BOB and, 29, 30; CFEP and, 126; on defense spending, 75; NSC and, 72; portrait of, 31
Dollar: balances, 127; confidence in, 128, 130; gap, 127, 131; glut, 132; value of, 127
Donovan, Robert: quote of, 139–40
Douglas, Paul, 38, 44, 135
Dulles, John Foster, 21, 22, 29, 74, 78, 97, 100, 101

Economic Report, 5, 124, 125, 138, 139, 141, 150; Burns and, 33, 34

Economy: management of, 4, 5, 50; political significance of, 4
Education, 49, 53, 91, 157, 161; Democrats and, 63; Eisenhower and, 16, 96–97; spending for, 90, 92–96
Eisenhower, David, 13
Eisenhower, Dwight: criticism of, 64–65, 75, 78, 98–99, 154, 157; election of, 56–61; goals of, 14, 18, 70, 72, 79–81, 83, 89, 103, 131–32, 155; leadership of, 11, 16–18, 54–56, 99, 155–61; organizational skills of, 42, 64–65; philosophy of, 14, 16–17; photo of, 25, 30, 33, 153; popularity of, 2, 54–56, 59, 61, 63, 99, 101, 116, 145, 155, 160; quote of, 10, 71; scholarly evaluations of, 1–3
Eisenhower, Edgar, 62
Eisenhower, Ida, 13
Eisenhower, John, 18
Eisenhower, Milton, 15, 23
Employment: freeze on, 83; full, 38, 68; growth of, 84; reducing, 71–72, 80, 84. See also Unemployment
Employment Act of 1946, 35, 43, 114, 124, 128; description of, 4–5
Engelbourg, Saul: on Burns, 135
Excise tax, 136; increase in, 137
Executive Office of the President (EOP), 28
Expenditures: accelerating, 140, 142; controlling, 85–87; domestic, 24; growth of, 90–91, 100, 102, 103, 138–39, 146; reducing, 24–25, 72, 80, 97, 99, 100, 102, 115, 131, 152, 156. See also Defense spending
Exports: decline in, 28; growth of, 127, 132; restrictions on, 128. See also Trade

Fair Deal, 17, 18
Farewell address, contents of, 85–86
Federal Aviation Agency, 80
Federal Housing Authority (FHA), 136
Federal Old Age Assistance program, 90
Federal Open Market Committee (FOMC), 109, 111; creation of, 107; tightening by, 122
Federal Reserve Act (1913), passage of, 106
Federal Reserve Bank, 107, 111, 112; deficits and, 125; description of, 106
Federal Reserve Board (FRB), 9, 11, 26, 52, 81, 117, 123, 128, 141, 144, 149; anti-inflation policies of, 116; bond crisis and, 120; CEA and, 136; description of, 106–8; Eisenhower and, 105, 108, 119, 121, 136; independence of, 108, 112, 114, 121, 158; inflation and, 115, 158; influence of, 6, 47, 107–8, 116; macroeconomic policy and, 112–14, 119–20, 131, 158; Martin

and, 109–11; members of, 106; monetary policy and, 41, 110–13, 118, 130, 136; Treasury and, 108, 119
FHA. See Federal Housing Authority
Fiscal responsibility, 130; guidelines for, 94
Flash, Edward: quote of, 138
Flemming, Arthur S., 104; on education, 94–95; on fiscal responsibility, 94; at HEW, 91, 93–96
Flexibility, 134, 139, 141, 143
Fluctuation, moderating, 35, 36, 38
Folsom, Marion B., 104; at HEW, 91, 92–93
FOMC. See Federal Open Market Committee
Food and Drug Administration, 92
Forecasting, 12; accuracy of, 38
Foreign crises, 60, 100, 129; impact of, 48
Foreign Operations Administration, 126
Foreign policy, 3, 126–27
FRB. See Federal Reserve Board
Friedman, Milton: on FRB, 112, 113; quote of, 120, 122, 125

Galbraith, John Kenneth: DAC and, 66; on FRB, 113
Gates, Thomas, 77
GNP. See Gross national product
Goldfine, Bernard, 60
Goldman, Eric: quote of, 16
Goldwater, Barry, 61, 160; criticism of, 62
Goodpaster, Andrew, Staff Secretary, 86
Gordon, H. Scott: on CGA, 124
Great Equation, description of, 76
Greenstein, Fred, 62; quote of, 3, 16, 20
Griffith, Robert: quote of, 13, 17
Gross national product (GNP), 50, 51, 118, 144; defense spending and, 76, 82; federal spending and, 80; growth of, 3; national debt and, 81
Growth, 50–51, 61, 67, 68, 102, 161; export, 127; importance of, 85; inflation and, 158; sluggish, 132, 150, 154, 155, 159; stimulating, 111; unemployment and, 145

Hargrove, Erwin, 40; quote of, 5
Harlow, Bryce, 44
Harriman, Averell: DAC and, 66
Hauge, Gabriel, 19, 34, 35, 40, 44, 119, 128, 133, 148; federal highway program and, 134; quote of, 115–16; work of, 42–43
Hazlett, "Swede," 26
Health issues, 91, 157; Democrats and, 63
Heller, Walter, 36; on Employment Act, 4–5; quote of, 7, 67
Henderson, Phillip: quote of, 87–88
HEW. See U.S. Department of Health, Education, and Welfare

Highway program, 134
Hobby, Oveta Culp: at HEW, 91–92
Hoffman, Paul, 126
Hoover, Herbert, 4, 8, 36, 56, 58, 68, 133, 142, 150
Housing: demand for, 136; subsidies for, 18
Housing Act of 1954, 136, 148
Hughes, Emmet John, 62; on Humphrey, 22; quote of, 19, 159
Hughes, Mrs. Rowland: photo of, 84
Hughes, Rowland, 91; BOB and, 29; photo of, 30, 84
Humphrey, George, 3, 26, 28, 40, 42, 44, 58, 74, 78, 87, 114, 119, 120, 121, 126, 131, 132, 134–37, 142, 149, 155; anti-inflation policies of, 116–17; balance of payments and, 129; on budgeting, 90, 152; and Burns, 34–35, 37; on confidence, 141; on defense spending, 75, 88, 97, 100; description of, 21; economic policy of, 24, 99–101; and Milton Eisenhower, 21–23; and NSC, 72, 88; photo of, 21; style of, 22–23, 25; on taxes, 73; work of, 20–25
Humphrey, Hubert: DAC and, 66
Huntington, Samuel: quote of, 78, 79

Independents, Eisenhower and, 60
Inflation, 4, 6, 10, 14, 28, 44, 47, 50, 73, 100, 123, 140, 144, 145, 149, 154, 155, 161; aggregate demand and, 36; Anderson on, 27; Burns on, 34; controlling, 5, 11, 37, 38, 41, 51, 52, 67, 105, 114–16, 119, 124–25, 130–32, 141, 157, 160; creeping, 80, 99, 110, 116, 124, 152; deficit and, 30–31; Democrats and, 115; Eisenhower and, 118, 133; fear of, 18, 102, 107–8, 118, 133, 137, 138, 148, 150, 151, 158; FRB and, 108, 113, 115, 157, 158; Saulnier on, 40, 41; Stans on, 32
Inflationary bias, 118
Inflationary psychology, 27, 117
Interdependence, 125, 128, 131
Interest rates, 105, 110, 114, 131, 158; drop in, 120; freezing, 148. See also Discount rate
Internal Revenue Code, 137
Internationalism, 75, 125
Intervention, 18–19, 35, 38, 50, 86, 154
Investment, 19, 40

Jacoby, Neil, 23, 38, 39, 44; quote of, 7
Japan, support for, 127, 129
Javits, Jacob, 62
Johnson, Lyndon B., 26, 59, 104, 156; DAC and, 66; Eisenhower and, 64, 65–66
Joint Chiefs of Staff, 87
Joint Committee on the Economic Report, 23
Joint Economic Committee, 5, 110, 135

Kefauver, Estes: DAC and, 66
Kennedy, John F., 3, 41, 54, 68, 81, 104, 130, 155, 156; DAC and, 66; election of, 61
Kettl, Donald: on FRB, 112, 120; on Martin, 110; quote of, 107, 111–12, 121
Keynes, John Maynard, 5
Keyserling, Leon, 43
Khrushchev, Nikita, 53
Korean War, 3, 53, 69, 71, 77, 119, 123, 133, 134; defense spending for, 81, 108, 145; growth during, 51; inflation during, 115; unemployment during, 52
Krasner, Stephen: quote of, 8

Larson, Arthur: on Humphrey, 22; quote of, 18, 19, 102
Lawton, Frederick, 29, 70
Lewis, Wilfred, 140
Liberal humanitarianism, 62
Liberalism: abandoning, 102; opposition to, 19–20
Lincoln, Abraham, 18, 86
Lodge, Henry Cabot, 140
Lora, Ronald: quote of, 49
Luxury tax, revenue from, 138

MacArthur, Douglas, 14
McCabe, Thomas, 108, 148
McCarthy, Joseph, 2, 17, 63, 159, 160
McDonald, David, 135
McElroy, Neil, 96, 98; as defense secretary, 77
Macroeconomic policy, 4; Eisenhower and, 3, 9–10, 13–20, 43; FRB and, 108, 112–14, 119–20, 131, 158; political significance of, 12. See also Policymaking
Maisel, Sherman, 108; quote of, 111
Manager of prosperity, 4–7; Eisenhower as, 7–10, 67, 154, 162; president as, 15. See also Prosperity, managing
Mao Tse-Tung, 74
Market economy theory, 125
Martin, John Bartlow: quote of, 59
Martin, Joseph, 90
Martin, William McChesney, 121, 122, 130, 136, 144, 148, 157; description of, 108–12; FRB and, 113–14, 119–20; on inflation, 158; monetary policy of, 131; photo of, 109; skills of, 110, 112
Medical research, spending for, 91, 93
Merriam, Robert: on BOB, 28; photo of, 89
Microeconomic policy, 43
Military: modernization of, 82; strength of, 76. See also Defense spending
Missile gap, 61, 98; Democrats and, 157

Mitchell, James, 96, 104, 124, 148, 149, 151; criticism by, 121; on tax cuts, 146
Mitchell, Wesley C., 32
Modern Republicanism, 101, 145, 152, 157, 159, 161; Eisenhower and, 94, 103–4; Flemming and, 94
Monetary policy, 47, 81, 104, 114, 135; Burns and, 36–37; Eisenhower and, 131, 158; flexibility in, 117; FRB and, 41, 110–13, 136; "honest," 116; inflation and, 157; loosening, 134, 154; relying on, 105–6; Saulnier on, 40; tightening, 105, 121, 122, 130
Money supply: fixing, 113; FRB and, 118; loosening, 108, 122; managing, 106; tightening, 51, 52, 112, 114, 131, 158
Moos, Malcolm, 86
Morgenthau, Henry, 107
Morley, Samuel: quote of, 5, 40
Murphy, Charles: quote of, 70

National Aeronautics and Space Administration, 80
National Bureau of Economic Research, 134; Burns and, 33; Saulnier and, 39
National debt, 28, 63, 107, 152, 160; increase in, 3, 70; reducing, 80–81, 103. See also Debt
National Defense Education Act (1958): passage of, 53; Folsom and, 92–93
National Institutes of Health, 93
National interest, 97; big business and, 58–59; Eisenhower and, 16, 153
National security, 85, 155, 157; balanced budgets and, 102; balance of payments and, 128–29, 131, 158; defense spending and, 76; Eisenhower and, 16, 42, 74–75; financing, 53, 83; significance of, 4
National Security Council (NSC), 9, 25, 87, 97; appointments to, 72
National Security Council memorandum 68 (NSC-68), 74, 75
National Security Council memorandum 162/2 (NSC-162/2), 78
Neustadt, Richard, 11, 102, 103; on Eisenhower, 98–99; quote of, 101
New Deal, 4, 15, 17, 35, 63, 142; Eisenhower and, 1, 18, 62, 160; Humphrey and, 24
New Economics, 68, 69, 145, 150; description of, 67
New Eisenhower, 102–4, 149, 150, 152; description of, 67–68; inflexibility of, 160–61
New Look, 87, 103; budget for, 81–82; criticism of, 78; modification of, 78–79
Nixon, Richard, 9, 33, 60, 104, 142, 149,

151; attacks on, 59; Burns and, 148; CCPSEG and, 124; on education spending, 96; money policy and, 123; photo of, 89; quote of, 54; on tax cuts, 146
Nourse, Edwin: resignation of, 43
NSC. See National Security Council
Nuclear weapons, 78, 79, 82, 97; development of, 98

O'Neill, William: quote of, 49–50
Offices of Management and Budget (OMB), 6. See also Bureau of the Budget
Okun, Arthur, 118
Open-market operations, 110, 120, 121, 123; description of, 111–12

Paarlberg, Donald, 40, 43
Personal income tax exemption, 138
Persons, Wilton, 45
Policymaking: Eisenhower and, 14–15, 42, 48; influences on, 10–11, 48–49. See also Macroeconomic policy
Population: growth of, 49, 90; budget and, 90
Pork barrel legislation, veto of, 89
Poverty, 50, 61, 161
Price controls, terminating, 115
Progress, postponing, 161–62
Progressive programs, 156
Prosperity, 55, 58, 59, 65, 67, 68, 71, 141, 155; managing, 12, 15, 18, 35, 46, 47, 128, 131, 132, 133, 154; threats to, 6–7; trade and, 132. See also Manager of prosperity
Public works programs, 135, 139, 140, 143, 149, 150

Quotas, eliminating, 130

Rabi, I. I., 86
Racial conflict, 61; impact of, 48
Radford, Arthur, 77, 78, 84
Randall, Clarence: work of, 126
Randall Commission, creation of, 126
Rayburn, Sam, 26, 59, 104; DAC and, 66; Eisenhower and, 64, 65–66
Readjustment, 134, 135
Reagan, Ronald, 33, 118
Recession, 9, 15, 46, 48, 50, 54, 59, 60, 68, 80, 89, 99, 100, 115, 122, 123, 137, 154, 159, 161; Burns on, 36; fighting, 11, 34, 37, 38, 67, 133–35, 138, 143–51, 158; FRB and, 113, 136; inflation and, 138
Reciprocal Trade Agreements Act (1934), 126
Recovery, 52, 122, 140, 143, 145
Rees, Albert: quote of, 111, 114
Reichard, Gary: quote of, 54

Republican National Committee, 93
Republican party: description of, 61–63;
  Eisenhower and, 14, 56, 58, 59, 61–62;
  majorities for, 56; recession and, 134;
  split in, 74
Reserve ratios, manipulating, 110–11, 136
Reuther, Walter, 38, 135
Revenue Act of 1951, 137
Revisionist scholarship, 2–3
Richardson, Elliott, 95
Richardson, Elmo, 20; on Eisenhower, 75;
  quote of, 16, 64
Ridgeway, Matthew, 78
Right to work, Republicans and, 94
Rising expectations, 154, 160
Rockefeller, Nelson, 44, 60
Roosa, Robert: on FRB, 114
Roosevelt, Eleanor: DAC and, 66
Roosevelt, Franklin D., 4, 16, 18, 36, 55, 98,
  150; leadership of, 1–2, 3, 159
Rossiter, Clinton, 4, 10
Rovere, Richard: quote of, 16, 54

Sanderson, Frank K.: photo of, 33
Saulnier, Raymond J., 47, 121, 125, 126,
  152; on balance of payments, 130; on
  CEA, 45; on centralization, 41; CGA and,
  124; FRB and, 119; on inflation, 117;
  money policy and, 123; philosophy of,
  40–41; photo of, 39; quote of, 119, 122;
  on recession, 143–44; on tax cuts, 148;
  work of, 39–42
Schools, construction of, 94–96. See also
  Education
Schwartz, Anna Jacobson: on FRB, 112;
  quote of, 120, 122
Securities. See Bonds
Shannon, William: on Eisenhower, 2
Smith, Adam, 125
SMSA, 49
Snyder, John, 108
Social responsibility, 55, 125, 155, 157, 161;
  spending for, 83
Social security, 15, 18, 91, 136, 137
Soviet Union: challenge from, 2, 61, 154;
  technology and, 156
Spending. See Expenditures
Sputnik: defense expenditures and, 145,
  156; impact of, 53, 54, 60, 76, 82, 84,
  103, 146, 148, 152, 155
Stability, 47, 73, 78, 102, 106, 121, 124, 138,
  143, 152; maintaining, 36, 141
Stabilizers, 150; using, 38, 144, 149
Stagflation, 145
Stalin, Josef, 53, 77
Standard metropolitan statistical areas
  (SMSA), growth of, 49

Standard of living, 155; growth of, 50, 154
Stans, Maurice, 84, 104; BOB and, 29, 30,
  32; on budgeting, 90; on education
  spending, 96; photo of, 89
Stassen, Harold, 142
Steel strike, impact of, 123
Stein, Herbert: on Burns, 36; quote of, 140,
  143, 149
Stevenson, Adlai, 56, 58, 60, 61; campaign
  of, 64–65; DAC and, 66; quote of, 59
Stewart, Walter W., 44
Strategic thought: budgetary considerations
  of, 87; revision of, 78
Strauss, Lewis, 97
Subtraction process, using, 72, 80
Suburbanization, 49, 50
Sundquist, James, 63; quote of, 66
Surpluses, 27, 30, 70, 80, 146, 160; produc-
  tion of, 90, 115. See also Deficits
Symington, Stuart: DAC and, 66

Taft, Robert, 14, 20, 44, 61, 63; quote of,
  73–74
Tariffs, reducing, 130
Taxation, 63; Burns on, 36; Eisenhower
  and, 138; limits on, 85
Tax cuts, 12, 19, 70, 72, 73, 78, 82, 87, 99,
  100, 134–37, 139, 142, 143, 148, 152, 159,
  161; proposing, 144; support for, 138,
  146–47; Treasury and, 149
Tax increases, 90; opposition to, 94
Tax Revision Act of 1954, 138
Taylor, Maxwell, 78
Taylor, Zachary, 60
Technology, 88, 98, 156
Ticket-splitting, 60
Time magazine, 58; on Eisenhower, 63
Trade, 126, 130; balance of, 127; free, 131;
  prosperity and, 132. See also Exports
Transfer payments, 80, 143
"Trickle down" effect, 135, 140
Truman, Harry S., 3, 16, 26, 29, 55, 56, 58,
  103, 108; budget crisis of, 69; DAC and,
  66

Unemployment, 4, 6, 10, 44, 45, 58, 60, 117,
  121, 123, 131, 139, 149, 152, 158;
  avoiding, 5, 18, 37, 116; Burns on, 34;
  Eisenhower and, 133; growth and, 145;
  growth of, 51–52, 122, 134, 135, 144;
  lowering, 52, 140, 144, 154. See also
  Employment
Unemployment insurance, 15, 18, 80, 135,
  144, 150
Urban renewal, 157
U.S. Council on Foreign Economic Policy

U.S. Department of Agriculture, budget of, 90
U.S. Department of Commerce, 6
U.S. Department of Defense: budget of, 103; growth of, 91; recession and, 139
U.S. Department of Health, Education, and Welfare (HEW), 13, 90; budget of, 103; growth of, 91
U.S. Department of Labor, 6
U.S. Interior Department, 83
U.S. Treasury Department, 12; ABEGS and, 46; FRB and, 108, 119, 120; role of, 6, 47, 116–17; tax cuts and, 149

Vatter, Harold, 118; quote of, 49, 50–51, 52, 80, 128
Veterans benefits, 80

Vetoes, 66, 88–89; overriding, 90
Vinson, Fred, 26
Voodoo economics, 73

Wage controls, terminating, 115
War, avoiding, 3, 17
Washington, George, 18
Weeks, Sinclair, 126; criticism by, 121
Welfare, 157; Humphrey and, 24
Welfare liberalism, 11, 35; economic conservatism and, 102, 160
Western Europe, support for, 127, 129
White House Conference on Education, 91
Wilson, Charles, 83, 88, 141; as defense secretary, 77
Woolley, John: quote of, 106
Wright, Robert: quote of, 161

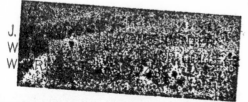